the
elephant
in the room

EXPOSING THE EVIL
OF ABUSE BY THOSE IN
SPIRITUAL AUTHORITY

Deborah G. Hunter

the
elephant
in the room

EXPOSING THE EVIL
OF ABUSE BY THOSE IN
SPIRITUAL AUTHORITY

Deborah G. Hunter

HUNTER ENTERTAINMENT NETWORK

Colorado Springs, Colorado

To order products, or for any other correspondence:

Hunter Entertainment Network
4164 Austin Bluffs Parkway, Suite 214
Colorado Springs, Colorado 80918
www.hunter-ent-net.com
Tel. (253) 906-2160 – Fax: (719) 528-6359
E-mail: contact@hunter-entertainment.com
Or reach us on Facebook at: Hunter Entertainment Network
"Offering God's Heart to a Dying World"

This book and all other Hunter Entertainment Network™ Hunter Heart Publishing™, and Hunter Heart Kids™ books are available at Christian bookstores and distributors worldwide.

Chief Editor: Gord Dormer
Book cover design: Phil Coles Independent Design
Layout & logos: Exousia Marketing Group www.exousiamg.com

ISBN: 978-1-937741-36-5 (Paperback)
ISBN: 978-1-937741-18-1 (Hardcover)
Printed in the United States of America.

DEDICATION

I dedicate this book to each person manipulated and violated by the insidious evil of spiritual abuse, hidden behind the mask of "good," and even "God". Humanity was created as "good" by the Creator of the Universe, yet there is a very present evil lurking in the darkness, hell-bent on destroying the *good* within us all. I challenge you to seek deep within; within your spirit, to find the true, authentic voice of healing, forgiveness, deliverance, restoration, reconciliation, and redemption. Much has been taken from you, stolen from you, and even killed within you, but let it not destroy the ultimate "good" you were created to experience and be, both here and eternally.

Understand that what was done *to* you had nothing to do *with* you. Abuse comes out of the heart of the abused. Rise above what was done to you, so you are able to live a life of freedom and to help someone else come out of their own darkness. Evil will not destroy you... you will emerge victorious!

Acknowledgments

I want to acknowledge every spiritual leader across the world that has not bowed to compromise; those that have held on to hard won integrity, moral compass, righteousness, and absolute love for God and God's people. Thank you for continuing to teach the Truth, while holding "loosely" those that have committed to serve alongside you in the Kingdom of God. Thank you for understanding that these are God's people, not ours. Thank you for accepting the call and assignment to lead God's people into spiritual maturity and to see them become all God has destined them to be in this life. Thank you for simply being a *vessel* that God can use for His glory. There *is* a Remnant in the Earth!

TABLE OF CONTENTS

Preface.. 1

Chapter 1: History of Spiritual Abuse 9

Chapter 2: The Call of True Spiritual Leadership 21

Chapter 3: The Great Deception.................................... 39

Chapter 4: Control, Manipulation & Intimidation.................. 57

Chapter 5: Verbal & Emotional Abuse............................. 83

Chapter 6: Mental & Psychological Abuse....................105

Chapter 7: Financial & Economical Abuse....................151

Chapter 8: Physical & Sexual Abuse............................177

Chapter 9: The Mass Exodus & Gathering of the Scattered 207

Chapter 10: The Truth Revealed: Exposing Spiritual Leadership...221

Chapter 11: Justice vs. Judgment....................................243

Chapter 12: Deliverance for the Abusers:

The Truth Shall Set You Free....................................261

Chapter 13: Authentic Repentance 281

Chapter 14: The Rebirth of the Gospel: The Remnant Arising! 311

Conclusion..325

About the Author...327

Bibliography...329

PREFACE

As I heard the voice of God three years ago to pen this message, I made every excuse in the book as to why I was not *qualified* to write such a weighty message. The message was absolutely a burden burning deep within my heart, as well as a fire ignited in my spirit over twenty years ago, as I began the journey and call of intercession for spiritual leaders in the earth. I would lie awake literally with my face to the floor for a period of five years, weeping and travailing for repentance and a *turning back* to the Lord for spiritual leadership, at times, until the sun would break forth across the horizon in the breathtaking Bavarian countryside. Some mornings, I would awaken on that very floor, not remembering half of what the Spirit of God prayed through me, as I wept almost incessantly for the spiritual climate of our world and prayed in my heavenly language.

As my time in Germany proceeded to wind down, I began to see more and more what God was revealing to me concerning the state of the Church and spiritual leadership around the world. After years of deep, intimate intercession, God began to share with me dreams and visions of particular spiritual leaders around the globe. One by one, He led me and my family in their pathway; some directly and some indirectly, through those we were sent to serve in the Church. The insidious things I began to see and witness as we transitioned from overseas back stateside confirmed the dreams and visions I had previously observed. Men and women in spiritual leadership positions, many of whom I had never seen before, except in my dreams/visions, I began to meet in one way or another. God was leading me in the pathway of these leaders through business, as well as ministry assignments.

I quickly began to discern the assignments God would send me and ultimately, my job was intercession. The evil I would witness, at times, would overwhelm me to the point where I asked God many times to stop speaking to me and to stop giving me dreams/visions. He did not relent; He continued to speak to me and awakened me often to pray and intercede for many different people and situations. It was not limited to the Christian church; I was seeing spiritual leaders from many different religions and spiritual practices, as well as governmental leaders, and the corruption and abuse taking place in each sect of society. He began revealing the truth and exposing the hidden darkness. He was shining light on the authentic and divulging the counterfeit. He started awakening within me a burning desire for truth and justice.

Subsequently, over the next ten years, I found myself being thrust into some of the greatest spiritual battles of my life. The dreams were now coming almost incessantly; they were clear and precise. I would hear His voice speaking specifically and distinctively concerning people and situations. Within months of me hearing and seeing these particular things, they were being openly revealed. God commissioned me several years before returning to the U.S. to share these very specific dreams/visions with people I could trust to intercede, as well as hold them in confidence. He was developing accountability for me, as I continued to see and hear by the Spirit of God. Someone has always had intimate knowledge of what God has shared with me, in order to be a witness as it was publicly revealed.

God's initial intention is not exposure. He provides us with limitless grace and mercy, a chance to repent and turn from darkness. 2 Chronicles 7:14 states: *"If My people who are called by My name will humble themselves, and pray and seek My face, and turn from their wicked ways, then I will hear from heaven, and will forgive their sin and heal their land."* If we refuse and reject His voice, whether it is through the truth of His Word, His Spirit, or even through those He is speaking and revealing things to, and continue in outright rebellion, He will remove His hand of covering from us.

My heartfelt prayer and earnest intercession over the years has been for authentic humility and brokenness to envelop the ranks of spiritual leadership in the Earth. The weeping and travail night after night and the grief in my spirit for those blinded by the darkness became my assignment. I have spent the last twenty years of my life covering spiritual leaders and praying for healing, deliverance, forgiveness, restoration, reconciliation, and redemption. Though I have had to complete some very difficult assignments, and have been ostracized, attacked, blacklisted, and threatened by many in the Church, I would do it again and again and again. God has allowed me to grow some very "thick skin," as it pertains to the call He has commanded me to fulfill.

In completing this book, I had to know for sure that I was releasing His heart, not merely my own feelings and opinions, or even simply my own experiences with spiritual abuse. I had to endure a process where God was healing and removing the frustration, hurt, pain, disappointment, bitterness, resentment, and yes, anger that had crept into my own life, unbeknownst to me, due to the many different assignments. He took me personally through some very difficult experiences, in order to know intimately what spiritual abuse produces in the lives of individuals. He began to heal me from within and planted inside of me not only His heart for the abused, but also for the abuser.

This message is not an all-out assault on those that have abused spiritually the people under their spiritual care and welfare. The purpose of this message is to bring justice for the abused, as well as accountability, responsibility, and yes, deliverance to the ranks of spiritual leadership, in order to release the fullness of God's love in the Earth through His Church, His *authentic* Ekklesia. Though the preface of this message is dealing with spiritual abuse from the lineage of Christianity and its denominations, you will, in fact, hear testimonies from people from different religions and spiritual practices, as well. I sensed a great urging from God to dig deep into the spiritual practices of our world to be able to see, intimately, why people choose to worship or practice certain religions and/or spiritual philosophies, and the abuse that stems from its origins.

As I submerged myself into getting to know others of differing beliefs, I found a deep commonality of humanity. Many others have and yet are experiencing much of the same abuses all over the world all in the name of their "religion," or "spiritual practice." I am writing from the foundation and basis of my faith, as a believer and follower of the teachings of the Bible and in Jesus Christ/Yeshua HaMashiach. My editorial stance of including other religions and/or spiritual practices does not diminish in any way, shape, or form my faith in or love for my Lord and Savior, Jesus Christ/Yeshua HaMashiach. In fact, it solidifies it beyond a shadow of a doubt.

Throughout this book, you will witness transparent, and yes, heart-wrenching testimonies from men and women all over the world that have endured many forms of spiritual abuse. Some will be noted as *anony-mous*, while others have chosen to use their initials and state/country. Some stories and names have been shared inconspicuously, so as not to divulge an individual's identity. These testimonies range from several months to some, over forty years ago. Their stories need to be heard, and if this book opens up some sort of healing for them to become free and be courageous enough to share openly, then all the warfare over the last several years writing will truly have been all worth it.

I initially sought out endorsements and even a foreword for this book, but as I sent out the final draft to many spiritual leaders all over the world, there were so many that did not want to *dig up* the secrets and abuse suffered by millions around the globe. They felt that it would harm the Church and cause a windstorm to sweep throughout Christendom. Many stated that most of these spiritual leaders have, indeed, repented and that they should not be subject to yet another book on spiritual abuse. I thank God for allowing me the opportunity to witness to many of these spiritual leaders through their rejection of this book. Many were healed, delivered, and set free from years of covering up sinister acts by their own peers. Through Holy Spirit, God was able to penetrate the hearts of some of the most religious leaders of our time. Many received the gift of Holy Spirit in prayer, as well as in person, as I have traveled over the world these last several years ministering and counseling spiritual leadership. Needless to say, I made the decision to leave out any and all endorsements in this book, even from those that approved of this crucial message. God Himself has endorsed it, and Holy Spirit has breathed the very words on these pages. After twenty years of interceding, praying, and sharing the heart of God on spiritual leadership, I have witnessed a shifting in the hearts of those called to serve humanity in the stead of Christ.

I pray for open hearts, open minds, open eyes, and open ears. I pray for open and honest communication to form conversations where these issues can be dealt with in a mature and responsible manner. I pray for Biblical accountability and integrity, as well as spiritual insight and revelation. I pray for keen discernment where there is blurred deception. I pray for wise counsel, seasoned elders, and time-tested, processed, and approved spiritual leadership to step into their rightful positions in the Earth. Those that will uphold the morals, values, and yes, commandments of God and bring justice for humanity. I pray for the healing and forgiveness of those caught in the snares and evils of spiritual abuse, and I pray for the deliverance of those perpetrating these evils upon God's children. I pray for authentic humility and repentance to break forth in our world, where we can look at ourselves in the mirror and examine our own evil ways and say, "No more! It stops here!" We all play a major role in the healing and deliverance of our world. We each are a part of a global body that has been ravaged, in some form or fashion, by an inaccurate and deceptive view of our Creator.

I introduce to you, *The Elephant in the Room: Exposing the Evil of Abuse by Those in Spiritual Authority*. Let's have the conversation!

Chapter 1

History of Spiritual Abuse

In the beginning, there was a force, a spiritual entity, hell-bent on deceiving, and ultimately destroying Creation in the belief that our Creator was "holding something from us." The deception of and the disobedience concerning the first man and woman is probably the greatest story ever conveyed in the history of mankind. It has shaped, whether good or bad, every culture upon the face of the Earth. Every sect of civilization has, in some manner, a piece of the Creation story embedded within their culture, religion, and moral compass. Each people group upon the face of the earth has had generational beliefs passed down from their ancestors, in an effort to carry on familial traditions, morals, and beliefs.

The very first instance in recorded history of spiritual abuse was that of our adversary, Satan, in the Garden of Eden when he questioned Eve, "Did God say…?" Adam and Eve both knew distinctly what the Lord had spoken to them, yet one was deceived, while the other outright disobeyed the Creator's commandment. Throughout this book, we will deal with both deception and disobedience, two of the major gateways of gross spiritual abuse that have affected billions upon billions of people throughout history.

Religion and spirituality is one of the most important aspects of our lives. Each of us, innately, holds deep-seated roots within us that point to something greater than ourselves. We all know there is something more than this life and seek our entire lives to find the answers to our existence in this world. We desire to know the "more," and sometimes, we seek out many paths along the way in an effort to find the *Truth*.

Religion is defined as the belief in and worship of a superhuman controlling power, especially a personal God or gods; a particular system of faith and worship; a pursuit or interest to which someone ascribes supreme importance. It comes from the Latin word *Religio*, meaning "restraint," or *Relegere*, according to Roman philosopher Cicero, meaning "to repeat, to read again," or most likely, *Religionem*, "to show respect for what is sacred." It is an organized system of beliefs and practices revolving around, or leading to, a transcendent spiritual experience.

In each culture in recorded human history, there has been some form of practiced religion or spirituality. Whether monotheism (belief in one supreme God, in the religions of Judaism, Christianity, and Islam), henotheism (the belief or worship of a single god in many different forms, while not denying the possible existence of other deities, in the religion of Hinduism), or polytheism (the worship of or belief in multiple deities, usually consisting of gods and goddesses, along with their own religions and rituals, practiced within ancient mythology, some forms of Hinduism, Buddhism, Confucianism, Taoism, Shintoism, and most forms of tribal religions originating in Africa, aboriginal Australia, as well as the early Americas.) There are many other "isms" that deny any existence of a higher power, being, or creator, or those that believe a "higher power" exists, yet has nothing to do with mankind, but we will not deal with those in this book, of course, because they see no reason for any form of spiritual authority.

Religion both now and in ancient times, revolves around the spiritual aspect of the human condition, gods and goddesses (or a single god or goddess), the creation of the world, a human being's place in the world, life after death, eternity, and how to escape from suffering in this world or the next.

Dating back to the earliest known recorded civilization in the world, debated by some, ancient Mesopotamia, or the "cradle of civilization," we see the origins of a polytheistic culture, whereas many gods provided for the many different needs of mankind. The beliefs were that mankind was created to be "co-workers" with the gods to bring order to the world. The first written records of religious practice date to around c.3500 BCE from Sumer, the southernmost region of ancient Mesopotamia, known as modern-day Iraq and Kuwait. The Sumerians called themselves "the black-headed people." Sumer, in biblical times, was known as the land of Shinar. There were earlier known inhabitants known as the *Ubaid* people prior to c.5000 BCE that lived along the banks and region of the Euphrates River. Because there is no recorded written history of their beliefs, the Sumerians are the people group that begins the research and study of ancient religion and spiritual practices of mankind, most likely carrying on the traditions of their forefathers. We know from Biblical accounts, as well as text from both ancient Jewish and Muslim manuscripts, that this region around the Euphrates River is considered the "birthplace of mankind". Even some newfound scripts from Asia and surrounding areas, within Hinduism and Buddhism, reveal the ancient lands bordering the Euphrates River as referencing "the beginning".

It is also very important to note that even in this post-modern civilization, there was the birth of *priesthood* from the beginning. This is the first recorded instance of spiritual leadership in human history. There was the existence of religion and/or spirituality amongst these early inhabitants. It wasn't until around c.2900-2334 BCE that there was a shift from the spiritual priesthood leadership to a more modern-day rule of a king over a nation. Much of the Sumerians' way of life, including religion, was overrun by this government-ruled dynasty, known as the First Dynasty of Lagash in c.2500 BCE. It shifted from being a spiritual kingdom overseen by priests to a worldly empire controlled by power-hungry kings. The Second Dynasty formed the Akkadian Empire c.2334-2218 BCE, the first multi-national empire in the world. We see the earliest known shift from a spiritual people/culture to spiritual practices controlled and manipulated by man. The spiritual decline of these early inhabitants came to an end around c.2047-1750 BCE when the Third Dynasty came into existence. It was known as The Ur III Period, named after the city of Ur. We have Biblical accounts of this city, the city where Abram was born, later named Abraham by God. It is widely

12

accepted that he was born c.1996 BCE. So, he was living in Ur during this time period known as "The Sumerian Renaissance," a great period of technological growth and expansion, but also the end of this ancient people group and their rich culture, language, and yes, spirituality/religion.

In Samuel Noah Kramer's book, *History Begins at Sumer*,[i] he lists thirty-nine "firsts" in history from the region among which are "the first schools, the first proverbs and sayings, the first messiahs, the first Noah and the Flood stories, the first love song, the first aquarium, the first legal precedents in court cases, the first tale of a dying and resurrected god, the first funeral chants, the first biblical parallels, and the first moral ideas."

The Bible, in Genesis 14, reveals to us that Abraham lived in the time of Melchizedek, king of Salem, but also considered by Biblical accounts as "the priest of God". Many theologians perceived Melchizedek as a "theophany," an appearance in human form, of Jesus Christ Himself. He revealed Himself to Abraham and blessed him, as the *High Priest* of God. The Bible likens Melchizedek to our Lord, a type and foreshadow of Jesus Christ Himself, considered our "High Priest," or our Great Shepherd.

"And Melchizedek king of Salem brought forth bread and wine: and he was the priest of the most high God." Genesis 14:18

The narrative of Melchizedek reveals to us the heart of God for His priesthood. This Biblical account makes known to us the sovereignty of God in carrying out His purposes for mankind through spiritual leadership. We no longer see mention of Melchizedek or the "priesthood," until the birth-line introduced through Abraham in the form of the Levitical priesthood through His great-grandson Levi, son of Jacob, later named Israel. The Levitical priesthood would inherit a lesser role of administering spiritual/religious ceremonies over Israel. The Levites' principal roles in the tabernacle, later Temple, included singing Psalms during Temple services, performing construction and maintenance for the Temple, serving as guards, and performing other services. Levites also served as teachers and judges, maintaining cities of refuge in biblical times. It was not until the birth of Aaron that God instituted the role of "High Priest" once again over Israel.

The role of High Priest, instituted by God at Mount Sinai, and the subsequent lineal descent from Aaron, provided the framework for God's authority in the tabernacle/temple of Israel. Though God rendered the blueprint of the construction of the tabernacle to Moses, the spiritual leadership role was allotted to Aaron. The High Priest was the chief religious functionary in the Temple of Jerusalem, whose unique privilege was to enter the Holy of Holies (inner sanctum) once a year on Yom Kippur, the Day of Atonement, to burn incense and sprinkle sacrificial animal blood to make amends for his own sins and those of the people of Israel.

On this occasion, he wore only white linen garments, forgoing the elaborate priestly robes worn during the year whenever he chose to officiate at services. The high priest had overall charge of Temple finances and administration, and in the early period of the Second Temple, he collected taxes and maintained order as the recognized political head of the nation. The high priest could not mourn the dead, had to avoid defilement incurred by proximity to the dead, and could marry only a virgin. The office, first granted to Aaron by his brother Moses, was normally of familial succession and intended for life. In the 2nd century BC, however, bribery led to several reappointments, and the last of the high priests were appointed by government officials or chosen by lot.

The first instance we see of recorded spiritual abuse in the line of Levitical, Aaronic, priesthood and the subsequent downward spiral of corruption and spiritual decline amongst God's chosen spiritual leadership was of Aaron's two eldest sons Nadab and Abihu. They were found desecrating the temple by offering "strange fire" to the Lord.

"Then Nadab and Abihu, the sons of Aaron, each took his censer and put fire in it, put incense on it, and offered profane fire before the Lord, which He had not commanded them. So fire went out from the Lord and devoured them, and they died before the Lord." Leviticus 10:1-2

The Bible says Aaron remained silent and kept his peace. He did not make excuse for the sins of Nadab and Abihu. He accepted the consequences his sons had to pay for their disobedience to God. We do not see any "mercy" offered by God for their disobedience; He immediately rendered judgment for their sin. God spoke to Moses to ordain their successors and younger brothers, Eleazar and Ithamar. Moses gave clear and direct instructions on how to prepare the food offerings and how and where to eat, as the priesthood offering sacrifices for the people's sin. They disobeyed direct orders and selfishly tainted the sin offering. Aaron made account for them by bearing the weight upon himself. He took responsibility for their disobedience. God spared them.

Why in once instance did God strike two priests dead, and in another, spare other priests from death? Again, we will deal later concerning deception verses disobedience, and God's judgment pertaining to each.

"I could no longer be a part of this church, as it was clear our pastors idolized and worshipped their children above God. It did not matter how many times they were caught in adulterous affairs, or how many people came forward as witnesses; these pastors kept releasing them back to preach, as if nothing happened. Sadly, each time they were placed back in authority, it happened again, and again, and again. I hold these pastors just as responsible as the perpetrators of this sexual and spiritual abuse. They led so many people astray. I was hurt so deeply and could not understand why God was not taking them out of these positions of authority. How could they continue to be allowed to sexually abuse people with no repercussions? I left the church for almost ten years and fell away from God altogether." ~*H.D., Ohio*

We see a pattern of continued spiritual abuse in the line of Eli with his sons, Hophni and Phinehas, who inherited the priesthood from Ithamar, Aaron's youngest son. The sons of Eli had little regard for the regulations of the law. The first perversion was that they did not handle and divide the meat of the sacrifice properly. Hophni and Phinehas looked upon the sacrifices not as a means of worshiping God, but as something which was there for their own personal use and pleasure. We see so much of this taking place in the spiritual leadership of today's church. As time went on, they became even more emboldened and began to send their servants to those who came to sacrifice, even before the sacrifice was brought to the altar. The servants would cut the choice portions off the animals before the animals were offered up. This meant that when the sacrifice was brought to the altar, it was only partially there... it was mutilated. This went against all the rules of the sacrifices. The sacrifice had to be brought to the Lord unbroken and not mutilated. For Hophni and Phinehas it was advantageous to take the meat when it was still raw, so that it could be sent to the marketplace and sold. They would keep the money for themselves. They became so bold that they started to take meat by force. The whole spirit of worship was destroyed. The true believers began to turn away due to the perversion they witnessed from these *priests*.

"Now Eli was very old; and he heard everything his sons did to all Israel, and how they lay with the women who assembled at the door of the tabernacle of meeting. So he said to them, "Why do you do such things? For I hear of your evil dealings from all the people. No, my sons! For it is not a good report that I hear. You make the Lord's people transgress. If one man sins against another, God will judge him. But if a man sins against the Lord, who will intercede for him?" Nevertheless they did not heed the voice of their father, because the Lord desired to kill them." 1 Samuel 2:22-25

Finally, it became known that these men were seducing and committing immoral acts with some of the women who came regularly to help in the service of the tabernacle. The tabernacle of God was beginning to resemble the pagan temples. The sons of Eli had corrupted the true worship of Jehovah. God sent Samuel the prophet to prophesy to Eli that he and his sons would suffer great consequences for their disobedience to His commands. Both Eli and his sons died, and subsequently, the Ark of the Covenant, *the presence of God*, was taken away by the Philistines.

"My heart grieves deeply for the Church today. So many have adopted the corruption and perversion witnessed in the early priesthood. I was a part of this church for over thirty years. I was one of the few that began with these pastors fresh out of seminary. We started the church in their home. Starting out, and well into twenty years of ministry, they were committed to the call of spiritual leadership. The humility and reverence for God and the work of the Lord was evident upon their lives. We walked with them through many hard and difficult times, yet they remained faithful to the cause of Christ. Around the year 2000, something drastically changed. Our pastors were now coveting the spotlight. They were bringing more *well-known* pastors to speak at our church, and with this came pride, arrogance, and what we termed a "Hollywood spirit". Instead of being co-servants along with our pastors, we were now seen as their "servants". We were commanded to serve these visiting pastors not in godly service, but like slaves. We remained in this church for another fifteen years, until we could take no more. This church had now become a *den of thieves*." ~*F.B.L. former pastor, WA.*

According to tradition, eighteen high priests served in Solomon's Temple (c. 960–586 BC) and sixty in the Second Temple (516 BC–AD 70). Since that time, there has been no Jewish high priest, because national sacrifice was permanently interrupted with the destruction of the Second Temple. It was also the end of lineal succession of spiritual and religious leadership. God's ordained spiritual seed was corrupted until the Great High Priest Himself, Jesus Christ/Yeshua HaMashiach, ascended to the throne of Heaven.

Many have since either accepted the call of true, authentic spiritual leadership or have seen an opportunity for financial prosperity and influence and accepted a career in preaching. Sadly today, there are more people seeking careers in preaching than those accepting their call as pastors/spiritual leaders. May God reveal His called and appointed, and expose the false and counterfeit, so His people can be led in His ways and walk in His will, that we may once again fear, reverence, the Lord our God.

Chapter 2

The Call of
True Spiritual Leadership

"Although He was a Son, He learned obedience from the things which He suffered. And having been made perfect, He became to all those who obey Him the source of eternal salvation, being designated by God as a high priest according to the order of Melchizedek." Hebrews 5:8-10

We expect those who call themselves spiritual leaders in our lives to uphold the sacred vows they took before God, as they accepted the "call" upon their lives to lead people in love and in truth. Spiritual leadership is one of the greatest calls, assignments, on Earth. Standing in the gap between God and man, as viewed through the role of the early high priest, is an honor and a privilege bestowed upon man by the Creator. Though our true High Priest ultimately broke down the middle wall of partition between God and man with His death, burial, and resurrection, we yet have men standing today in the stead of spiritual leadership in the earth realm.

Over the years, there have been many humble and selfless men and women that have accepted this earthly call to lead God's people. They never sought out fortune or fame, but simply desired to do the will of God. They lived their entire lives sold out and submitted to the Father.

"In over five decades of preaching the Gospel, I have never witnessed such gross disregard and disrespect for the anointing of God. Our houses of worship have turned into circus tents, "dog and pony shows," all to attract the crowds. This was never our example, and we are seeing a great decline is true spiritual leadership in the Church. Many of those called by God have walked away due to the evident apostasy in most churches today or have been run away or "voted" out by imposters and opportunists. We are in very crucial times. May God raise up His remnant in the Earth." *~A.J. Graham, retired pastor/North Carolina*

So many things vie for our attention. Voices from every corner of our lives are given so much space that we neglect the *still small voice* of our Lord. We were created to worship Him. Worship is not just singing a worship song, but it is intimate fellowship, relationship, with Father God. He longs to speak with us. He longs to sit with us and hear our voices. It gives Him great pleasure to commune with His children. As we take time to set ourselves apart, times of consecration, we enter into a realm where the heavenly meets the earthly. Supernatural communication is a necessary part of a Believer's life, especially those in spiritual leadership. We are spirit beings living in a natural world. Our spirits long for heavenly interaction, and when we don't receive it, we become almost lethargic in our everyday lives. David, in the Psalms, says it so beautifully:

"O God, thou art my God; early will I seek thee: my soul thirsteth for thee, my flesh longeth for thee in a dry and thirsty land, where no water is;" Psalm 63:1

Daily communion with our Lord is pertinent to our spiritual health. It is sustenance for the Believer. Just as our physical bodies need water, food, and exercise to live and be healthy, so, too, our spirits need daily intake from the supernatural realm. *Consecration* is defined as to make or declare sacred or holy; set apart, sanctify or to dedicate (one's life, time, etc.) to a specific purpose. In Biblical days, we often saw people consecrating themselves for the service of the Lord or for ordained times and seasons. Another word that is related to setting apart is *sanctify*, which means to make holy; set apart as sacred; consecrate.

"And Joshua said unto the people, Sanctify yourselves: for to morrow the Lord will do wonders among you." Joshua 3:5

Joshua encouraged the people to sanctify themselves, because God was ready to manifest wonders in their midst. It is extremely important for pastors/leaders to set themselves apart, to take quality time in the presence of the Lord, so one, they can be refreshed and hear clearly from the Lord, but also to hear clearly for those they have been called to lead. Joshua was able to hear pertinent instructions for the people. Not just a "catchy" sermon, but he was able to hear God's plans and purposes for the children of Israel, so he could prepare them for the journey.

The act of consecrating implies a process of preparation. We cannot rush time spent in the presence of the Lord. It is a time of refining, a time of purging, a time of renewal, and a time of restoration.... a *process*. In the days of the Levitical priesthood, much care was put into preparing oneself for consecration, even the specific instructions given by Moses on how to prepare the sacrifices. In making a commitment to set ourselves apart, God will give us clear and precise direction. He will tell us the what, when, where, who, why, how, and how long, as we seek His face. So many times, we act based upon our feelings, or what we see others doing, or what others advise us to do, instead of taking quality, intimate time away with the One who created us; the One who knows everything about us and has the answers we need.

"And ye shall not go out of the door of the tabernacle of the congregation in seven days, until the days of your consecration be at an end: for seven days shall he consecrate you." Leviticus 8:33

God gives specific instructions on how long the priests were to set themselves apart. We see this pattern all throughout the Bible. Each was prepared in some form, whether by consecration, sanctification, or separation. Here are a few examples:

- **Jeremiah**: "And it came to pass after ten days, that the word of the Lord came unto Jeremiah." Jeremiah 42:7
- **Noah**: "So he waited yet another seven days and sent out the dove, which did not return to him anymore." Genesis 8:12
- **Samson**: "And He said to me, 'Behold, you shall conceive and bear a son. Now drink no wine or similar drink, nor eat anything unclean, for the child shall be a Nazirite to God from the womb to the day of his death'" Judges 13:7
- **Ruth**: "So she kept fast by the maidens of Boaz to glean unto the end of barley harvest and of wheat harvest; and dwelt with her mother in law." Ruth 2:23
- **Samuel**: "And the child Samuel grew on, and was in favour both with the Lord, and also with men." 1 Samuel 2:26
- **David**: "And Samuel said unto Jesse, Are here all thy children? And he said, There remaineth yet the youngest, and, behold, he keepeth the sheep. And Samuel said unto Jesse, Send and fetch him: for we will not sit down till he come hither." 1 Samuel 16:11
- **Esther**: "Now when every maid's turn was come to go in to king Ahasuerus, after that she had been twelve months, according to the manner of the women, (for so were the days of their purifications accomplished, to wit, six months with oil of myrrh, and six months with sweet odours, and with other things for the purifying of the women;)" Esther 2:12
- **Job**: "And it was so, when the days of their feasting were gone about, that Job sent and sanctified them, and rose up early in the morning, and offered burnt offerings according to the number of them all: for Job said, It may be that my sons have sinned, and cursed God in their hearts. Thus did Job continually." Job 1:5

- **Daniel**: "Prove thy servants, I beseech thee, ten days; and let them give us pulse to eat, and water to drink." Daniel 1:12
- **Jesus**: "And when he had fasted forty days and forty nights, he was afterward an hungered." Matthew 4:2

Each of these Biblical figures had to endure their own processes in order to fulfill God's plan for their lives. They separated themselves apart for the Lord and each was used mightily by God. Purpose to set aside times of consecration for spiritual growth and intimacy with God, so you are able to hear His voice clearly, and so you will not be deceived.

Here are seven characteristics, or attributes (surely not exhaustive) of true spiritual leadership:

❖ Suffering   ❖ Submission
❖ Servant   ❖ Surrender
❖ Selfless   ❖ Sonship
❖ Sacrifice

1. Suffering

In today's modern church, especially in Western culture, we don't see the spiritual attribute of *suffering* any longer. Though the entirety of Scripture, from Old Testament to New Testament, reveals continual suffering for those that have followed God, pre-Resurrection and post-Resurrection, we do not see this teaching in the majority of churches around the world today. Many possess a theology that encourages prosperity and denounces any sort of suffering for the believer in Christ

26

Jesus. They attest that because Jesus/Yeshua suffered on the Cross for us, we in no way should suffer, yet is this biblical? The opening scripture reveals to us that though He was a son, He learned obedience through that which He *suffered*. Yes, He was sent into this world to suffer ultimately, on our behalf, but He was our example in every way. Suffering produces obedience in our lives. God desires each of us to be renewed and transformed from our old ways and mindsets into a new creation in Christ. This process comes with suffering, or in other words, denying our flesh, picking up our cross, and laying down our lives for Christ... *suffering*.

"Then He said to them all, "If anyone desires to come after Me, let him deny himself, and take up his cross daily, and follow Me." Luke 9:23

To follow Jesus/Yeshua, we are gifted with a life of suffering, or following by example His ways, His walk, and His will. It is not necessarily the suffering many think, but we are, indeed, as born-again believers, called to suffer for the Kingdom of God. *Suffering* is defined as the state of undergoing pain, distress, or hardship, to experience or be subjected to something bad or unpleasant. The Hebrew word is *penthos*, meaning mourning, sorrow, sadness, or grief. Jesus suffered greatly at the state of the world. He grieved deeply the sin of humanity, and He spoke out boldly, yet lovingly, for a turning away from evil and a turning toward the Father. In doing so, He suffered tremendously for the cause of the Gospel. So, too, we should pick up this cross of suffering and carry it in His name, especially those called to spiritual leadership. Just as Jesus/Yeshua was/is our ultimate example, those called to stand in His stead in the earth realm should exemplify the sufferings of Christ in their lives.

"Beloved, do not think it strange concerning the fiery trial which is to try you, as though some strange thing happened to you; but rejoice to the extent that you partake of Christ's sufferings, that when His glory is revealed, you may also be glad with exceeding joy." 1 Peter 4:12-13

In doing so, we reveal the glory of God through our lives and we lead others to a life lived for His ultimate glory.

2. Servant

Many titles have been bestowed upon those that feel God has called them in the area of spiritual leadership from preacher, pastor, bishop, prophet, apostle to reverend, but the Word of God tells us that the greatest title any spiritual leader can ever attain is that of a *servant*. *Servant* is defined as a person who performs duties for others, especially a person employed in a house on domestic duties or as a personal attendant. Strangely enough, as I studied the duties of the early high priests in the tabernacle/temple, domestic duties such as construction and maintenance were some of their primary roles. Why do we no longer see these principal duties performed by spiritual leadership today? Sadly, many feel they are "above" such roles and consider these positions beneath their "high calling". The Hebrew word for servant is *ebed*, meaning slave. The Greek is *diakonos*, referred to as a minister, an attendant, a waiter (at table or menial duties), especially a Christian teacher or pastor. Are these characteristics or attributes we see in or hear of concerning spiritual leaders in today's church? Unfortunately, we rarely see this carried out in the culture of the modern-day Western church.

"But Jesus called them to Himself and said, "You know that the rulers of the Gentiles lord it over them, and those who are great exercise authority over them. Yet it shall not be so among you; but whoever desires to become great among you, let him be your servant." Matthew 20:25-26

Jesus was the greatest servant in the history of the world. His entire public ministry centered on serving those around Him. He humbled Himself greatly and though He knew and was aware of His authority as the Son of God, and His calling as the Savior, He became "low" in an effort to reveal the love and compassion of the Father to humanity. He didn't seek to be served... He embodied *Servanthood*. This is the blueprint for true, authentic spiritual leadership.

"For even the Son of Man did not come to be served, but to serve, and to give His life a ransom for many." Mark 10:45

May we seek to serve those God has entrusted to our spiritual leadership with love, humility, compassion, and servitude.

3. <u>Selfless</u>

The true Gospel narrative is a *selfless* portrayal of absolute love. Our Lord laid down His life for us, so that we could live eternally with the Father. He took off eternity and put on humanity, standing in the gap between heaven and earth, and died on a cross for our sins. There is no single act of selflessness upon the face of the Earth that can compare to what Jesus/Yeshua did for the world. *Selfless* is defined as having or showing great concern for other people and little or no concern for yourself. There is a Hebrew word that typifies this attribute, and it is so fitting, especially in the life of someone that leads spiritually... *ahava*. Hebraically *ahava* is used as a verb and a noun; it is an act of doing, not simply a feeling. It means to give. It is more concerned with giving, than of receiving.

"For God so loved the world that He gave His only begotten Son, that whoever believes in Him should not perish but have everlasting life." John 3:16

God gave us His ultimate gift... His only Son, in exchange for our sinful nature, so that we may live eternally in unbroken fellowship with Him... the epitome of *selflessness*. How many of us can say we would give in such a way to others? As spiritual leaders, we are called to die to self and live in service to others. This reveals the character of Christ in our lives, so others may see Him through us. We have the greatest example of all in the birth, life, burial, and resurrection of our Lord and

Savior, Jesus Christ/Yeshua HaMashiach... *the selfless servant.* May we seek to daily imitate His way, His walk, and His will.

"Let no one seek his own, but each one the other's well-being." 1 Corinthians 10:24

4. <u>Sacrifice</u>

Leadership has always been, from inception and intent, an ultimate form of *sacrifice.* Those that seek or have even been ordained by God to lead people, must go through great testing, trials, and processes before taking on or receiving any sort of leadership role in someone else's life. This is not something to be taken lightly nor is it something to be flippantly accepted by those not prepared or purposed for such a role. Leadership requires great amounts of time, resources, prayer, and building. Whether secular or spiritual, leaders are the foundation of any business or ministry. They must *be,* before they can expect anyone else to *become.* They are the forerunners, the visionaries, the trailblazers... the pioneers. Their sacrifices pave the way for those coming behind them, those willing to "grab the baton" and "carry the torch".

As spiritual leaders, we are charged to live sacrificial lives before those we are called to serve. We are entrusted with the sacred role of living, by example, as Christ lived before us and gave His life for us.

"And walk in love, as Christ also has loved us and given Himself for us, an offering and a sacrifice to God for a sweet-smelling aroma." Ephesians 5:2

31

May your life, as one called of God, display the beauty of sacrifice not only to those you have been called to serve, but ultimately, to the One that sacrificed all to offer you eternal salvation.

5. <u>Submission</u>

One of the least taught and preached attributes of spiritual leadership is that of *submission*. We have donned this role upon women for centuries, ignorantly thinking this is only something God has commanded women to adhere to within the confines of marriage. Yet, submission is something God desires us all to walk in within every aspect of our lives. I wrote my first book entitled, *Breaking the Eve Mentality*[ii] on the subject of submission. As God began to give me His heart for this topic, and what it was originally intended to produce in our lives, this book progressed from being a treatise on submission for women, to a manual on how to live our lives entirely submitted to the will of God.

What is the *will*? The *will* is defined as control deliberately exerted to do something or to restrain one's own impulses. It also means the faculty by which a person decides on and initiates action, or a deliberate or fixed desire or intention. These definitions are from a human standpoint or from the view of individual choice, as it relates to making decisions in our own lives. The Hebrew word *davar* is translated as *word*, as well as *will*. It is defined as desire, intent, wish, want, have in mind, aim, testament, or order. Ultimately, God's will is His Word... the Holy Spirit inspired written Word of God found in the ancient writings of the Torah, as well as the Bible. Those that heard the voice of God, as well as walked with Jesus/Yeshua on the Earth, recorded these words for all of humanity to live under its teachings. This is God's desire... His intent, His wish, His aim, His order... His Word... His will!

We are to submit to the will of God in all areas of our lives. As spiritual leaders, we have made an oath to live by the very precepts of this Gospel. We have the words of life and eternity living within us, and we are to walk as living, breathing epistles of the Word of God. Our submission to His Word and to His Spirit gives us absolute assurance that we are living in His will. As we submit to the Lord, we are able to submit in every single area of life. This brings peace and order not only in our lives, but in the lives of those we have been called to lead. Ultimately, submission is obedience to God's Word, His will. Our Lord is the greatest picture of submission ever to walk the face of the Earth.

"And being found in appearance as a man, He humbled himself and became obedient to the point of death, even the death of the cross."
Philippians 2:8

May we heed the wisdom of God and walk in heartfelt submission to Him, so we can be true examples of love and light before this lost and dying world.

6. <u>Surrender</u>

The thought of *surrender* in most settings is definitely not what the majority of people would choose or even desire. This word encapsulates all of the aforementioned attributes of spiritual leadership: suffering, servanthood, selflessness, sacrifice, and submission. *Surrender* is defined as to cease resistance to an enemy or opponent and submit to their authority, to give up or hand over a person, right, or possession, typically on compulsion or demand, to abandon oneself entirely. The Hebrew word is *paradidomi,* which means to give into the hands of another, to give over into one's power, to deliver up one to custody, to betray, to cast, or to put in prison. As spiritual leaders, we are called and commanded by God to "surrender" to His will. We must abandon ourselves entirely to the cause of Christ in the earth, and ultimately "betray the world," if you will, in order to walk with Him. Just as Paul and Peter were thrust into prison for the sake of the Gospel, so, too, we must surrender all to accept the sacred call of God upon our lives.

Sadly, many spiritual leaders in our pulpits today don't know at all what it means to surrender in this manner, and if they were strictly held to these standards, would most likely quit their jobs and find a new career path. Therefore, the call to true, authentic spiritual leadership is so crucial and something that is not to be taken lightly or callously.

"I have been crucified with Christ; and it is no longer I who live, but Christ lives in me; and the life which I now live in the flesh I live by faith in the Son of God, who loved me and gave Himself up for me." Galatians 2:20

7. <u>Sonship</u>
In Hebrew tradition, there was an appointed time where every Hebrew boy was determined to be a "full grown" son, with all the rights and privileges of sonship. It was at this crossroad that the young man

would no longer need an overseer to watch over him and keep him in check. There was now a natural understanding between father and son that he was no longer a child, but a full-grown son and no longer under the law, but under grace. This transition period is very important in the life of every Believer. We are deemed "sons" of God through a process of maturation in the Word of God and by the Spirit of God living within us, causing us to live as sons and not slaves to the sin that once held us in bondage.

"And because you are sons, God has sent forth the Spirit of His Son into your hearts, crying out, "Abba, Father!" Therefore you are no longer a slave but a son, and if a son, then an heir of God through Christ." Galatians 4:6-7

Unfortunately, many spiritual leaders in today's church were never processed as *sons*, but rather skipped this crucial course and took on positions that some were never ordained to operate in and others, simply not ready or prepared to fully carry out. Sonship is a pertinent key to walking in discernment and wisdom, especially as a spiritual leader. When we reject this process, we ultimately reject God as our Father. May we all humble ourselves under His loving care and allow Him to transform us into true sons of God.

"I was raised in the church. My father, grandfather, and great-grandfather were preachers. I believe it went back even further, but I don't have records to verify. Church was *in my blood*. I was groomed to preach at an early age, and I preached my first sermon at twelve-years-old. As I matured, I began to see things that I just could not believe being done to people in our church, and yes, by my father and grandfather. I have to believe they *inherited* this from my great-grandfather and those before him. I knew enough of the Bible to understand what they were doing was definitely not of God. They would go to people's homes that had not given in the offering plate and force them to give whatever they had, threatening them that if they didn't, God would punish them. There was mental, emotional, and yes, physical abuse that took place from the pulpit and it was passed off as the correction of God. Our church was not a church of love, but of control, and sadly, I witnessed my own family carry it out.

I confronted my father and was ex-communicated from my church and family at the age of seventeen. I knew God called me to preach, and I knew He was showing me this was not of Him. I got under a godly church and served faithfully, until being released to preach. I have been preaching for over forty years and I have witnessed God's true servants and I have run into opportunists. Sadly, there are not many true servants still preaching today." ~*Rev. W.D., Virginia*

The pathway of true, authentic spiritual leadership, as well as the walk of any true Believer in Christ Jesus, is narrow. We are called to the ministry of suffering, servanthood, selflessness, sacrifice, submission, surrender, and sonship. These very attributes, our Lord Jesus Christ embodied. He personified the role of headship; He is our greatest example of spiritual leadership; He is our High Priest. His very life, death, burial, and resurrection centered around and culminated in the very act of laying down His life for mankind. He is our Great Shepherd, and has, indeed, ordained a company of *under shepherds* to lead, guide, direct, and serve His people in the earth realm.

"And Jesus, when He came out, saw a great multitude and was moved with compassion for them, because they were like sheep not having a shepherd. So He began to teach them many things." Mark 6:34

As we imitate and emulate the life and leadership of Jesus Christ/Yeshua HaMashiach, people's lives are blessed, and they are prepared through discipleship. I was once under the leadership of a pastor that spoke this phrase often, "Follow me as I follow Jesus. If I ever stop following Jesus, stop following me and run as fast as you can." Sadly, and unfortunately, he stopped following the ways of Jesus and made some very disturbing choices, which led me and many others to run as far as we could in the opposite direction of his leadership.

"For God is not unjust to forget your work and labor of love which you have shown toward His name, in that you have ministered to the saints, and do minister. And we desire that each one of you show the same diligence to the full assurance of hope until the end, that you do not

become sluggish, but imitate those who through faith and patience inherit the promises." Hebrews 6:10-14

We are encouraged as spiritual leaders that God will not forget the heartfelt labor of love, we offer freely to His people in service to Him. We are admonished to continue in this same service to the Father to the end, through their example. This is a beautiful scripture given to us by God that reveals the heart of true spiritual leadership and its impact upon humanity. It also implies that if we do not follow this blueprint, as spiritual leaders, then we can surely have a negative impact on those we lead. Please notice that this scripture says to *imitate* those who through faith and patience inherit the promises. The King James Version does say to *follow*, but we must understand it does not mean to follow man, but to imitate the ways of God in and through those that lead. We are living in a very dangerous time where people are following men, instead of God.

We are grateful to God for the true, authentic spiritual leaders still standing for righteousness, holiness, integrity, and truth. Your obedience to preach the incorruptible Word of God and truly lay down your lives for the cause of Christ in such deceptive times is to be honored and commended. May we wholeheartedly cover and intercede for these precious servants of God.

Chapter 3

The Great Deception

"No one can serve two masters; for either he will hate the one and love the other, or else he will be loyal to the one and despise the other. You cannot serve God and mammon." Matthew 6:24

Spiritual deception has been around since the Beginning, because evil has been present since the fall, at the inception of Creation. The Bible speaks of the curse being pronounced in Genesis 3:15 upon the woman and the serpent as being a *protevanglium*, or the "first mention" of the Good News of salvation. It is God prophesying the coming Messiah and the war, if you will, between the seed of Satan and the seed of the woman. This *war* is the battle between good and evil… between the children of God and the children of Satan. Read this verse:

"And I will put enmity between you and the woman, and between your seed and her Seed; He shall bruise your head, and you shall bruise His heel." Genesis 3:15

THE ELEPHANT IN THE ROOM

The word *enmity* is defined as the state or feeling of being actively opposed or hostile to someone or something; animosity, hatred, conflict, or malice. The deception enacted in the Garden by way of the serpent carved a path of darkness for humanity that we have been trying to rectify ever since. The absolute hatred of God's Creation, a spiritual people, true worshipers of the Creator, led to a cycle of deception that continues to this day. Throughout history, we have seen and witnessed moral compass (spiritual laws and guidelines) recorded in every civilization on the face of the Earth. Each tribe, community, across the globe has had some sort of code of ethics engrained within their heritage, passed down from generation to generation, and the head of every one has been a spiritual leader of some sort, whether priest, shaman, imam, rabbi, monk, or pastor.

Even when governmental entities began to take over nations, there was still reverence for the spiritual leadership in each governing territory. There was deep respect and honor given to the one, or groups of individuals, that were known as the ones, that heard from heaven... the ones that could see and hear on behalf of the people. These people were set apart and sanctified for the work of God. They consecrated themselves to this work and committed their lives to daily service unto God and humanity. These spiritual leaders understood their *lot* and forsook the pleasures and riches of this world to take on such a revered and humble existence, in service to the Creator and the created. What happened? Where did the breach occur causing this once holy call to become corrupted and perverted?

"I had known my pastor since we were in high school. He grew up in the church and ever since I can remember, he said he was going to be a pastor one day. In the time we were raised in the church, there was no "celebrity" spirit; the call was feared and reverenced. We knew what holiness meant and it was preached heavily in our denomination. Upon the turn of the twentieth century, something really shifted, and he began to shift with it, adopting practices and a lifestyle never seen by a pastor in our church. It was like Dr. Jekyll and Mr. Hyde... he changed so quickly into this monster demanding us all to worship him and then back into this humble servant in an instant. I knew if he did not humble himself and accept correction, in love, he was heading for ultimate destruction. Regrettably, that is exactly what transpired in our church. He would listen to no one, and eventually, he was removed as pastor of our church. The spirit of mammon overtook this man's life, and he is still running from city to city trying to find someone to let him preach. This is truly the most evil spirit I have witnessed in the church today."
~Elder J.R., COGIC denomination, Hattiesburg, MS.

THE SPIRIT OF MAMMON

The *spirit of mammon* mentioned in the Bible, as well as other ancient texts, reveals the root and ultimate stronghold so prevalent today amongst spiritual leadership worldwide. *Mammon* is defined as wealth regarded as an evil influence or false object of worship and devotion. It was taken by medieval writers as the name of the devil of covetousness. Biblically, in ancient Aramaic, it simply means "riches" or "greedy gain". God states that we cannot serve two masters for we will love one and hate the other. Its implication is that if we seek one, we cannot be loyal to and will ultimately despise the other.

From the earliest of spiritual texts, we see the *spirit of mammon* in operation. As stated in an earlier chapter, one of the greatest commands for spiritual leadership is to be set apart, or consecrated, for the work of the Lord. Priests and other spiritual leaders were hidden, to an extent, and found separated from the masses in solitude to hear from God, as well as in worship and meditation. We saw this in the life of Moses, Abraham, and yes, even in the life of Jesus Christ/Yeshua HaMashiach. They were frequently seen going *out*, in seclusion, from the people and making themselves available to God. When we stray away from this blueprint, we subsequently open the door for the enemy to come in and corrupt and pervert that which was meant to be holy.

"... but we will give ourselves continually to prayer and to the ministry of the word." Acts 6:4

In today's spiritual culture, we see the tendency for leaders to constantly seek the spotlight. They have forsaken the holy *vestments* and replaced them with worldly *garments*. With the emergence of mega churches in the last few decades, and the celebrity spirit that has subsequently followed, we have noticed a drastic shift in the way the role of a pastor, or spiritual leadership of the Church, has transformed. Mind you, the idea of a "mega" church has been around for centuries. We saw Jesus feed five thousand men, not including the number of women and children present with them. This number is said to have possibly been close to ten thousand or more. It is not the number of people that is the ultimate issue; it is the *spirit* behind the mega church culture that is destroying the spiritual legacy of the Church.

We have a very real enemy that desires to corrupt and pervert the holiness and sanctity of the Church. His desire is to distract, deceive, and ultimately, destroy the seed of Christ in the earth realm. Many believers ignorantly perceive Satan as this horned, red devil so prevalently displayed on television and in the media. Remember, he transforms himself as an "angel of light" (2 Corinthians 11:14). He comes to tempt and to persuade us to follow that which "looks good". He twists and perverts Scripture, in order to pull us into his web of deceit.

So many spiritual leaders have fallen into this trap and have disobeyed the voice of God to separate and consecrate themselves to this higher calling. This did not happen overnight; it was a subtle progression of choices made throughout their service to God. Each time Holy Spirit would warn them not to do certain things or not to covenant with certain individuals, they disobeyed His voice. The voices of others became louder than the voice within. The promises of wealth, fame, and influence overshadowed the ultimate promise of God for eternity. In their disobedience, they opened the door to deception.

Spiritual leadership has traded loyalty and servanthood to God for their name in lights. They have taken on the spirit of this world. Sadly, this *spirit of mammon* has so penetrated the modern-day church that it no longer looks, sounds, or even feels like church any longer. The state the church is in today is very disturbing. Surely not some great epiphany, as the writers of the Bible prophesied it thousands of years ago. Yet, it doesn't ease the sting of its effect on society. The Church should be a place of great humility, compassion, and love, but the "riches and fame" of this world has stifled the presence of God and left us with entertainment, instead of anointing; itching ears, instead of convicted hearts. Holiness has all but dissipated into jumping and shouting (an outward appearance), instead of the inward transformation of a heart submitted and surrendered to the Lord.

"My heart breaks deeply for the state the Church is in today. No more do we see the moral compass and sacred humility once lived out in the majority of churches in the past. So many are seeing and seeking the opportunities and advancements now available to pastors/ministers that were not accessible many years ago. Masses are now claiming this as the *favor* of God upon His people, but this is not the favor of God; it is the deception of our enemy. I have witnessed humble, heartfelt servants of God transform into harsh, egotistical power-driven monsters. Many of these were peers of mine. When I refused to *jump on the bullet train* of the wealth and prosperity gospel, I was blacklisted among my fellow pastors/ministers. They claimed I had a poverty mindset and purposed to separate themselves from me and my family, so our toxic thinking would not stain their "faith". Truly sad, right? I left the organized church and now do extensive missions work around the world. I did not know how blinded I was by the enemy and "Christendom," until I actually stepped out of the four walls of the church into the world and began spreading the true Gospel of Jesus Christ.

Sad to say, many of my dear and once closest friends are so caught up in the fame, the wealth, the influence, and the power that they refuse to hear the authentic voice of God, Holy Spirit. I have tried to minister the truth of this deception to many of them, and yet they continue to build their precious earthly empires. They are still purchasing their million-dollar mansions and private jets. Unfortunately, they no longer know the true meaning of the Gospel." ~A.W., *Former Pastor, now missionary of the Gospel, TX*

"For what will it profit a man if he gains the whole world and lose his soul." Mark 8:36

We have confused going "out" into the world to let the light of Jesus shine through us with mingling "in" and "with" the world. We have played the harlot all in the name of winning the world to Christ. We walk on their red carpets, stand in front of their billboards, entertain their demonic events, pose for photos, invite them to sing worldly music in our sacred services, let them speak across the pulpit and "tweet" across social media about how wonderful they are and how enticing are their sinful lifestyles. We promote sinful music, television shows, and other media outlets, and are watering down our messages, so as not to offend them or run them away. Many give huge amounts of money to the church, so this "paralyzes" the leaders, as they no longer trust in God to provide, but man. They are now under the control of the enemy of their souls. Compromise has now bred disobedience *and* rebellion...subtle witchcraft.

"For rebellion is as the sin of witchcraft and stubbornness is as iniquity and idolatry. Because you have rejected the word of the Lord, He also has rejected you from being king." 1 Samuel 15:23

God is calling us to repent! He has sent prophet after prophet to warn God's shepherds to humble themselves and repent. The stage lights have all but blinded them to holiness and the true Gospel of Jesus Christ. Holy Spirit no longer moves them; money, status, and fame have consumed them. But the lights are beginning to fade away. The soul longs for pleasure, but the spirit thirsts for righteousness. The two cannot coexist cohesively.

THE GREAT DECEPTION

God is calling us to separate from the world. We are called to be *in* the world, but not *of* the world. All throughout scripture, we saw men and women whom God placed in the world to shift it, not to become a part of it. The Church has backslidden so far away from its purpose, because the *love of money* and *fame* has overtaken it. The Bible says it's the "root of all evil." I have witnessed much evil all in the *name of Jesus* in churches all over the world. The things I have seen with my natural eyes, as well as in prophetic dreams from the Lord, has sent me to my knees in prayer and intercession many times. I would weep incessantly for hours upon hours and cry out to God to open the eyes of our shepherds. He continued to show me several spiritual leaders, specifically, to cover and pray for over years of intercession.

One by one, He would lead me across their paths. He began to give me specific words to prophesy to them. One by one, they would ignore me or attack me. One by one, the words began to manifest in their lives and in their churches. Churches split, marriages were defiled, and many people were hurt. This "celebrity" spirit God had shown me years ago was manifesting in the Church. The lusts of fame and fortune, disguised as *favor*... the spotlight, is consuming the modern-day church and its spiritual leaders. No longer are they seeking the Lord for direction, but they are now hiring consulting firms and marketing strategists. Multi-million-dollar deals are being made with the world. They no longer need God! They have slept with the devil himself! They are totally self-sufficient now; and will tell you, "You can do this too!" What have we done? We have created a new *church culture* that is independent of

God's leading and anointing, and interdependent within the confines of this new *church system*.

What happens when the lights fade? What happens when your voice is replaced with a new, fresh, young voice? What happens when your face is no longer on all the flyers, billboards, conference "line-ups," or television screens? What happens when you are no longer gracing the New York Times Best Seller list? What happens when you no longer see your name on the list of "America's Top 100 Churches?" What happens when you become *washed up* and they are no longer making money off of you and the "Gospel"? Let me tell you, *exactly* what they do in the world to those celebrities who sell their souls for fame and fortune. Please don't think you can make a pact with the devil, get what you want, and get out! The enemy's main goal is not money and fame, it is your soul. This "celebrity" spirit in the church is the most demonic spirit I have seen. It is, indeed, the *spirit of mammon*. And, as we see every day, it is ravaging the most gifted and talented singers, actors, and musicians in our world today. These precious people have sold their souls to the devil. And he is now coming **boldly** after the Church: pastors, psalmists, ministers, musicians, prophets, and whoever else he can tempt with fame and fortune, *mammon*.

Our spiritual leaders are being *pimped* across national television. The Gospel of Jesus Christ is being mocked and ridiculed, because we sold out for "thirty pieces of silver!" Our Christian artists are being played like a fiddle by the machine of the music industry, promising a platform, but they will suck the Spirit of God right out of you. They will dangle gifts in front of you and draw you in to taint the Christ in you, and in the end, you are singing the devil's tune. It is time for us to WAKE UP!!! This world doesn't want our God! They want to make money off you, and then spit you out. The spotlight will fade. The question is, when it does, will there be any *light* left in you? There is Good News! Jesus Christ/Yeshua HaMashiach, the Son of the Living God, came to die for you and for me. Humble yourself, repent, and turn back to your first love. This world has nothing to offer us! The day is coming, and very soon, when the LIGHT OF THIS WORLD, will be the only spotlight we see. His Light will pierce every bit of darkness and we will stand "naked" before Him once again. It is not worth losing our souls. I don't know about you, but I do not want to be the one to whom He says, "I never knew you, depart from Me." Matthew 7:21-23

Our biblical blueprint clearly reveals this is neither the heart nor the example of true, spiritual leadership coined by Jesus' earthly ministry. Our Lord strayed away from such debacles to reserve the glory for all earthly signs, wonders, and miracles released through Him to Father God. He humbled Himself and pointed others to the Father. May we follow His example and turn away from this deception and turn back to Him wholeheartedly.

WOLVES IN SHEEP'S CLOTHING

The progression, or "shift," within the Church over the last 10-20 years is not one that we can boast about. We have adopted a *marketable* prototype, instead of a God-breathed, Holy Spirit infused movement of God. There are many different finds and several statistics that have been done on church growth over this time span. In fact, much of it is done from within, not without. Churches now have strategizers, businessmen and women that are paid to *sell* the Church to the world. They brainstorm to locate the right demographic and its culture to determine who to bring to a service or conference. They bring the best, if you will, to pack out churches and auditoriums in an effort to get the most they can in offerings and/or ticket sales. The efforts are honed in the area of financing first, instead of counting the costs of *who* ultimately, they are drawing to these 'spiritual' settings.

"But he that is an hireling, and not the shepherd, whose own the sheep are not, seeth the wolf coming, and leaveth the sheep, and fleeth: and the wolf catcheth them, and scattereth the sheep." John 10:12

I was a part of the mega church culture for almost seven years and the things I witnessed were absolutely demonic in nature. Notwithstanding what is seen in the highways and byways of the foyers or entrances with people held waiting to enter these events who are cursing one another and physically fighting each other to get to seats, there is also the hidden casualties of the celebrity culture at work behind the scenes. I have witnessed some of the most heart-wrenching acts of demonic influence in church offices, side rooms, and hallways where the outside world is not privy to observe. Worship leaders who fight for leads, and tear down another brother or sister before ministering and go out on the platform as if nothing just happened? Pastor's wives with the ugliest of attitudes prancing around like they are *Queens* and belittling the people they are called to serve. I have witnessed meeting a pastor's wife for the very first time, in an intimate setting of someone's home and at first; I was completely ignored for over an hour of being there. Once the time came where we were in the same room, the nastiness of attitude that came out completely threw me off because one, I did not even know this woman and two, I said to myself, "Is this the pastor's wife???" I don't care where we are or who we *think* we are, always share kindness and love to people, especially if you are "called" to shepherd God's people! But sadly, the pride and arrogance that I witness in these cultures is very far from godly anything.

This celebrity culture has done so much damage in the Church. Not only are we prancing our pastors in like they are gods, but we are also seeing the elite of society walking in during Worship like they are walking on a red carpet in front of their 'fans' and given the *best* seats in the house (if there even is such a thing). When I first witnessed this, my spirit was grieved, really grieved. Entourages of celebrities, their families, and security led down from a side door, not behind the congregation and up to their seats, but *directly* in front of the pulpit and to the "VIP" seats. My heart sank as I watched people stop worshipping to see who the celebrity was and cameras snapping pictures of them. I have literally wept in many of these services. This is supposed to be the house of prayer and the house of God, but let me promise you, we have made it a *den of thieves and wolves.*

"I have become sick to my stomach with what we call "church" today. Much of what is taking place in church buildings all over the world is an outright circus, sometimes literally! I have witnessed acrobats dangling from ceilings on scarves, snakes and other reptiles in cages, a pastor hanging on a cable swinging through the sanctuary, and so much more! What are we doing??? We have made a mockery of the Gospel! Instead of trusting God's Word to do what is has successfully done over centuries in billions of lives, the modern-day church has hired marketing teams to tell them what will *draw* people to the altars. Sadly, they are not being drawn to holy altars in repentance, but wooed to altars of Baal worship, idolizing these wolves disguised as shepherds."

"God help us!" *~S.M., former children's church worker, Longmont, CO*

We have allowed secular artists to come and sing and perform for God's people and celebrities who have outright denied Jesus/Yeshua as the Son of God and the ONLY way to the Father to *impart* to the Church! What is wrong with us? Do we know what we are doing? Holiness is being replaced by carnality, secularism, and perversion! Anything to gain exposure, influence, and wealth. Nothing is sacred anymore. Our spiritual leaders are bought with a price and paraded across television, radio and yes, even motion picture. We ignorantly call this *favor*, when it is, in reality, the most ultimate form of deceit upon the Church today. We are allowing the world to make money off the "Gospel," but not the true Gospel; the watered down, hypocritical, whitewashed gospel of degradation of God's people and our Lord's name. Wake up people! This is NOT of God! We are singlehandedly turning our Lord over again into the hands of His accusers to crucify anew. (Hebrews 6:6) They don't want your Gospel; they want your money and to mock you before the world! We must wake up, repent, and turn back to God! We have fallen away from our first love. We have become lukewarm in our service and love towards God. We no longer possess the true, authentic anointing and authority of God.

"But know this, that in the last days perilous times will come: For men will be lovers of themselves, lovers of money, boasters, proud, blasphemers, disobedient to parents, unthankful, unholy, unloving, unforgiving, slanderers, without self-control, brutal, despisers of good, traitors, headstrong, haughty, lovers of pleasure rather than lovers of God, having a form of godliness but denying its power. And from such people turn away!" 1 Timothy 3:1-5

Pastors are now marketable commodities and are auctioning themselves off to the highest bidders. Many aren't even considering ministering, unless you are ready to dish out a minimum of $10,000.00 per event or appearance. No longer are we being led by the Spirit of God; we are being led by our flesh. The sad reality is that our leaders, and now many of us who have followed and imitated their ways, have accumulated such wealth, power, and influence that it is almost impossible to turn away from it all and back to the Lord. But glory to God, with Him all things are possible! I am interceding almost incessantly for our pastors, leaders, and the Church of our Lord Jesus Christ, as are many others.

Our spiritual leaders must humble themselves and return to God. We must turn this around and get back to preaching the uncompromising Word of God, the fear and reverence of/for God, holiness and Christ-like living, and get this fleshly, carnal, worldly spirit out of God's Church.

These times are the absolute most deceitful. Even the very elect of God is being deceived and deceiving. Many have made pacts with the world and have compromised the Word for worldly gain. Guard yourselves, know the Word of God for yourselves, and if you hear or see anything that goes against His Word and His Spirit... *RUN*, run as far as you can away from it! Remaining under such manipulative and controlling spirits will cause you to stray from the Truth. Jesus/Yeshua is being taken not only out of our society, but out of the Church, as well. When you see this (watch extremely close, as it will be so gradual, many will not notice it) know that *apostasy* has arrived, and already has in many churches around the world.

Apostasy is the formal disaffiliation from, abandonment of, or renunciation of a religion by a person. It can also be defined within the broader context of embracing an opinion that is contrary to one's previous religious beliefs. It will progress into services surrounding self-help, (no need for Jesus, YOU are the way) entertainment (itching ears), money-driven (greed), focusing on what others are doing to you (contention and strife), movements (cult-like manipulation), secular influence being incorporated in speakers, musicians, singers, and performers (releasing worldly spirits into people's lives) and the outright abuse of God's grace by allowing anything and everything in leadership and in the pulpits of our sacred meetings without spiritually judging it, casting out and setting those *spirits* down.

Pray church that we open our eyes and set our houses in order. Guard your hearts and your minds and seek the Father greater than you ever have before. The greatest gift we have to keep us from falling into deception is that of *discernment*. Seek the Spirit of God and His voice in these evil times. He will reveal His Truth and keep you from falling in this age of apostasy. You may feel you are alone in your efforts, but please remember that *many* are called, but *few* are chosen, and you are definitely not alone.

"Enter by the narrow gate; for wide is the gate and broad is the way that leads to destruction, and there are many who go in by it. Because narrow is the gate and difficult is the way which leads to life, and there are few who find it." Matthew 7:13-14

Chapter 4

Control, Manipulation & Intimidation

"However, when He, the Spirit of truth, has come, He will guide you into all truth…" John 16:13a

The spirit of the Church is, in essence, the Spirit of Christ, or the Spirit of Truth. His presence, His peace, and His power should be operative in every church, and should be the focus of every spiritual leader called by God. His attributes are what the Church must be built upon, and every one that calls themselves a Christian, a Believer, a follower of Christ and especially those in spiritual leadership, ought to be found living and operating in Truth.

Our Lord, Jesus Christ/Yeshua HaMashiach embodied truth, love, and compassion, and laid down His life for His Church to continue walking in this manner. When these traits are corrupted and perverted, all manner of evil becomes present and subsequently, *spiritual abuse* is inevitable. As spiritual leaders, we must understand that His people are not our property. He entrusts spiritual leadership in the Earth to teach, train, disciple, encourage, equip, and empower His people with His Word. We are mere vessels and stewards of that which has been placed in our earthly care. God gave clear instructions in His Word of how *not* to treat His children.

"The elders who are among you I exhort, I who am a fellow elder and a witness of the sufferings of Christ, and also a partaker of the glory that will be revealed: Shepherd the flock of God which is among you, serving as overseers, not by compulsion but willingly, not for dishonest gain but eagerly; nor as being lords over those entrusted to you, but being examples to the flock; and when the Chief Shepherd appears, you will receive the crown of glory that does not fade away." 1 Peter 5:1-4

Control

When we don't understand our position in someone's life, we erroneously and sometimes ignorantly, usurp authority not divinely authorized to us by God. He says to us in this passage of scripture not to *lord* over those entrusted to us. Lording over someone implies a spirit of control over them and/or a particular situation. This is a very dangerous position to find ourselves. Again, these are God's people, not ours. A spiritual mentor of mine once stated, "The more loosely we hold people, the better. Our fingerprints should not be upon them, only His." This statement so profoundly impacted me and revealed how we can be called to teach, preach, and even prophesy, but ultimately, it is still HIS Word and HIS voice that penetrates and transforms the hearts of mankind, not my proclamation of its truths.

"But Jesus called them to Himself and said, "You know that the rulers of the Gentiles lord it over them, and those who are great exercise authority over them. Yet it shall not be so among you; but whoever desires to become great among you, let him be your servant. And whoever desires to be first among you, let him be your slave—just as the Son of Man did not come to be served, but to serve, and to give His life a ransom for many." Matthew 20:25-30

"From the young age of five, I remember clearly giving my life to Jesus and knowing in my heart of His absolute love for me. I never needed anyone to tell me where to serve; it just came naturally for me. I found a need and filled it with no complaining or grumbling. I served faithfully in honor to my Lord and Savior. I was not a man-pleaser and I have never served to be seen by anyone but my Father in Heaven. It was His approval that I sought. As time progressed, well into my twenties, and the older generation began transitioning, new leadership was hired. I submitted myself to the appointed leaders. I understood that it is God that places those in authority as it pleases Him. I continued to serve wherever I was needed, and absolutely loved the house of the Lord.

THE ELEPHANT IN THE ROOM

After a few months under this new leadership, things began to change tremendously. There was no longer a spirit of love, compassion, and servitude. It quickly escalated into a storm of pride, arrogance, and control. I prayed daily asking God to help me to continue to serve with joy, but I can honestly say my joy was turned to mourning and grieving. The abuse suffered at the hands of these *pastors* was more than I could bear. I literally became a slave to these leaders, instead of the servant I had grown up to be in the Church.

I was ordered to come to their home and clean: doing their laundry, ironing their clothes, cooking, taking care of their children, and literally waiting on them hand and foot. They would harshly shout out scripture to me when they thought I was disobeying their direct orders. I didn't know anything else but the church I grew up in. My parents had passed away and the only family I had lived halfway across the country. It wasn't until I met an *angel* sent by God that my eyes were opened to the truth that this was not His will for my life.

I confronted these imposters and let me tell you, the evil that proceeded out of these people was unlike anything I have ever witnessed before in my life. These were not God's servants… these were opportunists seeking power and control. Praise God my *angel* was with me, and her boldness and authority put those demonic spirits in their place! I am eternally grateful that His true love and compassion was revealed to me at such a young age or else I don't where I'd be today." ~*Anonymous, Chicago, IL*

The spirit of control is rooted in *witchcraft*. Its desires are carnal, worldly, and yes, demonic in nature. It is a work of the flesh, and not of the Spirit. So, how is it possible for a spiritual leader, one that surrendered his life to the cause of Christ, to fall into this deception? First, by neglecting to obey the Word of God they preach. You cannot preach what you do not live, yet we find so many spiritual leaders today living completely outside of the will of God. Secondly, by falling into the very same temptation of the enemy... to be like God. The scripture above in Matthew states that even the Son of Man, Jesus/Yeshua did not come to be served, but to serve. Control serves only one purpose... dominance. The one controlling seeks to dominate in every area of their lives. This is a narcissistic trait and has absolutely no place in the lives of spiritual leadership. I will deal with narcissism in a later chapter.

Manipulation

A controlling spirit will eventually lead to manipulation. *Manipulation* is defined as to control or influence (a person or situation) cleverly, unfairly, or unscrupulously. Unfortunately, as controlling spiritual leadership progresses, the desire to suppress and oppress God's people becomes more prevalent. Below are several ways in which a manipulative spirit manifests:

- It makes you feel guilty... for everything.
- It forces insecurities on you.
- It makes you doubt yourself.
- It makes you responsible for the other's emotions.
- It makes you believe that you want what they want.

The Spirit of Christ that rests, rules, and abides within the born-again, Spirit-filled believer cannot and should not house these evil thoughts, ways, and ideas. Something else is at work here, and we understand its origin. It is from the pit of hell... from the evil one... Satan himself. We have a true enemy and his desire is to twist, confuse, corrupt, and pervert the very Word and Spirit of God within the Body of Christ. One of the greatest manifestations of manipulation in spiritual leadership is the twisting of the Word of God to suit the self-centered motives of the manipulator. The Bible gravely warns of the consequences of such:

"For I testify to everyone who hears the words of the prophecy of this book: If anyone adds to these things, God will add to him the plagues that are written in this book; and if anyone takes away from the words of the book of this prophecy, God shall take away his part from the Book of Life, from the holy city, and from the things which are written in this book." Revelation 22:18-19

Spiritual manipulation will try to control people by using their weaknesses, or vulnerabilities, against them. They exploit these vulnerabilities to achieve their own goals, regardless of the harm they do to individuals. This takes place by the pastor/spiritual leader manipulating scripture, believing the person/people will take their spiritual authority as *gold*, or in other words, the spiritual leader is always right. I have witnessed this more times than I can count where a spiritual leader has been in direct rebellion to the Word of God, but refuses to be corrected by that very Word. They will outright tell you not to question their authority, and if you do, there are grave spiritual consequences. One of the most manipulated scriptures used by rebellious spiritual leaders is found in 1 Chronicles 16:22 and Psalm 105:15:

"Saying, "Do not touch My anointed ones, And do My prophets no harm."

These scriptures are meant for true, authentic spiritual leaders and believers that remain grounded in humility and purity; those that have surrendered and submitted their lives in service to mankind, not those that choose to trample upon and defame the name and character of our Lord and Savior for their own selfish motives and benefit... classic manipulation. Spiritual leaders that twist and pervert scripture in an attempt to manipulate believers are operating in outright witchcraft! You are partnering with Satan to deceive and ultimately destroy the seed of Christ in the hearts of those you have been called to lead.

You may have experienced a pastor(s) that has used and manipulated scripture in an effort to keep you, or someone you know, from leaving their church. No matter how much false doctrine, corruption, or perversion you witness, if you threaten to leave, these spiritual leaders love to manipulate by throwing the Word of God, out of context of course, in your face in an effort to keep you in bondage. They will call you a rebel and say that you are out of order. Many will tell you that God will judge you for leaving, and sadly, many pronounce curses upon you if you try to even attempt to leave. Again, this is witchcraft!

"I had attended this church for about four years. It was a church that had been in this community for years but had been taken over by an out of town pastor from another state. The preaching was electrifying and the pastor very charismatic. He won the hearts of the congregation immediately, and so many things were being "changed" within the church. It was happening so fast that many were becoming fearful of what this pastor's true intentions were here in our city. It became evident that he was manipulating us by some things he would *mistakenly* say across the pulpit. He would completely contradict himself many times but excuse it away quickly with his charm and stage antics.

Sadly, on more than one occasion, he was exposed by his own untamed mouth. He outright admitted to deceiving and manipulating the congregation to give towards a project that had already been completely funded. I could no longer follow this man's leadership and eventually left the church. I still cannot wrap my mind around these spiritual leaders

that think they can get away with such deception and manipulation."
~*B.J., Atlanta, GA*

Unfortunately, this is happening more often than not in our pulpits. Entire sermons are constructed around a pastor/spiritual leader's motives, instead of led by the Spirit of God. False doctrines have infested the Church to the point where most Believers cannot even rightly discern between the authentic Word of God and counterfeit motivational and inspirational messages built upon deception. This is a hard pill to swallow, but many pastors/spiritual leaders today are banking upon people not reading their Bibles. They want you to come to church every single day, Monday-Sunday, to hear *them* teach and preach, so that they can persuade you to believe what they want you to believe.

Each of us has a responsibility to read, learn, and grow an intimate relationship with the Father through His Word and through quality time spent in His presence in prayer, worship, and meditation. The only way we can be controlled and manipulated is if we do not know the Word of God for ourselves and have an intimate relationship with Him. We can address the spiritual abuse, but if we are not holding ourselves accountable to know this Word for ourselves, then we, too, must take part of the responsibility, as well.

Spiritual Fathering/Mothering

One of the greatest forms of manipulation I have personally witnessed, as well as from the revealing of Holy Spirit, is that of *spiritual fathering/mothering*. Please do not get me wrong, I firmly believe in spiritual mentors, as well as the fathering/mothering spirit needed for spiritual growth and maturity in the Body of Christ. In fact, God has placed a spiritual father and mother in my life to cover me and impart spiritually into and over me for close to twenty years. I value and honor them both deeply and thank God for their example in my life. What I have witnessed and experienced on a grander scale in this new *church culture* is not true, authentic spiritual covering, but a perverted and twisted form of idol worship.

"You shall have no other gods before Me." Deuteronomy 5:7

Sadly, many spiritual leaders have allowed these spirits to overtake and overpower the very Word of God they preach. In seeking fame and fortune, they have forsaken this very scripture. They have taken on the role of "god" in the lives of those they have been called to lead, not *lord over*. The more spiritual "sons and daughters" they can bring under their umbrella, the more they are worshipped and held in high esteem. It is not about a spiritual covering; it is, indeed, deception aimed at gaining a massive following of worshippers. It is not an atmosphere of servant-hood; it is modern-day spiritual bondage and slavery. I have witnessed this personally and it is truly one of the most deceptive practices going on in the Church today. A pastor boldly and unashamedly lashed out at me once and commanded me never to put his *spiritual father's* name in my mouth ever again. He told me I was not worthy to even mention his name! He proceeded to give me a rundown of his "spiritual DNA" and that I could never even begin to understand his level of authority and rank in the spiritual realm. In fact, this pastor was captured in a photo kissing the ring on his *spiritual father's* hand… deception.

"I truly thought I was supposed to submit to this man as my spiritual father because I had joined the church and committed to serving God in this city. I only knew a little of the Bible, and he would constantly bring up scriptures that would imply my absolute need to come under submission to him. Even if I did not agree with many of the things I was seeing take place, I humbly submitted, because I did not want to disobey God's Word.

As time passed on, things became progressively worse and he began asking me and others to lie for him and cover up his messy situations. I refused and told him this was not of God. He got right up in my face, his eyes turned very dark, and he told me that he owned me. He told me that I had made a spiritual covenant with him that could not be broken. I knew at this point that I needed to leave this church and leave fast. I played it off as if I was apologizing for my rebellious behavior, so he could calm down. He did, but I never returned. I learned months later that he was arrested, and the church was shut down. It took me years to get over this spiritual abuse and trust again." *~A.D., London, UK*

We must spiritually discern the grave error we are teaching and showing this new generation of Believers. Idol worship is one of the most dangerous practices any born-again follower of Christ could fall into… it is written:

"You shall not make for yourself a carved image—any likeness of anything that is in heaven above, or that is in the earth beneath, or that is in the water under the earth; you shall not bow down to them nor serve them. For I, the LORD your God, am a jealous God, visiting the iniquity of the fathers upon the children to the third and fourth genera-tions of those who hate Me, but showing mercy to thousands, to those who love Me and keep My commandments." Deuteronomy 5:8

Regrettably, this is exactly what we are witnessing en masse in the modern-day church culture. It has spread far and wide, and even in what we consider *third-world* countries, this deception is bringing with it every form of demonic perversion you can possibly imagine. People are being brainwashed by these deceptive spiritual leaders. This is no harmless honor or reverence… this is not authentic spiritual fathering and mothering… this is an all-out onslaught and overtaking of divine authority… this is a replacing of the One true Father God, our Divine Creator.

"Do not call anyone on earth your father; for One is your Father, He who is in heaven." Matthew 23:9

This scripture was written to guard us and warn us against the very manipulation we see so prevalent in today's Church. Too much authority in the hands of any man is sure to lead to a perversion of truth. We see this most prevalent in the Catholic Church where priests are given the title of "Father," or in the instance of a pope being referred to as "the Holy Father". This is in direct defiance to the Word of God. No man is holy, but God. Many may debate that the scripture *"… be ye holy, for God is holy"* contradicts this statement, but when we manipulate scripture and use it to benefit our selfish and carnal desires and motives, we can make it say whatever we want. This scripture, in essence, describes the character and posture Father God commands us to walk in here on earth, not the divine attribute and authority of our true Holy Father. He is God and He will share His glory with no man! The word *Father*, spiritually speaking, denotes divine authority, eminence, superiority, sovereignty, a right to command, and a claim to a particular honor and respect. Though we are commanded to honor our earthly fathers and mothers, and even respect our spiritual leaders, true fear, reverence, and godly honor is eminently reserved for our Father in Heaven alone, not man.

"I did not grow up with a father; in fact, I did not even know who my father was until I was well into my forties. I carried a lot of bitterness, resentment, anger, and yes, hate in my heart for a man I had never even met. When I was finally introduced to the Church, it took me quite a while to trust anyone. After several years, my heart was being softened and opened up to trust again. Our pastor was a very reserved man. He definitely knew the Bible like the back of his hand. He wasn't a loud preacher; he mostly taught the scriptures like a high school teacher would teach a class. After beginning counseling with him concerning my childhood and lack of fathering, he offered to step in and be a "spiritual father" in my life. I was very hesitant, at first, because I did not want to talk about my father at all. Secondly, I did not want or need a *father* in my life. I had learned to block out this "need" and live my life not even acknowledging this void.

As the counseling broke the walls down in my life, I began to trust my pastor tremendously. I even began calling him "Dad". Our relationship grew in leaps and bounds. One day at church, there was a visiting pastor that came from Africa. He was highly revered in his nation, and counseled dignitaries all over Africa. I served as an armor bearer for my pastor's wife, and I was placing a glass of water on her table that was next to him. He jumped up and began yelling at me, stating I had no authority to walk past him and that I needed to learn proper protocol.

Mind you, I had NO IDEA what this pastor was referring to, but my pastor ran up to us asking what happened. As I began to speak, the visiting pastor cut me off again and said to me, "SILENCE! LEARN YOUR PLACE WOMAN!" I was now drenched in tears not understanding what I had done wrong. I turned to my pastor and said, "Dad, what is going on?" My *spiritual father* looked at me and said, "Don't you ever refer to me in that manner again. I am not your Dad; I am your pastor."

My heart broke into a million pieces. I could not believe what was taking place right before my very eyes. I thought I was dreaming. I could not breathe. I ran out of this church and never looked back. I have tried unsuccessfully, several times, to take my life. Someone was always there to find me and get me to a hospital. It was in one of those hospitals where I truly found the Father I was always seeking inwardly. A chaplain would come into my room every morning and just sit and read the Bible and pray with me. I was extremely angry and withdrawn, wishing they would have just let me die. In a brief moment of prayer when the chaplain asked me if I had ever received the Holy Spirit into my life, something shifted inside of me. He led me in a prayer to receive the Gift of Holy Spirit, and the love and acceptance I felt within me was something I had NEVER experienced in my life!

I found my true Father and I have promised to never call another man on the face of this Earth father again. No man is capable of holding such a holy position. We must stop giving men such weighty titles that they will never be able to fill in our lives. It is very careless and very dangerous, especially to those just coming into the Church that are naïve to the things of God." ~*Martha, Iowa.*

We will delve deeper into this form of spiritual manipulation in a later chapter.

Intimidation

As spiritual leadership is allowed to continue to operate in these evil ways with no consequence of any sort, you will begin to see their desires and motives even more clearly. When they feel they cannot be corrected or "touched," their plans will eventually begin to unfold. No longer will you see great control or manipulation, but now you will begin to witness the spirit of intimidation coming from spiritual leadership. *Intimidation* is defined as intentional behavior that would cause a person of ordinary sensibilities to fear injury or harm. It is not necessary to prove that the behavior was so violent as to cause mean terror or that the victim was actually frightened. How can we possibly be speaking of intimidation within the confines of spiritual leadership? Why would pastors/spiritual leaders want to intimidate anyone, let alone those that have been entrusted to their spiritual care and covering? Again, they are no longer operating in the Spirit, but are being consumed by their flesh and its desires. These are what the Bible calls *works of the flesh*:

"Now the works of the flesh are evident, which are: adultery, fornication, uncleanness, lewdness, idolatry, sorcery, hatred, contentions, jealousies, outbursts of wrath, selfish ambitions, dissensions, heresies, envy, murders, drunkenness, revelries, and the like; of which I tell you beforehand, just as I also told you in time past, that those who practice such things will not inherit the kingdom of God." Galatians 5:19-21

Spiritual Bullying

Intimidation can lead to any one of these works of the flesh, and in most cases, is progressive in nature, as no accountability or responsibility is rendered to these spiritual leaders. They perceive themselves as untouchable, and resort to *spiritual bullying*. I have witnessed firsthand the most evil of attacks spewed across pulpits all over the world. The place we deem the most holy and sacred has now become the launching pad for some of the most heinous and insidious spiritual attacks. Unfortunately, they are not coming from our enemy, Satan, or even from those that say they don't believe in God; they are proceeding out of the mouths of those that proclaim they are *called* of God to lead His people.

"But no man can tame the tongue. It is an unruly evil, full of deadly poison. With it we bless our God and Father, and with it we curse men, who have been made in the similitude of God. Out of the same mouth proceed blessing and cursing. My brethren, these things ought not to be so. Does a spring send forth fresh water and bitter from the same opening? Can a fig tree, my brethren, bear olives, or a grapevine bear figs? Thus, no spring yields both salt water and fresh." James 3:8-12

73

THE ELEPHANT IN THE ROOM

This is devastating on a level that is indescribable! I have witnessed it range from *insignificant* joking and personal attacks from a pastor concerning the authenticity of a wedding ring a man purchased for his wife, of which it was all he could afford, to another pastor literally yelling across the pulpit telling a man to get his wife, their kids, grab their coats, and leave his church. This spirit is NOT of God and has no place in the Church! The wounds that are caused in the hearts and minds of these precious people, by the very ones that are supposed to be God's messengers, are sometimes irreversible. Flesh-filled, piercing words cut like knives into the hearts of those seeking God's voice and His truth. Sadly, because many lack spiritual maturity and discernment, they will not only run away from the Church, but ultimately, God Himself due to the erroneous spiritual attacks from their pastors/leaders.

On the more serious end of spiritual bullying, we are witnessing the Church become a *mob-like* entity, instead of a sanctuary for the lost and hurting of the world. These pastors/spiritual leaders are taking part in some of the most scandalous attacks not only on many of their congregants, but also against other pastors/leaders that don't agree with their corruption. When someone speaks out against the corruption and/or perversion in a church, these people are *silenced* through many different tactics, including being blacklisted by their pastors, called names ranging from divisive all the way to being referenced as a witch, a sorcerer, or a warlock. These leaders bully their congregation into separating themselves from these individuals and their families, even to the extent of issuing gag orders, so that no one is allowed to even mention their names or anything dealing with confronting spiritual leadership. Yes, this is absolutely taking place in churches all over the world!

I personally have been bullied to the point of actual physical threats from pastors and their "followers". I have been threatened with arrest due to *slander*, as well as have had my life threatened by spiritual leaders to stop talking about spiritual abuse. This happens more often than most Believers even know, and it is devastating to witness in what is called *God's house*.

"We pastored a church for over twenty years in the very community we both were raised. We loved our church and those that God allowed us to serve. After placing a board over the authority of our church business affairs, it all went downhill. A very well-known pastor was instated as our board director. We respected and honored this pastor greatly, as he was highly revered all around the country, and even in other countries. We immediately felt as if they were trying to kick us out of our own church. Our brothers and sisters, friends and colleagues, were being turned against us, and some, we later found out, were threatened that if they did not stay away from us, their lives and livelihoods would be in danger.

We could not believe this was happening to us! Sure enough, after one year, we were "voted out" as pastors of our own church. Horrendous lies and accusations were hurled at us by some of the very people we have known all our lives. We were crushed! Another pastor was brought in to replace us. This pastor was from an entirely different state than us. We found out much later, after multiple court cases to get our church back, the reason all of this had taken place.

If you think the Church could never act as "the mob," you better think again. There are many *takeovers* happening in churches everywhere. It is business for them, not about God." *~Anonymous,* Texas

The modern-day church culture and structure is operating as a corporate business, and at times, even imitates many illegal worldly operations, like mob families and drug organizations. As Believers, we have not been called to protect a brand, a movement, an organization, or a leader. All of this is sure to crumble, as it is not founded on the Rock, our Savior. We are called to freedom in Christ Jesus where we are *led* by His Spirit, Holy Spirit. God has allowed me to see a lot in the last twenty years concerning the modern-day church and its ways. I have been literally interceding for years with outlandish attacks launched at me not only from the enemy, but from spiritual leaders, leadership staff, and yes, even once trusted friends and fellow believers that were intimidated and bullied to silence. I have experienced attacks on my body, my family, my children, my finances, my business and yes, my mind. I went through one of the greatest seasons of my life literally begging the Lord to stop speaking to me and showing me dreams. He was revealing so much to me.

I knew what He was calling me to, but I did not want it! I was sick of being labeled a *rebel* by those He was calling me to prophesy to in the Church. There was always a way for them to twist a prophetic word into judgment or questioning of their motives, instead of actually stopping for a moment to hear the voice of God, as well as the love from the heart of the one prophesying. We are a rebellious people, just as the children of Israel were wandering in the wildernesses of the Bible, refusing to hear the voice of the Lord and desiring what they had back in Egypt, because they "desired the benefits of God while rejecting the process." They did not want to obey the Lord and be renewed in their mind; instead, they went back to slavery 'in their minds' as *better* than God leading them through the wilderness. Many died in the wilderness, but I see an even greater tragedy in today's church.

We are trying to enter our "Promised Land" at any cost, without going through the preparation, or process, by heeding the voices of our pastors, instead of the voice of God. We constantly hear how God wants us to be blessed, and prosperous, and to get all He has for us, but refuse to preach on transformation and Christ-like living. The character is no longer important, and this leads to a perversion of power, influence, and wealth. It is no longer about building God's Kingdom, but about building earthly empires.

It is time to break the chains of bondage off God's people. This is oppressive and disturbing to say the least. My heart bleeds for people who go to church 3-4 times a week, but still hunger and thirst for an authentic encounter with the Lord. They have not been taught how to hear His voice, only to give, give, and give some more. They hear a pastor go on and on about his/her travels and who he/she was able to meet for almost an hour. Which celebrity is coming to the church to "preach" and what singer is coming to "minister"? God says, "This is not my Church; I am nowhere in this!" He has commanded many of these pastors to get this mess out of His Church, but they have refused. He has sent them prophets, and they have rejected them. Many will die in the wilderness of Egypt, "the world." *What will it profit a man if he gains the whole world, and lose his soul?* We are seeing many spiritual leaders falling into the hands of the world. True pastors are taking their lives at alarming rates, because they are being bullied and tormented by rogue spiritual leaders. They are fighting many forms of temptation due to the corrupted and perverted *church culture* we now see as the forefront of "Christendom". Worldliness and carnality consume our Sunday morning services. I hear in my spirit even now the cry of God through the mouth of Abraham to Pharaoh, "Let My people go!"

"Why do ye such things? For I hear of your evil dealings by all this people. Nay, my sons; for it is no good report that I hear: ye make the LORD's people to transgress. If one man sin against another, the judge shall judge him: but if a man sin against the LORD, who shall intreat for him? Notwithstanding they hearkened not unto the voice of their father, because the LORD would slay them." 1 Samuel 2:23-25

God directs His words of rebuke toward Eli the priest. Eli was at fault before God. What he said to his sons was true. The sins they committed were heinous; they were sinning against God. Eli made clear the serious nature of their sins, and then dismissed them back to their priestly duties. Eli's sin was a failure to discipline his sons. This was a sin typical of Israel throughout the period of the Judges and later again after the time of the captivity. Eli knew the difference between good and bad and taught his sons, but did not follow through on his words. He did not punish them according to priestly law. His sons needed to be excommunicated from the priesthood and put out of the temple. They showed no sign of repentance. They repeatedly returned to their same sins. The Old Testament law would have required that the sons be driven out of the city and stoned for their blasphemous actions in the tabernacle of Jehovah.

We see this same lack of discipline and true spiritual authority in the Church today. Many spiritual overseers are refusing to correct and rebuke the sin of those under their spiritual covering. They are sweeping their indiscretions under the rug and sending them right back out into the pulpit with absolutely no consequence.

"Those who are sinning rebuke in the presence of all, that the rest also may fear." 1 Timothy 5:20

Unfortunately, because these spiritual leaders are not being corrected and/or rebuked, it leaves the door open for them to not only do these things again, but it gives others the green light to simply do as they please, as well. We see the harsher judgment in the days of Eli the priest concerning his sons, as well as the sons of other priests, because God understood the magnitude of influence. He stated in Timothy to rebuke in the presence of all, *that the rest may also fear.* When godly correction and rebuke is laid as a foundation in the Church, it sets the atmosphere for godliness, integrity, holiness, and morality. When others witness the consequences of sin, they are more apt not to make those same mistakes. Sadly, today's church has no real solid foundation of biblical accountability and responsibility when it comes to spiritual leadership. It is almost non-existent.

Why is today's Church so lackadaisical with the sin of spiritual leadership? Why do we turn a blind eye to the rebellion, deception, corruption, and perversion of those standing before hundreds, thousands, and even millions of Believers all around the world as "God's messengers"? It is past time to clean God's house of the unholy and profane dealings of rebellious spiritual leaders, or He will do it Himself. It is time to reinstate holiness and purity back into our sacred pulpits. It is time to proclaim the Good News of the Gospel once again throughout the world and eradicate these false doctrines rooted in control, manipulation, and intimidation.

"Then the Lord spoke to Aaron, saying: "Do not drink wine or intoxicating drink, you, nor your sons with you, when you go into the tabernacle of meeting, lest you die. It shall be a statute forever throughout your

generations, that you may distinguish between holy and unholy, and between unclean and clean, and that you may teach the children of Israel all the statutes which the Lord has spoken to them by the hand of Moses." Leviticus 10:8-11

Chapter 5

Verbal & Emotional Abuse

"Therefore, as the elect of God, holy and beloved, put on tender mercies, kindness, humility, meekness, longsuffering;" Colossians 3:12

Abuse of any kind in the Church goes completely against the nature of our heavenly Father. God is love. His thoughts toward us are good. His Word is filled with His thoughts concerning us, and even when He must correct us or chastise us due to our continual sin; it is always administered in His *agape* love. Unfortunately, as spiritual leaders gravitate more and more away from the Word and towards worldly influences, we see a greater tendency to abuse their authority.

The most common form of abuse in the Church today is ***verbal abuse***. It happens more often than not and has the capacity to inflict deep wounds in the psyche of people. Verbal abuse is absolutely detrimental to the spiritual growth of any human being, whether child or adult. Though we may not *see* the actual wounds as we would with physical abuse, verbal abuse causes deep, internal wounds that last much longer than any visible physical abuse ever could reveal. There is a popular slogan that states, "Words cut deep." This is a powerfully true statement and it is biblical.

"A wholesome tongue is a tree of life, but perverseness in it breaks the spirit." Proverbs 15:4

The role of spiritual leadership is to reveal the heart of God and the nature of God into the lives of those under their authority through the inherent teachings of Christ. When what is spoken out of the mouths of pastors/leaders contradict what they teach from the Word of God, believers find themselves torn between the message and the messenger. Many equate a rogue spiritual leader's actions with the love of God. Some will submit to this oppression in the name of "love," while others end up hating God, because if this is how God treats His children, then they want no parts of Him. The Word is intended to build up the spirit, not tear it down. Sadly, many in the Church today are being verbally assaulted by the very one's standing in the "stead" of Christ.

<hr />

"I was my pastor's wife's armor bearer for five years. We were friends before I took on this role in her life. I admired and respected her greatly, not simply because she was our "First Lady," but because she and I had history together. We went through so much during our high school years and were, in my eyes, family. The first year was good. She still had a very humble spirit and continued to extend all glory to God. It seemed like everything shifted overnight. She was a very conservative dresser and grew up in a very strict church when it came to what virtuous women should wear and how to carry themselves as women of God. Her modest apparel turned to tight dresses and stiletto heels at the suggestion of her new *stylist*. She went from barely any facial makeup to hiring a make-up artist to have her face done before every service. It was not only her outward appearance that changed drastically; her spirit went from kind and gentle to harsh and nasty instantaneously towards most people in our church.

She would walk in barking orders at everyone and demanding that she be *served* as the queen she had been ordained by God (she literally spoke these words). If her water was not ice cold, she threw it on the person that brought it to her and demanded they bring her ice-cold water, or they can "get out of her church". I witnessed this demeanor every time I was in her presence. Having to be right by her side at all times, I saw some of the most evil actions I have ever witnessed by a *spiritual leader* in my life! I finally could take it no more, and I prayed to ask God for the words to say to her. I waited until we were in a private setting outside of "church," and I confronted my friend in a loving spirit. Well, what happened next fully knocked me off my feet. My friend since high school, my sister, my family... cursed me completely out, called me a "Judas," told me I was replaced, and never to step foot in *her* church again.

It took me a very long time to heal from the verbal abuse from someone I truly respected and honored. Sadly, this seems to be the *norm* of many pastor's wives all over the world." ~*Anonymous,* Washington, D.C.

The blatant disregard and disenfranchisement of a body of Believers by someone trusted with the attributes and characteristics of Christ is unfathomable. How dare we treat God's people with such disgust and disdain? Who do we think we are? The Bible says, "God resists the proud but gives grace to the humble." (James 4:6) It is apparent that the spirit of mammon has enabled the deception of these pastors/leaders. Taking on worldly spirits will bring with it worldly responses. What many in the Church today are experiencing is no better, and sometimes worse, than being in the world. We expect this from non-believers, those that are ignorant to the teachings of Christ and the intimate knowledge of God's love, not from those that say they have been called by God to shepherd His people.

"Death and life are in the power of the tongue, and those who love it will eat its fruit." Proverbs 18:21

As spiritual leaders, we have the power to impart death or life into the lives of those in our spiritual care. We must examine ourselves to test whether or not our motives are pure in regard to holding this most crucial position in people's lives. This is not a game nor is this something to take lightly. God will hold you accountable to how you have treated and handled His people. Don't allow your pride and ego, and your desire for wealth and influence to move you out of divine position. What will it profit you to gain this power and lose your soul?

"Let no corrupt word proceed out of your mouth, but what is good for necessary edification, that it may impart grace to the hearers." Ephesians 4:29

We are to make sure our words are *seasoned with salt*. In other words, all that we say and do in regard to those under our spiritual care should be offered as a means of imparting grace, as the scripture above states, to the hearers. We are called to build them up, encourage them, equip them, and empower them to walk in their God-given purposes and destiny. Verbal abuse tears down self-esteem, confidence, and identity in people's lives. It seizes the will of people in order to control, manipulate, and intimidate them to do what we want them to do for us. It's a lot more calculating and insidious than most choose to acknowledge, causing people on the receiving end to question themselves, wonder if they are overreacting, or even blame themselves. Verbal abuse rarely takes place out in the open, because the abuser desires to keep up his/her façade in the eyes of others. Verbal abuse can be isolating since it chips away at your sense of self-worth, making it more difficult to reach out to anyone.

As children, we either heard or were the progenitor of speaking the phrase, "Sticks and stones may break my bones, but words will never hurt me." This saying originated from an English-language children's nursery rhyme. It is used as a defense against name-calling and verbal bullying, but research shows that in most cases, words absolutely cause long-term and sometimes lasting wounds. Especially in the case of verbal abuse being initiated by spiritual leadership, similar to that of a parent verbally assaulting their child/children, it tends to be much more concerning, as well as devastating, in the lives of those on the receiving end. Verbal abuse leaves lasting scars in the hearts and minds of people and affects every area of their lives. It is very difficult for a follower of Christ to reconcile God's love in their hearts, while being torn down verbally by trusted spiritual leadership.

"And the tongue is a fire, a world of iniquity. The tongue is so set among our members that it defiles the whole body, and sets on fire the course of nature; and it is set on fire by hell. For every kind of beast and bird, of reptile and creature of the sea, is tamed and has been tamed by mankind. But no man can tame the tongue. It is an unruly evil, full of deadly poison. With it we bless our God and Father, and with it we curse men, who have been made in the similitude of God. Out of the same mouth proceed blessing and cursing. My brethren, these things ought not to be so." James 3:6-11

"I have loved the local church my entire life. I have served from my heart *in the shadows* with no expectation of accolades or acknowledgement. My service is to God and His people, and it has been the most fulfilling aspect of my entire life. At the age of twenty-five, I was prophesied to by my pastor that God was calling me as a missionary to serve in Africa. I always dreamed of going to Africa and serving God's precious children. My pastor's new wife (his first wife had passed away) immediately began treating me harshly. The people in our church, most of which watched me grow up, rallied behind this prophecy over my life and began praying for me and sowing into my future mission's trips. She was livid. On multiple occasions, she would tell her husband, my pastor that he did not hear from God concerning my life, and that I would not be ordained as a missionary to represent my church in Africa.

I was called a Jezebel even though I was not even seeking this title/position and attacked verbally on a continual basis. She kicked me off the prayer team I had been a part of since I was fifteen years old and openly told the congregation that I was oppressed by a demon and needed deliverance. She stated that I was praying against her and wanted her husband, her title, and her church. My pastor was like a father to me since I was a little girl. This man was over twice my age and there was absolutely NO foundation for her to think this was ever the truth! Those that knew me well understood that there was something absolutely wrong with this woman.

Needless to say, I found out that she had been accusing *many* women in the church of the same thing. Sadly, our pastor had become blinded by her deception and began treating the people in the same harsh manner.

Many of us left, and though they are still in the Church, it is merely a handful of people recycling in and out.

Today, ten years later, I am serving as a missionary in Africa and live amongst the very people God called me to love and serve." ~*Hope, Tanzania, East Africa*

There are multiple ways in which verbal abuse can manifest. Here is a list, surely not exhaustive, that you can identify in your life, or in the lives of others you may know dealing with verbal abuse.

1. Name-calling
2. Condescension
3. Manipulation
4. Criticism
5. Demeaning comments
6. Threats
7. Blame
8. Accusations
9. Withholding

VERBAL & EMOTIONAL ABUSE

1. <u>Name-calling</u>

One of the most evident forms of verbal abuse is that of *name-calling*. Verbal abusers can quickly tear down any individual by calling them names, in order to diminish their identity. Sadly, it is the deep scars of the abuser's childhood and/or fractured life that causes them to attack others to make themselves feel good and to have a sense of control. It somehow makes them feel better about themselves, which is toxic and self-absorbing. As Believers, our identity should come from the love of God through His Son, Jesus Christ/Yeshua HaMashiach. A spiritual leader should imitate that love and impart that love, not destroy it in the lives of God's people. Unfortunately, I have witnessed this more times than I would like to remember, both personally and towards others.

2. <u>Condescension</u>

The Bible tells us, as spiritual leaders, that we are to make ourselves as servants to those under our spiritual care. We are never to "lord over" those God has entrusted to us. *Condescension* is the act of usurping, or assuming, an air of superiority over someone. One of the fruits of a condescending spirit is sarcasm. Sarcastic people are very harsh and love to make jokes out of everything and towards almost everyone. Condescension is the act of belittling people in an effort to make them look or feel bad, in order to make the one spewing it *appear* superior. Again, this is an attribute of a very noxious and broken individual. This kind of person should not be in a position of spiritual authority.

3. **Manipulation**

We spoke in the last chapter concerning *manipulation*, but to delve further, especially regarding verbal abuse, this type of spirit seeks, subtly, to pronounce blame on the abused from the abuser. This kind of individual will try, at all costs, to persuade the recipient of this verbal abuse that it is their fault and that the abuser's acts are warranted. Manipulators like this tend to turn situations completely around in their favor, in order to suppress and oppress the other's rightful feelings and concerns. This demonic act of twisting the truth is a form of witchcraft.

4. **Criticism**

The act of finding, or pointing out, fault in others is defined as *criticism*. Instead of building someone up through their weaknesses, those that criticize look for any and every fault within you to tear down your self-esteem. The Bible warns us of the spirit of condemnation. Condemnation is the act of "damning" someone without any reservation whatsoever. The Word of God tells us that Jesus was not sent to condemn the world, but to save it. Those that are comfortable with criticizing people are, in essence, condemning those He came to save. This is very dangerous and should not be named amongst those in spiritual authority.

5. **Demeaning comments**

The word *demean* is defined as causing someone to lose their dignity and the respect of others. *Demeaning* someone is to insult, degrade, humiliate, or shame someone. Why would any spiritual leader choose to demean anyone, let alone someone under their spiritual covering? Sadly, this happens more often than not in today's church settings, as well as in many spiritual circles all over the world. It can commonly come out in the form of race/ethnic background, gender, religion, and background in general. Many denominations and religions target people by the color of their skin as inferior. Also, women are the object of much degradation not only in Christianity in terms of not being free to minister the Gospel, but also in Islam, Hinduism, Buddhism, and other religions that suppress and oppress women incessantly. Both people of color and women have been subjected to the most inhumane of spiritual practices around the world. Another most notable act of demeaning and degradation can be attributed to the religion of Judaism in the atrocities of the Holocaust. To demean another human being is to insult God who created them in His own image.

6. **Threats**

We have seen many movies and television shows where *threats* are common practice amongst the evil of this world. To threaten someone is to state one's intention to take hostile action against someone in retribution for something done or not done. Yes, threats take place every day in spiritual institutions all over the world. I have witnessed this in every way, shape, fashion, and form in the Church, but in regards to verbal abuse, threats can come in the manner of threatening to take someone's title or position because an individual refuses to agree with corruption and/or perversion. This is rogue abuse of spiritual authority and happens frequently in many spheres. I, myself, was threatened by a former pastor and told to *leave his church* because I was not in agreement with "he and his staff."

There are multiple testimonies from churches all over the world where pastors have placed gag orders on entire staffs, so they will not expose the corruption and/or perversion going on in these places. People are threatened to either sign them or leave their churches. Some have even been threatened with lawsuits for slander, because they have courageously stood up and spoken the truth against these corrupt spiritual leaders. I tell people often the Church, over the last few decades, has progressively turned into a *mob-like* culture. As we saw in one of the earlier testimonies, even pastors are being ousted out of their own positions and churches taken over by "pastors" in higher positions.

7. <u>Blame</u>

Blame is one of the most common forms of verbal abuse and involves constantly placing the blame for one's actions on others, instead of taking responsibility for them. It is assigning the accountability, and even guilt, of one's actions on another blameless individual. In the cases of many people I have interviewed over the course of almost three years in writing this book, most have had spiritual leaders try to cover up their indiscretions by placing blame on them and making them look like the perpetrators. They are called rebels, rogues, divisive, witches, warlocks, sorcerers, Jezebels, and every other evil name you can think of other than a child of God. These innocent people are lied on and blacklisted not only within their own fellowship of believers, but many have also been ostracized by those close to these pastors/spiritual leaders. Unfortunately, many of these pastors/spiritual leaders are in cahoots with one another doing the same corrupt/perverted things, so they will gladly come in agreement with their *friends* and ignore the truth. Many innocent believers in the Church and in spiritual institutions all over the world are finding themselves the victims of *blame*, while their abusers get off scott-free.

8. **Accusations**

An *accusation* is a statement by one person asserting that another person or entity has done something improper. We can see the progression of blame leading to the evil and wicked point of accusations against innocent souls. To accuse someone is to indict them, charge them, and arraign them in the court of public opinion. In this case, amongst their fellow believers, their peers. I myself, as well as many othe rs I have spoken to, were *marked* by many pastors/churches due to the false statements/accusations made by professing spiritual leaders. Not too long after I was told by my former pastor to leave his church, we found a beautiful gathering of believers in our city. A pastor from my previous church contacted my new pastor *warning* him of me and my family. I am very grateful to God that He kept my heart and my mind intact during this season, because many people have walked not only away from Church due to such egregious spiritual abuse, but God altogether.

The pastor that shifted his blame on and spewed false accusations concerning me and many others, several years later, lost not only his marriage, but his position in the church, as well. I don't say this to gloat; it is devastating and was absolutely preventable. Hundreds, even thousands, of families were affected and some even destroyed for his actions. The Bible calls Satan the *accuser of the brethren*. Let us not, as spiritual leaders, be named as such. We are called to be ministers of love, compassion, truth, and reconciliation.

9. <u>Withholding</u>

Withholding is the act of refusing to give someone something they are in need of or seeking from you. In the sense of verbal abuse, this word seems to be an oxymoron to many. How can withholding be considered an act of verbal abuse? In the case of the abused, some seek out accountability and retribution from their abusers. In more cases than not, the abusers go *silent* and will ignore, at all costs, facing their victims. This is seen as the second stage of abuse, or a re-abuse, of the victim. Many pastors/spiritual leaders believe that if they remain silent, the issue will simply go away. They will, by no means, entertain the victim's truthful accusation and will silence everyone around them, as well. This is one of the most insidious acts of verbal abuse, because it seeks to keep hidden what eventually will be exposed.

Verbal abuse, if committed over a long period of time, has the power to damage the emotional state and well-being of an individual. Harsh words have now penetrated the spiritual fabric of a person and changed their emotional DNA. They are no longer the same individual. ***Emotional abuse*** is all about "taking" from one person for your own benefit. When you are emotionally manipulated, you lose your power and become vulnerable for exploitation. Many falsely accused people end up being bullied into believing they are the victimizers. They are so berated for speaking up and lose so many friendships and relationships that they begin to question their initial seeing and hearing from God.

Emotional manipulation can manifest in many ways. Here are just a few so you are able to recognize when you are being emotionally abused:

❖ **They invite you to their space.**
   People who are emotionally abusive tend to draw or *invite their victims into their space*, or close in proximity, so they can usurp their control and authority over them. They feel that since they "let you in," they now have some sort of power in your life. This need for *power* in someone's life is a direct attribute of an emotional abuser.

❖ **They listen first.**
   Those seeking emotional power over an individual will play the role of *listening first* as if they are truly interested in your feelings and emotions. They will be the ear to hear and the shoulder

to cry on; until they have accumulated all the information they need to draw you into their web of abuse. Be very mindful of who you let in your space, as well as how much information you provide to them. Setting boundaries is very important to combat against emotional abuse.

❖ **They twist the facts.**

This attribute is mostly self-explanatory, but a few things to keep in mind concerning the *twisting of facts* is one, they tend to make you feel as if you know nothing and they are your source of information. Secondly, they will try to persuade you to do the same. One of their goals is to pull you into their twisted mindset, in order to discredit you when you call out their abuse.

❖ **They inundate you with information.**

Not only will emotional abusers seek to be your only source of information, but they will also *inundate you with information* in an attempt to keep you in a state of confusion. They will divulge so much information to you that they can ultimately use against you if you turn against them. They will back you into a position where you cannot deny you were already privy to certain issues, but chose to keep it in confidence, even if it is corruption and/or perversion concerning them or others. The abuse leans towards overwhelming someone to the point of knowing "too much".

❖ **They block you with red tape.**

Though many emotional abusers draw their victims close to them, when the abused begin to stand up, the victimizers will use a tactic called *"red tape,"* to hinder them in their efforts to expose the abuse. In a spiritual setting, this will take place by the pastor/spiritual leader placing others in authority to "vet" those trying to gain access to the said pastor/spiritual leader/abuser. In other words, the victims must go through the *proper channels* and submit to the *spiritual protocol* set in place by spiritual leadership. Unfortunately, while the abuse was taking place, these channels and protocols were unnecessary.

❖ **They speak louder.**

Again, another self-explanatory tactic, but crucial in determining the attributes of emotional abusers. These people are overbearing. They love to overpower in conversations. They will over talk you to make you feel less than or inferior to them. Emotional abusers also *speak loud*, or yell at others in public to belittle and berate their victims to keep them subservient.

❖ **They are negative.**

Emotionally abusive people rarely have anything positive to speak over others' lives. Everything they speak is laced with *negativity*. Their nature is pessimistic and cynical, and they tend to display these characteristics in every area of their lives, not only towards those outside, but many times in their own marriages and families.

❖ **They use ultimatums.**

Power-driven abusers seek absolute control of their victims. One way they abuse their authority is by issuing ultimatums to those that refuse to submit to their emotional abuse. An *ultimatum* is a final demand or statement of terms that if not met, leads to retaliation or the threat of suffering harsh consequences or punishment.

❖ **They make fun of you.**

When someone *makes fun of* someone else, it is an outward issue of insecurity that has yet to be dealt with inwardly by the one enacting the emotional abuse. They make fun of others to make themselves *look* better. These are emotionally broken individuals that seek out vulnerable people to abuse. There is a common saying that "hurt people, hurt people".

❖ **They judge you openly.**

One of the greatest ways in which people are *judged openly* using emotional abuse is through character assassination. Emotionally abusive people will use everything in their power to tarnish your character and make you look bad in the sight of others. Please understand that now; you are not the only one being emotionally manipulated. These abusers emotionally manipulate others into believing their lies.

❖ **They're your "friend" only when it's convenient.**

As long as you are complying with and in agreement with an emotional abuser's toxic behavior, they will be your *best friend*! Many victims don't even know they are being emotionally victimized until it's too late, and when they do finally stand up and speak out, the friendship is terminated. The relationship is only active when it is beneficial to the abuser.

❖ **Trivializing.**

The act of *trivializing* means to make something, or someone seem less important, significant, or complex than it really is/they really are. When emotionally abused people desire to talk about their feelings and emotions, they are accused of overreacting and overreaching in their concerns. Their feelings and emotions are minimized and downplayed as unimportant and insignificant.

Many find it extremely difficult to heal, be delivered, and recover from such offensive verbal and emotional abuse from those in spiritual authority. How can people trust the teaching, preaching, and leadership of spiritual leaders that overtly abuse their power and authority? How do we reconcile God's ultimate love for us, while being violated verbally and emotionally by those claiming to be His messengers? This is very difficult for new believers, as well as spiritually immature believers. May we seek to offer *open doors* and *safe places* for the spiritually abused to share their stories and learn to heal without the threat of continual verbal and emotional abuse, as well as isolation.

"My life was shattered by someone that called himself a pastor. My family served this man and the Church since we were teenagers. I picked up my family and followed him, as he was assigned not only in a new city, but an entirely different state as head pastor. He called me his *son* and entrusted me with much dealing with the transition and move to the new church. We ate together, fellowshipped together, cried together, laughed together, prayed together, and built this church together. After about four years into our move, things began to change drastically. He was bringing in *new faces* and *new voices*, and he was rubbing elbows with the rich and famous. Subtly, our communication and fellowship began to fade. He began to cut me out of conversations and meetings. Anytime I would preach for him and the Church was ministered to greatly by the Lord, he would pull me into his office and tell me to "tone it down". He accused me of trying to be him and imitating his preaching style to *woo* his people.

I was dumbfounded, as he was the man that encouraged me, equipped me, and empowered me to accept the call of God to preach. I was broken by his callousness toward me and my family. Eventually, I was no longer allowed to minister within the church or preach anywhere someone knew him. He made sure that no pastor in this city would accept me as an authentic minister of the Gospel. My family was ostracized by our fellow members and church family and we silently left the church.

It has been a long road of healing and forgiveness that had to take place in our lives. Power changes people. He is no longer the man I once knew. The emotional abuse we suffered at the hands of this man I once called "Dad" is indescribable! We were tossed away like trash. We pray every day for him to repent and turn back to God. May this evil cease to exist in churches all over the world and may true shepherds rise up and bring healing to God's people." ~ *K.D.*, Arizona

Verbal and emotional abuse within the trusted authority of spiritual leaders is beyond our natural understanding. There is something much more evil than we can fathom lying beneath the surface that would cause and therefore lead someone that calls themselves a pastor, preacher, priest, or spiritual leader to carry out such spiritual abuse. If this is not dealt with expeditiously, more grave spiritual abuse is inevitable.

Chapter 6

Mental & Psychological Abuse

"An evil man seeks only rebellion; Therefore a cruel messenger will be sent against him." Proverbs 17:11

We understand that abuse progressively develops in terms of cycles or stages. Abusers are very patient and calculating individuals. They make it a point to study the people they prey upon, in order to gain complete an utter power over them. As verbal and emotional abuse progresses, abuse victims are now in danger of becoming entangled in *mental and psychological manipulation*. It transforms from spiritual bullying into religious slavery. These abusers not only want to control your heart; they now desire to gain power over your mind. Many find this type of abuse extremely hard to believe amongst spiritual leadership, but it is taking place en masse all over the world and in every religion upon the face of the earth.

THE ELEPHANT IN THE ROOM

Mental and psychological abuse are forms of abuse characterized by a person subjecting or exposing another person to behavior that may result in mental/psychological trauma, including anxiety, chronic depression, or post-traumatic stress disorder. This kind of manipulation is a type of social influence that aims to change the behavior or perception of others through indirect, deceptive, or underhanded tactics. By advancing the interests of the manipulator, often at another's expense, such methodology could be considered exploitative and devious. Mental and psychological manipulation is viewed as the exercise of undue influence through mental distortion and emotional exploitation, with the intention to seize power, control, benefits and/or privileges at the victim's expense.

How does this play out in the confines of our sacred institutions? What benefit do spiritual leaders gain by subjecting those under their spiritual care to mental and psychological abuse? In the context of verbal and emotional abuse, we were able to gather that, in most cases, it is merely the deep, embedded emotional insecurities of the abusers desiring to inflict upon others what they, themselves, may have experienced in their own lives. Within the boundaries of mental and psychological abuse, if there is such a thing, these emotional insecurities morph into an insidious desire to "own" people's thoughts, and ultimately their minds, in an attempt to enslave them mentally to do their bidding.

In most of today's modern church settings, we are witnessing a more corporate-like structure, building and empowering entrepreneurs and business-minded people, focused upon wealth, status, and influence, instead of a spiritual gathering of like-minded believers in Christ, seeking and serving to save the lost of this world and discipling as the early church forefathers, and our Lord Jesus Christ, commanded in the Great Commission... the Gospel. I have been a part of several corporate church structures where these practices were commonplace. Conferences aimed at building wealth and creating business and entrepreneurial streams of affluence and influence have replaced worship, relationship with God, salvation, and discipleship. So many are deceived into believing this is God's will, because false teachers are twisting and perverting scripture in an effort to make it say, and agree with, their selfish and evil motives. Unfortunately, many are deceived and will continue to be deceived, because they do not have an intimate relationship with the Lord and with the Word of God themselves. They have fallen prey to the *lights, cameras, and action* of modern ministry and the celebrity of their spiritual leaders. In essence, they are trapped in idol worship.

Mental and psychological abuse is imminent in atmospheres such as this and thrives on the spiritual immaturity and ignorance of its victims. These spiritual leaders know full well when boundaries have been crossed and the once devoted allegiance and worship of God is transferred to a mere man. We cannot expect to imitate the world's ways and not take on the *spirits* of this world. The celebrity and entertainment-driven church culture of today is breeding ground for idol worship and cult-like activity.

"You shall have no other gods before Me." Exodus 20:3

THE ELEPHANT IN THE ROOM

The word *cult* is defined as formal religious worship, a system of religious beliefs and its body of adherents, a religion or social movement regarded as unorthodox or counterfeit, great devotion to a person or idea as well as persons united by devotion or allegiance to an artistic or intellectual movement or figure. A typical cult has a charismatic, unaccountable leader that persuades by coercion and exploits its members, financially, sexually, or in some other way.

"I honestly cannot remember how or when it shifted, but I found myself brainwashed by the man I highly honored and respected. We served alongside of one another fighting for civil rights in the community we were both raised. He was a born preacher; me, a social activist. He was a man of the greatest integrity and though we disagreed on much, our commonalities prevailed over our differences. He led me to Christ after ten years of standing arm and arm against deep-seated racism in our city. We vowed to serve God and our community side by side, until we took our last breaths.

Progressively over the next ten years, he became well-known and sought after in *preaching circles*. He began traveling incessantly and when he returned home to preach, his "doctrine" began to subtly change. He would speak about the spiritual leaders he met in other countries and how God was shifting his mindset and giving him deeper revelation of the Bible. His *extravagant charisma* and *quiet demeanor* captivated all that graced his presence. He was not a shouting preacher or a *make you stand up on your seat* kind of pastor. He was reserved and almost calculating now that I look back and see clearly what he was devising in his heart and in his mind. It was like we had been hypnotized over a period of time by his wisdom, knowledge, understanding, and revelation. Though I questioned much of this "revelation," I know now it was the Spirit of God warning me; his charm and countenance always lured me right into agreement with this deception. We called ourselves *soldiers for life*. Why would I question his intentions or motives? He loved me, he loved God, and he loved God's people, right?

That day came when he called an altar call for our entire church. He had just returned from Africa with a prominent church leader in the country he ministered, and he *gave us a word from God*. He told us that he received a visitation from Jesus, and he was commanded to have his entire church kneel before him, and kiss and pour out expensive oils upon his feet. We were to *anoint* him for the high calling he received from God during this "visitation". It was as if I was instantaneously awakened by God out of this trance this man so deceptively lured me and so many others into to worship him.

I refused! As I watched our entire church kneeling at this man's feet and yes, kissing and pouring oil upon them, I literally felt as if I was going to vomit! I got out of my seat and began to walk out. He openly rebuked me and called me a demon. The visiting pastor from Africa summoned his security to get me and bring me over to them to be "delivered". This stuff was literally like a scene out of some sort of diabolical movie. I was in outright disbelief! My *social activism* came out of me and I literally punched one of his security guards and demanded to call the police if they did not let me go. They did, and my pastor, my friend, my "soldier for life," told me to never set foot in his *holy* presence ever again. Not only did he *excommunicate* me from his church, but he told me I was condemned to hell for my rebellion against "his holiness".

You simply cannot make this stuff up… after years of spiritual counseling and yes, some psychiatric therapy; I found my way back to the truth. I have traveled to Africa and other countries around the world, and this kind of "ministry" is widespread… they are cults. It is absolute mental and psychological manipulation… it is witchcraft at its finest! I am so grateful to God for literally *opening my eyes*." ~*Brian*, Alabama

"And he said to Him, "All these things I will give You if You will fall down and worship me." Then Jesus said to him, 'Away with you Satan!' For it is written, "You shall worship the Lord your God, and Him only you shall serve.'" Then the devil left Him, and behold, angels, came and ministered to Him." Matthew 4: 9-11

MENTAL & PSYCHOLOGICAL ABUSE

Psychiatrist Robert Jay Lifton, who once taught at Harvard Medical School, wrote a paper titled *Cult Formation*[iii] in the early 1980s. He outlined three primary characteristics, which are the most common features shared by destructive cults.

1. "A charismatic leader, who increasingly becomes an object of worship as the general principles that may have originally sustained the group lose power. That is a living leader, who has no meaningful accountability and becomes the single most defining element of the group and its source of power and authority."

2. "A process of indoctrination or education is in use that can be seen as coercive persuasion or thought reform commonly called *brainwashing*."

3. "Economic, sexual, and other exploitation of group members by the leader and the ruling coterie (small exclusive group)."

We have witnessed a prevailing insurgence in the modern-day church culture of cult-like, charismatic leaders that are worshiped and idolized by hundreds, thousands, and even millions of followers all over the world. How can this be? How have so many strayed so very far away from God and His truth? Simple… they have been deceived through mental and psychological manipulation and abuse. The Bible says, "Let this mind be in you which was also in Christ Jesus." (Philippians 2:5) As we develop a personal relationship with Jesus, through His Word, our thoughts are transformed, literally, by the renewing of our minds.

(Romans 12:2) We can safeguard against deception as we guard our hearts and our minds IN the Word of God.

"Be anxious for nothing, but in everything by prayer and supplication, with thanksgiving, let your requests be made known to God; and the peace of God, which surpasses all understanding, will guard your hearts and minds through Christ Jesus." Philippians 4:7

Unfortunately, many refuse to meditate upon the Word of God for themselves and fail to develop an in-depth relationship with Him, while totally relying upon their "pastor" to teach them in the *ways of God*. Remember, these spiritual leaders may be abusing their authority and deceiving, but we, too, have a responsibility, through the Word, to guard ourselves, as well. When we allocate our freedom in Christ to mere man, and not the Spirit of the Living God, we hand over hearts and minds to mental and psychological abuse. The Father states that He will guard us through His peace, but we must obey His Word. Here are three effects of mental and psychological abuse that many Believers all over the world have suddenly found themselves facing and battling due to deception, oppression, and ultimately witchcraft, in our pulpits:

1. **Anxiety**: The Bible says be *anxious for nothing*! Anxiety is defined as intense, excessive, and persistent worry and fear about everyday situations. Here are several symptoms of anxiety:

❖ Feeling nervous, restless, or tense
❖ Having a sense of impending danger, panic, or doom
❖ Having an increased heart rate
❖ Breathing rapidly (hyperventilation)
❖ Sweating
❖ Trembling
❖ Feeling weak or tired
❖ Trouble concentrating or thinking about anything other than the present worry

2. **Chronic depression**: The Bible says, *"Let this mind be in you which was also in Christ Jesus."* Chronic depression is a mental health disorder characterized by persistently depressed mood or loss of interest in activities, causing significant impairment in daily life. Here are a few symptoms associated with this disorder:

❖ Sadness or depressed mood most of the day or almost every day
❖ Loss of enjoyment in things that were once pleasurable
❖ Major change in weight (gain or loss of more than 5% of weight within a month) or appetite
❖ Insomnia or excessive sleep almost every day
❖ Being physically restless or rundown in a way that is noticeable by others
❖ Fatigue or loss of energy almost every day
❖ Feelings of hopelessness or worthlessness or excessive guilt almost every day
❖ Problems with concentration or making decisions almost every day
❖ Recurring thoughts of death or suicide, suicide plan, or suicide attempt

3. **Post-traumatic stress disorder**: The Bible says, *"He will keep us in perfect peace as our minds are stayed on Him."* Better known as *PTSD*, this is a disorder in which a person has difficulty recovering after experiencing or witnessing a terrifying event. Several signs of PTSD include:

- ❖ Intense feelings of distress when reminded of a tragic event
- ❖ Extreme physical reactions to reminders of trauma, such as nausea, sweating, or a pounding heart
- ❖ Invasive, upsetting memories of a tragedy
- ❖ Flashbacks (feeling like the trauma is happening again)
- ❖ Nightmares of either frightening things or of the event
- ❖ Loss of interest in life and daily activities
- ❖ Feeling emotionally numb and detached from other people
- ❖ Sense of a not leading a normal life (not having a positive outlook of your future)
- ❖ Avoiding certain activities, feelings, thoughts or places that remind you of the tragedy
- ❖ Difficulty remembering important aspects of a tragic event

Due to our lack of wisdom concerning mental health in the Church, as well as the deception of our enemy concerning the Word of God, we find ourselves trapped in these mental and psychological battles, because we refuse to believe that our spiritual leaders are, indeed, battling these disorders themselves, as well using them to manipulate and control people under their authority. I understand that these disorders are a part of many people's lives, even those outside of the Church, but I am speaking to the spiritual abuse carried out by those entrusted to the care and well-being of those they committed to serve spiritually, which directly contributes to severe anxiety, chronic depression, and yes, post-traumatic stress disorder (PTSD).

When a Believer is manipulated by someone they have entrusted spiritually, this tends to be more mentally and psychologically destructive in his/her life, because the spiritual leader is held to a trusted position in the *stead*, or role, of God. Though we fully understand that no man can or should hold this weight of authority in anyone's life, it happens more often than not in the Church, as well as other religions around the world. People tend to equate the spiritual abuse with God Himself and develop a severely distorted and deceptive view of their Creator. This is highly destructive. We usually only hear of PTSD in the ranks of our military servicemen and women, due to the stress and trauma of being sent to war zones, of which many have actually gone through intense battle and have seen death and destruction. Many of whom have come home severely wounded, not only physical, but emotionally, mentally, and psychologically. But we fail to recognize the very same symptoms revealed in the lives of those that have suffered mental and psychological abuse from spiritual leadership.

I have interviewed hundreds of people around the world that have experienced mental and psychological abuse in the Church. This book cannot even begin to contain the stories of people all over the world that suffer daily trying to reconcile what took place in their lives. The guilt, shame, and yes, blaming themselves for not being able to see the deception of these spiritual leaders is a reality in these people's lives. Many no longer go to Church, some have even questioned their faith, and others have walked completely away from God. The repercussions of spiritual abuse are astronomical! Sadly, because we have refused to address this abuse in the Church, though this is shifting drastically, we are seeing mass casualties in Christendom.

***

"I have battled with drug addiction most of my life. I struggled with health issues since birth and the drug use started in high school, because the pain was just too unbearable. When I gave my life to Christ, I was able, progressively, to get deliverance from the drugs. I was never really close to my mom, and never knew who my dad was, until later on in life. The Church really became my family and I was beginning to heal in many areas of my life, physically, emotionally, and mentally. The church I was a member of was well-known in my city, and around the country. Our pastor traveled all over the world and was pretty sought out by other pastors/churches. I loved my pastor. He was so energetic and passionate when he preached. When news of his corruption and infidelity surfaced, I was broken. I had been at this church for four years, and I never saw this coming.

So many people began to the leave the church and there was so much division in the leadership. People were gossiping, some against him and some for him. I was lost. I honestly got really angry. I left the streets to get away from the world and all the chaos and confusion in it. I stayed for a while after all of this took place, and he was still preaching. I did not recognize this man. He became very arrogant and nasty. Instead of humbling himself and repenting before the Church, he abused the pulpit to attack other people. Every Wednesday and every Sunday, my spirit was becoming more grieved. People continued to leave the church, and there was a heavy spirit over us all. Unfortunately, I was becoming angrier and angrier by the day. I fell back into drug use, but this time, it was heavier. Not only was I using more; I was now using heavier drugs than before. No one in the church would discuss what was happening. I had so many emotions and the one place I assumed would help me pretty much ignored me. The leaders were all stunned themselves, and really didn't know what to say. Some became just as arrogant as the pastor, and so much changed. I felt all alone, once again. I did not feel God in this church anymore. It became a show.

I am not proud of my decline back into drugs, and I am not placing blame on this man. What I am saying is that it affected me tremendously, as well as many others. I eventually left and spiraled out of control. I tried to take my life several times, but I guess God was not ready for me. Though I am not currently in a church, I am in therapy and getting stronger by the day." ~*Sean*, Atlanta, GA

Thoughts of Suicide

Anxiety, chronic depression, and post-traumatic stress disorder, if not addressed and dealt with can and will lead to thoughts of suicide and unfortunately, the carrying out of this most devastating ending of one's life. It is taking place in churches all over the world. Christians are not exempt from falling into this destructive cycle. Unfortunately, it is happening far too often in the Church amongst lay members, as well as pastors/spiritual leaders. Something in particular is taking place spiritually; something has shifted over the last decade that has caused a major spike in suicides not only in the world, but in the Church, as well. There is a great spirit of oppression that has been released, and the casualties are growing by the day. We know the Bible prophesies these specific times taking place in the last days.

"For false christs and false prophets will rise and show great signs and wonders to deceive, if possible, even the elect." Matthew 24:24

False teachers/prophets are growing by the day. Many did not start out this way but gradually, over time, became deceived themselves, and in turn, began deceiving. With social media so widely available at our fingertips today, even in the most remote of areas, these false teachers/prophets have amassed followers that sit in front of their computers for hours every day being deceived. Due to the decline in church attendance because of the celebrity/entertainment-driven culture, many have chosen to pick their favorite preacher(s), free of relationship and human

118

interaction, and accept this as "church". Unfortunately, many of these people do not understand that even this is a trick of our enemy, Satan. His desire is to isolate us and strip us of any and all human interaction, and because of this, many fall into deep depression and loneliness, leading to suicide. We must seek God for keen discernment in these last days. Deception is at its highest!

Through all of this, we are able to distinguish between the true, authentic spiritual leaders called by God to serve in this capacity and the counterfeit, opportunity-seeking false teachers/prophets out for self-centeredness and self-gratification. One of the most notable of traits revealed through these false spiritual leaders is *narcissism*. Let's delve into this insidious trait and learn of its origin and its purpose.

Narcissism

Narcissism is defined as the pursuit of gratification from vanity or egotistic admiration of one's idealized self-image and attributes. This includes self-flattery, perfectionism, and arrogance. The term originated from Greek mythology, where the young Narcissus fell in love with his own image reflected in a pool of water. Narcissists typically come from families where the parent/parents seek conformity in their children, rather than offering a healthy, loving, and maturing environment where children can grow and learn without callousness and criticism. Sadly, most pastors/preachers grow up in these rigid environments due to steeped and staunched religious upbringings. Depending upon their denomination, or sect, this can very well determine the levels of narcissism in a spiritual leader's life. Though we see the mental and psychological abuse carried out by spiritual leaders, we must understand that they, too, suffer or have suffered from it themselves.

Narcissism is a mental health condition characterized by:
- an inflated sense of importance
- a deep need for excessive attention and admiration
- lack of empathy for others
- often having troubled relationships

People with a narcissistic personality are walking on very dangerous ground when it comes to leading in a spiritual capacity. The spiritual well-being of hundreds, thousands, and even millions, in some cases, is as stake. There must be a system of accountability and responsibility within our church structures to righteously and rightfully deal with these issues, so masses of people can be protected from mental and psychological abuse and manipulation.

The most recent edition of the *Diagnostic and Statistical Manual of Mental Disorders*[iv] lists nine criteria for diagnosing narcissism, but it specifies that someone only needs to meet five of these standards to clinically qualify as a narcissist.

❖ grandiose sense of self-importance

❖ preoccupation with fantasies of unlimited success, power, brilliance, beauty, or ideal love

❖ belief they're special and unique and can only be understood by, or should associate with, other special or high-status people or institutions

❖ need for excessive admiration

❖ sense of entitlement

❖ interpersonally exploitative behavior

❖ lack of empathy

❖ envy of others or a belief that others are envious of them

❖ demonstration of arrogant and haughty behaviors or attitudes

I have personally encountered numerous spiritual leaders with all these characteristics combined, unfortunately. It is devastating to witness God's name being used and abused alongside of these self-centered attributes, but I have come to understand that God is nowhere in these gatherings any longer. It ceased to be about Him the moment these narcissistic traits surfaced and were allowed to manifest in His Church.

"The church I attended, and was a member of for thirty years, has become inundated with narcissists. It was a staple in our community for so many years, but rapidly began declining as preachers from all over the world began visiting and sharing their false doctrines across the pulpit.

THE ELEPHANT IN THE ROOM

Our pastors went from reserved and humble friends to arrogant and entitled associates. Sadly, I now count many of my *not-so-close* associates as more of friends than I do these pastors. Their air of newfound *self-importance* reeks of pride and arrogance. Their children are even worse, unfortunately. They all walk around the church as if they are *gods*. They look down on you as if you are beneath their acknowledging. I know this sounds harsh, because it is absolutely reprehensible! I was a pastor in this church! The lead pastor of this church would often say, "Eagles don't associate with chickens." Who was he speaking of? This is a church! A sacred place of worship for God's people! I was slowly beginning to see where this church was heading, and I did not like it one bit!

As people began to speak up and speak out, he would make it a point to open up each service with this phrase, "We have a lot of jealous haters amongst us church. Let God deal with them. He will avenge us." His arrogance grew and grew, until I could take it no more! I confronted my once dear friend about my deep concerns and there was no response other than, "You're fired! Get out of my presence!" The desire for fortune and fame will turn even the humblest of people into narcissistic madmen. I not only grieve the death of a friendship, but I mourn the loss of God's authentic Church. We are in dark times." ~*Tom*, California

The narcissistic personality has no place in the confines of our sacred assemblies. How can light dwell with darkness? How can good fellowship with evil? How can love mingle with hate? How can humility coexist with pride? How can truth exist with lies? We all understand fully that these contradictions are not plausible in the house of God. Godly fruit and spiritual maturity cannot blossom in these demonic gatherings. These spiritual leaders are deceived and deceiving.

Here is a list of ten warning signs of narcissistic leadership.

- Absolute authoritarianism without meaningful accountability
- No tolerance for questions or critical inquiry
- No meaningful financial disclosure regarding budget or expenses, such as an independently audited financial statement
- Unreasonable fear about the outside world, such as impending catastrophe, evil conspiracies, and persecutions
- There is no legitimate reason to leave, former followers are always wrong in leaving, negative or even evil
- Former members often relate the same stories of abuse and reflect a similar pattern of grievances
- There are records, books, news articles, or broadcast reports that document the abuses of the group/leader
- Followers feel they can never be "good enough"
- The group/leader is always right
- The group/leader is the exclusive means of knowing "truth" or receiving validation, no other process of discovery is really acceptable or credible

We will never really come to terms that our spiritual leaders can maneuver in such devious and deceptive ways. It is hard to believe, and in many cases, we refuse to believe that the very people we entrusted as God's messengers could consciously, or even unconsciously, do such things. Understand that there are spiritual entities at work seeking to destroy not only God's people, but ultimately God's name and His image in the Earth, and what better place to start than in spiritual leadership.

A common tactic of narcissism most prevalent in today's church culture is a phrase coined as *Gaslighting*. Gaslighting is a form of psychological manipulation in which a person or a group covertly sows seeds of doubt in a targeted individual, making them question their own memory, perception, or judgment, often evoking in them cognitive dissonance (conflicting ideas, beliefs, or values) and other changes, such as low self-esteem. In essence, they cause their victims to question their own sanity. Below are several ways in which Gaslighting manifests through mental and psychological abuse:

- You no longer feel like the person you used to be
- You feel more anxious and less confident than you used to be
- You often wonder if you're being too sensitive
- You feel like everything you do is wrong
- You always think it's your fault when things go wrong
- You're apologizing often

- You have a sense that something's wrong, but aren't able to identify what it is
- You often question whether your response is appropriate
- You make excuses for the abuser's behavior

"My life was destroyed serving people I thought were true shepherds of God. I poured my life into this church and into these pastors that took me in off the streets. Yes, I am forever grateful, but I often wonder if I was better off in the streets. I was a former prostitute struggling to take care of my daughter. I was abused as a child and my mother was a drug addict. It was an endless cycle of destruction. I met these pastors at an outdoor outreach during the winter. They were giving out coats, blankets, hot food, and toiletries. After receiving the items, they asked if they could pray with me. They did and invited me to their church. I was really hesitant, because there were so many that came into the city that were only out for a *photo op*. They would come with cameras and video cameras to document what they were doing. Very few were ever really concerned about those of us in the streets.

I was at the end of my rope at this point, so I went to the church. I gave my life to Jesus and began going every Sunday. I was immediately told that I needed to join as a member, as this was God's order. I didn't question it, because they were the pastors, they knew better than me. I became a member and of course was immediately told that members should tithe. I didn't have two coins to rub together, but everything I received, I gave ten percent to the church. I was told I had to serve in some sort of ministry, so I did. I began greeting those that would come into the church. It was awkward, as I was very standoffish, but I did it anyway.

I really did not know what "church" was supposed to be like. I did not go to church growing up and didn't know anyone that did, either. My perception through this experience was that you did what God asked with no questions and this went for our pastors, as well. I honestly believe now that these pastors were preying on the weak and abused of society. They knew we were vulnerable and "easy prey". They figured they could reel us in with their outreach and make us slaves in their church. I was told, not asked, to clean the bathrooms, the kitchen, and the sanctuary, if I wanted food. I was still on the streets during this time. Again, I did not know any other way. Our church had about twenty people, very small, all of which were from the streets: drug addicts, prostitutes, drug dealers, and the homeless. We all had jobs to do to keep the church up.

After about a year of being at this church, I got a job. My life seemed to be turning around for good. I told my pastor's wife that I was blessed with a job and would need to pull back from the cleaning, because it would interfere with my work hours. Whew! Let me tell you, the response she gave was like I had met the devil himself! She cursed me completely out and told me, "First of all, you don't simply go out and *find a job* without asking your pastors, first. Your job is here in this church that you committed to serving. We own you and you owe us." Secondly, she told me, "And who do you think we have to clean this church? We are going to have to go back out and find someone else. Not only are you going to give us ten percent of your check, but you are going to pay us extra for the hours you are losing cleaning, until we find someone else." I could not believe what I was hearing! I told her that I was not under a legal contract to do this work in the church and that I was doing it out of love and service. She proceeded to tell me that they were feeding me and my daughter and giving us at least a warm building to be in for hours during the day, whereas we would be in the cold streets… that we owed her.

I could not take it anymore. I told her I would rather live on the streets, than be treated like a slave in this church. This woman called me a whore and said I would always be a whore, and that my child was a bastard. She proceeded to tell me that I would never be anything else in this life and to get out. Mind you, I had been abused all my life. I lived on the streets and prostituted my own body. The mental and psychological abuse this woman and her husband put me and many others through is beyond comprehension. My life was already "bad" before I met these people, but to know that there are some in this world that will use God's name to abuse and enslave is absolutely evil and disgusting.

I don't even know who to trust anymore. I avoid these "street preachers" and "outreaches" as much as I possibly can. ~*Toni*, New York

God does not tear down His people with His words; He builds them up. God does not twist and pervert the truth to destroy someone's emotional well-being; He plants, He waters, and He gives us increase. God is not a control freak, a master manipulator, or an irrational intimidator; HE IS LOVE! God is not a psychotic tyrant, determined and resolute to destroy the mental and psychological state of His people; He gives them His peace and the mind of Christ. God is not a raving manic, hell-bent on destroying "mere sheep;" He is the Lamb sent as a sacrifice and the Lion, coming to avenge His people!

When will we, the Church, finally stand up and say, "ENOUGH!" When will we choose to demand accountability and responsibility in our pulpits? When will we boldly stand in the face of evil and lift the standard of our Lord Jesus Christ? The time is now.

Cultural/Ethnic Abuse

Mental and psychological abuse guised under the umbrella of spiritual authority has been around since the beginning of time. Masses of entire cultures have been the target of spiritual abuse in the name of "religion". The tearing down verbally, emotionally, mentally, and psychologically of entire groups of people in the name of God, or any kind of *god*, may very well be the greatest of evils and atrocities committed upon the face of the Earth. It is diabolical to believe that any ethnicity of people is superior to another created human being.

We have witnessed through the centuries entire nations slaughtered *in the name of God* or *in the name of a leader*. Whether it may have been in the ancient scrolls, earliest of biblical texts, historical accounts, and even other spiritual or mystical writings throughout history, we are keenly aware of the ethnic/cultural *cleansing* of entire groups of people in the name of superiority of race, underlined by religion or spirituality. Here is a list of several well-known in history (not exhaustive):

- ❖ Hebrew Genocide of all male boys under 2-years-old (37-4 BC)
- ❖ Nubia Genocide (12,000-10,000 BCE)
- ❖ Sarai Nahar Rai, India (2140-850 BCE)
- ❖ Volos'ke, Ukraine (7500 BCE)
- ❖ Roman Genocide of Carthage (146 BCE)
- ❖ Athenian Massacre at Melos (416 BCE)
- ❖ St Brice's Day Massacre, Vikings (1002)
- ❖ The Crusades (1095-1492)
- ❖ The Mongol Invasions (1206-1405)
- ❖ African Slavery/The Atlantic Slave Trade/Black Holocaust (1444-1865)
- ❖ Taiping Rebellion, China (1850-1864)
- ❖ The War of Triple Alliance, Paraguayan War (1864-1870)

- ❖ Native American Genocide, Wounded Knee Massacre (1890)
- ❖ Herero and Namaqua Genocide, Namibia (1904-1908)
- ❖ The Albanian Genocide/Balkan War (1912-1913)
- ❖ The Armenian Genocide (1915-1917)
- ❖ The Soviet Great Terror, Russia (1932-1933)
- ❖ The Jewish Holocaust, Germany (1933-1945)
- ❖ The Bangladesh Genocide, Pakistan (1971)
- ❖ The Cambodian Genocide (1975-1979)
- ❖ Omarska/Prijedor Massacre, Bosnia/Herzegovina (1992)
- ❖ The Rwandan Genocide (1994)
- ❖ The Kosovo Genocide (1998-1999)
- ❖ The Darfur Genocide, Sudan (2003)
- ❖ Nigerian Genocide/Boko Haram, Nigeria (2014-present)
- ❖ Christian & Yazidi Genocide, Iraq/Syria (2014-present)
- ❖ The Rohingya Genocide, Myanmar (2015-present)
- ❖ The Kurdish Genocide, Turkey/Syria/Iraq (2018-present)

The first session of the *United Nations General Assembly* affirmed the crime of genocide describing it as "a denial of the right of existence of entire human groups, as homicide is the denial of the right to live of individual human beings." [v]

Unfortunately, though much of this mass genocide/ethnic cleansing is a result of tyrannical regimes, its underlying evil stems from religious and/or spiritual perversion and/or corruption. The twisting of religion for the mass manipulation, control, intimidation, mental and psychological warfare, as well as eradication of entire ethnic groups has been recorded all throughout our history.

There are two reigning mindsets that allow these atrocities to happen. One is *dehumanizing*, where you consider other groups of people less than human. Then there is *demonizing*, where you consider them to be fully human, which makes them all the more contemptible because of the evil choices that they've made. Here are some well-known quotes and facts concerning the dehumanizing, demonizing, and obliteration of entire ethnicities:

Jews:

"Don't be misled into thinking you can fight a disease without killing the carrier, without destroying the bacillus. Don't think you can fight racial tuberculosis without taking care to rid the nation of the carrier of that racial tuberculosis. This Jewish contamination will not subside; this poisoning of the nation will not end, until the carrier himself, the Jew, has been banished from our midst." ~ *Adolf Hitler,* German Chancellor, Nazi Party

- "It is the mission of the Islamic Republic of Iran to erase Israel from the map of the region." ~*Ayatollah Ali Khamenei,* former Supreme Leader of Iran

- A fellow Nazi reported Eichmann once said, "… he would leap laughing into the grave because the feeling that he had five million people on his conscience would be for him a source of extraordinary satisfaction." ~*Otto Adolf Eichmann*, Austrian German Nazi SS Officer

Yazidi:

"Our psychological, social, and religious identity has been destroyed. People are living all over the place, and they don't know what the future is. There have been no initiatives from the Iraqi government to help the displaced people return back to Sinjar; no national reconciliation process; no attempt to rebuild ruined infrastructure." ~ *Khider Domle*, Yazidi researcher

- "Researchers said families who failed to escape were rounded up en masse and divided up as part of the "systematic" genocide that saw men and boys above the age of twelve separated and massacred if they refused to convert to Islam." ~ *Dr. Valeria Cetorelli*

Christians:

"Islam is not willing to be a peaceful religion. It has the goal of conquering all religions into acceptance or subordination. This is why there is so much violence in Islam. The Sunnis are killing the Shia and the Shia are killing the Sunnis. Both types are killing other "heretical" Muslim groups. The killing of Coptic Christians in Egypt has been a result of the drive for conquest. The killing of Christians in Africa, the Middle East, and other Islamic countries has the aim of *eradicating*

Christians or *forcing their conversion* to Islam." *~Dallas Roark*, Answering Islam

- The number of Christians in Iraq is especially stark: Before the American invasion, as many as 1.4 million Christians lived in the country. Today, fewer than 250,000 remain—an 80 percent drop in less than two decades. *~The Guardian*

- "The government of China has orchestrated a campaign to '*Sinicize*' Christianity, to turn Christianity into a fully domesticated religion that would do the bidding of the party. Bibles are being destroyed, churches are being demolished, Christians are being imprisoned, and crosses are being removed from buildings all over China." *~Lian Xi*, Professor at Duke University

Muslims:

"As grim as the situation is for Rohingya (Muslim) refugees in Bangladesh... their prospects back in Myanmar (Buddhist) are even worse." *~Joshua Kurlantzick*, Senior Fellow for Southeast Asia

- By 1875, the French conquest of Algeria was complete. The war had killed approximately 825,000 indigenous Algerians since 1830. A long shadow of genocidal hatred persisted, provoking a French author to protest in 1882 that in Algeria, "We hear it repeated every day that we must expel the native and if necessary, destroy him." As a French statistical journal urged five years later, "The system of extermination must give way to a policy of penetration." *~Ben Kiernan*, Australian genocide expert

Africans/African Americans/People of Color:

"Our clear goal must be the advancement of the white race and separation of the white and black races." *David Duke*, former Grand Master/Ku Klux Klan

- In *Mein Kampf*, Hitler described children resulting from marriages to African occupation soldiers as a contamination of the white race "by Negro blood on the Rhine in the heart of Europe." He thought that "Jews were responsible for bringing Negroes into the Rhineland, with the ultimate idea of bastardizing the white race which they hate and thus lowering its cultural and political level so that the Jew might dominate." He also implied that this was a plot on the part of the French, since the population of France was being increasingly "negrified". *~Adolf Hitler*, German Chancellor

- Perhaps, one of the greatest genocides in history, collectively, through the mass pillaging of the African continent by British, Arab, and other nations led to the transcontinental slave trade of Africans to the Americas (Central & South American islands, The Americas, and Canada.) Many records show that around 12.5 million Africans were enslaved, and around 1.8 million perished on the ships (or were thrown overboard) during the Middle Passage from the 15th through 19th centuries. Several human rights groups, as well as historians, believe these numbers are erroneously inaccurate and could very well have been in the tens of millions enslaved with close to ten million lost to genocide.

Native American Indians:

"Damn any man who sympathizes with Indians! I have come to kill Indians, and believe it is right and honorable to use any means under God's heaven to kill Indians. Kill and scalp all, big and little; nits make lice." ~*Col. John Milton Chivington,* U.S. Army

- "U.S. history, as well as inherited Indigenous trauma, cannot be understood without dealing with the genocide that the United States committed against Indigenous peoples. From the colonial period through the founding of the United States and continuing in the twentieth century, this has entailed torture, terror, sexual abuse, massacres, systematic military occupations, removals of Indigenous peoples from their ancestral territories, forced removal of Native American children to military-like boarding schools, allotment, and a policy of termination." ~*Roxanne Dunbar-Ortiz*, Native American Studies Professor

"The abuse runs deep in Native American families. I am old enough to remember much more than most of us. I was born in 1921. Our identities were completely stripped away, our land was stolen, and our minds, brainwashed. There is a deep hatred within Native American communities and reservations for the "white man". My parents would share horrific stories passed down from their parents and grandparents of how our livelihood and humanity were stolen *in the name of religion*. I remember a story my father told us of a preacher that said, "It was God's will for us to come and secure this land. It was God's will for us to come over and "civilize" this land. It was God's will for us to build America. It was our destiny." Many of us know our Creator deeply and though some of the "spirituality" of our ancestors was pagan, our people have always been a spiritual and peaceful race. We understand what God's will is and what is the will of evil men that use His name for their own gain.

It wasn't until 1924 that Native American Indians were "allowed" citizenship in a land where we were indigenous. Many of our brothers and sisters living on the reservations today are so isolated and broken, living in dire poverty and steeped in alcoholism, drug use, and suffering mental illness. The suicide rate amongst Native Americans is extremely high, a statistic the government refuses to address or even acknowledge. Our culture was wiped completely out! There was a genocide of our people! I can't speak for any other ethnic group or race of people; I can only speak for mine. Our entire way of life was destroyed. Our entire land mass was stolen. Our entire language was bastardized. Our people are on the brink of absolute distinction.

Over 90% of the Native American Indian population was destroyed by colonization. This was not a progressive totality over decades or even centuries; this took place almost immediately upon seizure of our land.

From the mass murder of entire tribes, disease infested immigrants, building of structures that pushed out our natural habitats of wildlife and agriculture, Natives were all but *spirits of the past*. Our population pre-colonization was reported at close to 115 million (I believe it was much higher). Today, it is reported at 5 million (I believe it is much lower than this), or 1.5% of the United States population. What a difference 500 years makes… pray for our people. I have lived a long life and suffered much, but my people today are suffering greater. They are slowly disappearing." ~*B.W.*, Wyoming

3 Causes of Genocide:

1. **Fractionalization, grievance, and dehumanization**: This group of theories collectively argue that genocide can be predicted by higher ethnolinguistic or religious fractionalization within a country combined with grievances between groups. The final important dimension is dehumanization of the victim group. This theory is associated with the sociologist Leo Kuper, who conducted some of the earliest studies in comparative genocide.

2. **National crises**: Here, catastrophic events such as war, economic depression, or revolution are the triggers for genocide or other types of mass killing. This causality is motivated by one of two theories, the scapegoat theory and the political opportunity theory. The first theory suggests that a particular group is identified

as the cause of the crisis and that the solution is to eliminate the group. The second theory instead argues that the crisis creates the opportunity for a group to consolidate their power.

3. **Government power**: This theory is largely due to Rudolph Rummel and is referred to as the power principle. Rummel argues that, "The more power a government has, the more it can act arbitrarily according to the whims and desires of the elite, and the more it will make war on others and murder its foreign and domestic subjects. The more constrained the power of governments, the less it will aggress on others."

10 Stages of the Genocidal process[vi]:

1. Classification
2. Symbolization
3. Discrimination
4. Dehumanization
5. Organization
6. Polarization
7. Preparation
8. Persecution
9. Extermination
10. Denial

These are the most inhumane acts forced upon humanity that seek to enact both mental and psychological abuse upon those they deem *weaker*, *subservient*, and even *less than human*. Yet, from the Beginning, we see even the division between brothers: Cain and Abel; Esau and Jacob (fraternal twins); Ishmael and Isaac (half-brothers); and the twelve sons of Jacob: Joseph, Simeon, Levi, Zebulon, Issachar, Dan, Gad, Asher, Naphtali, Reuben, Judah, and Benjamin. The inept hatred and jealousy ran deep in each of these families, even to the point of murder. It's not ultimately the color of a man's skin, or even the family we are inherently born into; it is the evil of man's heart... the sin of man that persuades us, tempts us, and forces us to enact hatred upon our fellow man.

Unfortunately, we have a true and real enemy that distracts, disconnects, deceives, and destroys us with futile arguments and surface-level disagreements. How we receive the spiritual wisdom of God our Creator verses responding to fleshly and carnal feelings will ultimately determine our humanity. When we experience racism or cultural abuse of any kind, do we reciprocate (is it inherently within us, as well) or do we rise above it, knowing with confidence that we were all created in the image of God Almighty, Creator of every living being on the face of the Earth? Do we have to tear down another human being to feel good about the pigment of our skin? Do we believe the level of melanin in our skin, or lack thereof, distinguishes superiority? This level of ignorance is what our true enemy banks on... he desires to keep us at each other's throats, not understanding that we are, indeed, descendants of one another. We all possess a level of melanin in our skin, some more, some less, and in rare cases, none at all (albinism), but again, does this equate to superiority or inferiority?

Each culture upon the face of the Earth has a spiritual viewpoint of who our Creator is, and yes, what physical attributes He possesses. There are even disputes of who the *original* people are, and whether there is a superior or subservient ethnicity/race/culture of people. This has been going on since the beginning of time, and sadly, will continue until the end of time.

The Greek philosopher Xenophanes of Colophon (c.570-478 BCE)[vii] once wrote:

"Mortals suppose that the gods are born and have clothes and voices and shapes like their own. But if oxen, horses, and lions had hands or could paint with their hands and fashion works as men do, horses would paint horse-like images of gods and oxen oxen-like ones, and each would fashion bodies like their own. The Ethiopians consider the gods flat-nosed and black; the Thracians, blue-eyed and red-haired."

Many different ethnicities ascribe God to be in their own image, instead of us all being formed and created in His image. Because of the innate and gross spiritual abuse over the centuries, people have been exposed to mental and psychological manipulation in the form of religious bondage and slavery. They are programmed to believe that God has made them a subservient race of people. Then, there are others that have also been victims of mental and psychological abuse in the form of superiority complexes in religions that teach that the color of their skin gives them privilege above another ethnicity of people. Over the years, this complex has shifted back and forth, reciprocally, between cultures and ethnicities all over the world. Please note, in our not so distant history, the last countries to abolish slavery were Saudi Arabia in 1962, and Mauritania in 1980. This is only on record; there are many countries that continue this practice *in the dark.*

"There is neither Jew nor Greek, there is neither slave nor free, there is neither male nor female; for you are all one in Christ Jesus." Galatians 3:28

"I grew up in one school throughout my entire childhood. It was a Christian academy and it was connected to the actual Church that ran the school. I was one of very few black kids in this school, as well as the Church. Our family was accepted wholeheartedly with no qualms about us being "black;" they loved us, and we loved them. My brothers and I excelled in school, joined sports, traveled on mission's trips, and served in our church just like all the other *church kids*. It was a non-denominational church with more of a contemporary Christian flare. Our worship was definitely not what most black churches, or even Pentecostal churches, were used to hearing. As I graduated and began in the workforce, I interacted more with those of my own ethnicity. I always got joked on, because they said I was acting too "white". My clothes, my hair, my talk, and my style, to them, were not *ethnic* enough. One of my friends at work invited me to his church. I was all for it! Any chance to worship Jesus, especially in a new setting, was exciting to me. It was a traditional Baptist church, and it was an entirely African American congregation. I enjoyed the praise and worship, even though it was not what I had grown up experiencing. The preaching was definitely more upbeat and fiery than my church, but the Word was explosive!

My friend wanted to introduce me to his pastor after the service, so we waited in line to speak to him. I shook his hand and he asked me my name. I told him and he had a strange look on his face. He asked me where I grew up and where I went to school. I proceeded to tell him about the Christian academy and my church. His demeanor shifted intensely. He asked me how I could live around, go to school, and worship with "white people". I was definitely taken back, but I boldly said to him, "Why not?" This was his response, "So your family must be their "token black family"? I was truly trying my best not to get offended, but I could not believe I was having this conversation with a pastor! I said, "Sir, with all due respect, my family is not a *token* anything, and my Dad works with many of the people in my church. They are friends, but more importantly, they are brothers and sisters in Christ." He literally laughed in my face! He said, "Okay, you keep believing that son. You're one of the sell-outs." And he walked away.

My heart grieved deeply as we left. I asked my friend how he could be in a church, and underneath of a pastoral covering, that hated white people? He explained to me that there is deep-seated anger against them in the *black church* and that all white people are the same. I interjected and explained to him that this was simply not true. I was a living witness to this, spending all of my life in the same church and with the same church family. I tried telling him that this was not God's thoughts and that He created us all in His image and likeness, and that yes, there is racism in the world, but the Church should not be one of those places. He laughed at me and said, "You must be living in a fantasy world." It was at this point that I realized how divided the global church really is, and that there was a huge gap between what I thought and what is really taking place in the Church. I vowed to God at this point that I would be a part of changing this narrative." ~*W.D.,* Massachusetts

Sunday mornings, all across the United States of America, is probably the most segregated day of the week. From the North to the South and from the East to the West, people gather together in small town family churches and storefronts, to multimillion-dollar mega church facilities and everything in between. In most small town, rural areas, you see most ethnicities worshipping with their own people. Their traditions and cultures influence them to be more "comfortable" with their own *kind* and you very seldom see someone of another *race* as a member. In the mega church setting, though there is more of a likelihood for integrated worship and fellowship, there is still a *dominant* culture apparent, whether black, white, Spanish, Asian or otherwise. This "culture" will determine the overall atmosphere of the church, from worship to prayer. There are many mega churches that are all of one *race*, with no integration whatsoever.

I have been a military spouse for almost twenty years, but more intricately, a part of a multiracial family. I was raised a Methodist and my husband, Baptist. We have traveled all over the world and been privileged to worship with many nationalities and denominations from English, German, Dutch, Italian, African, Spanish and Korean, to Baptist, Methodist, Pentecostal, A.M.E., Anglican, and many non-denominational fellowships. Our scope of worship and fellowship is broader than most people. We have never "sought out" a church, God has always led us where He needed us to be and we learned to adapt to each culture of worship and fellowship. It allowed us to see the many facets of God's creation and how they loved and honored the Lord.

This is not easy for many to do. Sometimes, when I walk into a fully black church, I get stares. I can worship anywhere that lifts up the name of Jesus! But it is uncomfortable for many to cross these lines. Much has to do with race, but some of it is embedded deep within tradition and religion. Some feel they absolutely cannot worship unless it is to traditional Gospel hymns played on organs or pianos. This is their culture, their tradition... all they know. Some require dress codes and if someone new walks in off the streets and is not dressed "appropriately," they are usually met immediately with judgment, instead of love, because of *tradition*. We run a lot of people away from church due to our strict rules, traditions, and religion, and in many cases, mental and psychological abuse.

I often ask myself, "If we all believe the Bible and believe in Jesus Christ/Yeshua HaMashiach, how is it that we, the Church, are so divided?" How is it that a white preacher can preach the same message as a black preacher, same scripture reference and all, but some would not receive simply because of the manner in which it was preached? Some preachers are very calm and reserved, while others are very loud and boisterous. Some churches don't respond much in *Amen's* or *shouts*, but receive in a more reserved manner, while others will jump, shout, throw their hands up, and dance. Is any of this the right or wrong way? Absolutely not! The Bible reveals all kinds of ways to praise and worship our Lord, yet many seem to think their way is right and all others wrong. Again, because of my being exposed to the *world of worship*, I can walk into any Christian church that loves Jesus and worship with my brothers and sisters, no matter ethnicity, culture, or language. Even if I cannot understand the language, I am connected to them by the Spirit of God.

I traveled to Germany in May of 2014 to minister at a conference and there were so many countries represented. There were translators when I ministered, but after the service, I was just standing worshipping and a beautiful woman from Curaçao walked over to me. She could speak no English, but just looked into my eyes and tears began to roll down both of our faces. We knew one another by the Spirit of God, not by the flesh: our skin color, our language, or our culture. It was so breathtaking. Before I left the conference, she came to me and held my face and said, "Sister." I will never forget this moment in time. This is what God desires for His people! The Bible says in Psalm 133 that it is good and pleasant for brothers (sisters) to dwell together in Unity. This should be the mark of the Church.

People are calling for the Church to be the voice of reconciliation for the racial upheaval we are seeing in the U.S. and around the world, and we absolutely should be, but we can't speak what we are not living. It must start with us first. We must begin to unite in one common cause: JESUS/YESHUA. We must learn to love one another, respect one another's traditions and cultures, and "hold the face" of our brother/sister, even if we don't fully understand them or know their "culture". Purpose in your heart to get to know people of other ethnicities, cultures, traditions, and denominations. Find out how they worship God and respect and honor it. Pray for your brothers and sisters. Start with the Church closest to you that is not *like* yours. Reach out, pray with them, and build relationships. Our ultimate love for one another will allow humanity to see the light of God and begin to heal and reconcile this nation and the world at large. It starts with YOU! What will you do today to begin the healing and bridge the gap? When we all begin to see our distinct commonalities and that we are all created in His image and in His likeness, this spirit of mental and psychological abuse, manipulation, and warfare will cease to exist. We, the Church, the people of God/Yahweh must reconcile this in our hearts *first*, before we are able to minister to this lost and dying world. Spiritual leadership must be the example!

"I thought I was losing my mind. The things I was seeing and hearing from God concerning the spiritual leadership in my church just did not seem real. I battled back and forth, trusting what God was showing me in one instance and then rebuking it, thinking it was the enemy, in the next. I was constantly rebuked by my "pastors," told I was mentally ill, and placed in counseling to deal with my *rebellious spirit*. The mental and psychological torture I was enduring in "church counseling" literally led me to check myself into a mental hospital. After a few days of intense therapy with my psychiatrist, she asked me, "Why are you here? There is nothing wrong with you." As I began to share with her the events that led up to me admitting myself into this mental hospital, she shook her head and told me I was a victim of mental and psychological abuse, concealed under the banner of *spiritual counseling*.

She explained to me that this happens more than people want to admit in the Church and that many are truly scarred and cannot come out of this dark place. My therapist understood spiritual warfare and was able to discern the spirits that were trying to deceive me into thinking I was mentally ill. She proceeded to tell me that over half of those in mental hospitals were dealing with *spiritual issues*, instead of mental and psychological illness. She also stated that unfortunately, many of our pastors/spiritual leaders are bound spiritually themselves and have no idea they are practicing witchcraft. Sadly, it is an epidemic in the modern-day church.

I knew deep within my spirit I wasn't crazy. I knew I was hearing the voice of God. I now understand that the enemy did not want me to speak the truth to my pastors. He wanted to keep them bound in spiritual, mental, and psychological darkness, so they could keep us there, as well. I went back to school for my degree in Pastoral Counseling. I now counsel pastors and have found my purpose in life. The enemy's desire, his goal, is to kill, steal, and destroy, but God came to give us life, and life more abundantly. That for me, literally saved my life! I am eternally grateful for the *angel* He sent to open my eyes. Now, I am able to help *open the eyes* of others." ~*April*, Texas

So much evil has taken place in the name of religion. Millions of people all over the world have been the victims of mental and psychological abuse by those claiming to stand in the stead of God or under the banner of religion. These abuses run very deep in people's lives and, in

many cases, delve into the fabric of entire nations/groups of people. Powerful strongholds have rested upon masses of people for centuries, causing ripple effects throughout our generations. We must have the conversations and begin the healing process, so that deliverance and freedom can manifest in the lives of the abused.

Chapter 7

Financial/Economic Abuse

"Therefore if you have not been faithful in the unrighteous mammon, who will commit to your trust the true riches?" Luke 16:13

The desire for wealth brings with it some of the most demonic of spirits. Modern Christian ministry today is mostly money-driven and success-motivated. It is no longer about souls, or discipleship. It is "big business!" Statistics reveal pastors are leaving the ministry by the droves, and yes, those who see what it has become have left the confines of the structured church. Many are being 'kicked out' because they refuse to bow down to the unrighteous spirit of "mammon," but then you have many more who are 'anointing' themselves and becoming pastors who have not been called by God, all in an effort to become wealthy and famous... *wolves in sheep's clothing*. They seek money, money, and more money from you, manipulating and intimidating you into believing the more you give, the more you will get back from God.

Unfortunately, so many preachers have mastered the art of manipulation and have learned to twist and pervert scripture for their own benefit and motives. The spirit of today's church is *the bigger, the better*. They manipulate with worthy "causes," all the while bleeding the pockets of those who just want to do the will of the Lord. These givers cannot for the life them understand why they are still struggling financially. I have witnessed pastors beg for offerings for almost thirty minutes, giving 1% scripture and 99% persuasion, even to the point of collecting an offering for a project and 'slip up' during the service to say it was already paid off. This is deceit! I have always been a tither, and a generous giver, but I learned very early on to hear the voice of God regarding giving. If God didn't say give, I didn't give. But so many believers are not trained to hear the voice of God for themselves, and they are bait in the hands of manipulative spiritual leaders. I understand now why Jesus/Yeshua was targeted by the high priests. He began to *mess with their money*. He was healing, *really healing*, physical bodies. He turned over the tables of the moneychangers in the temple, and He exposed their deceit with Truth.

"No one can serve two masters; for either he will hate the one and love the other, or else he will be loyal to the one and despise the other. You cannot serve God and mammon." Matthew 6:24

Financial abuse by spiritual leadership has been going on since the inception of spiritual authority. We saw from the story of the sons of Eli that they stole the altar sacrifices to go and sell them in the marketplace.

FINANCIAL/ECONOMIC ABUSE

Pastors/spiritual leaders are preying upon the people of God in an effort to "maintain" the lavish lifestyles they have made for themselves, as well as to maintain spiritual control. They will do anything, even if that means compromising the Word of God and aligning with the devil to keep it. They continue to beg for money even while knowing their church leaders/staff are struggling, those refusing to say anything because they are afraid to let people know what they are going through. This is bondage! Church leaders are trying to 'keep up with their pastors' and have built this façade of wealth and prosperity (an outward *appearance* of blessing). Many are giving *publicly* their alms (offering) coercing others to do the same when the Word of God explicitly says to give in secret. This goes against the Word of God!

"Take heed that you do not do your charitable deeds before men, to be seen by them. Otherwise you have no reward from your Father in heaven. Therefore, when you do a charitable deed, do not sound a trumpet before you as the hypocrites do in the synagogues and in the streets, that they may have glory from men. Assuredly, I say to you, they have their reward. But when you do a charitable deed, do not let your left hand know what your right hand is doing, that your charitable deed may be in secret; and your Father who sees in secret will Himself reward you openly." Matthew 6:1-4

Pastors are boasting across the pulpit what they are giving, what they have done for the poor, telling people God is saying give a 'certain amount' (lies) and manipulating people to give what God has not told them to give. This brings shame on those who cannot give by making others stand up to 'reveal' their tithes or offerings and use them in schemes to make others feel bad for not giving. This, too, is bondage. Pastors/spiritual leaders are bleeding the people of God for money to build "their own empires," yet tell them to have *faith* that God will bless them. Where is *your* faith in God? What happened to taking what He tells His people to give and asking Him to multiply it? We don't even believe God like this anymore! Our pastors/spiritual leaders have truly been deceived and refuse to open their eyes and ears to the voice of God, as well as those sounding the alarm. They are trading the true riches of God's Kingdom for worldly riches (mammon). *"For what profit is it to a man if he gains the whole world, and loses his own soul? Or what will a man give in exchange for his soul?"* (Matthew 16:26) We have seen, at alarming rates, pastors taking their lives over the last decade. In times of great intercession, the Lord has revealed this very spirit as the culprit (mammon). We need money to build the Kingdom: to feed the poor, look after the widows, and take care of the orphans. Money is not evil; it is the LOVE of money that is the root of all evil.

*"For **the love of money** is a root of all kinds of evil, for which some have strayed from the faith in their greediness, and pierced themselves through with many sorrows. "*1 Timothy 6:10 (emphasis mine)

FINANCIAL/ECONOMIC ABUSE

What starts out as a genuine love for God and love for God's people ends up a *chain around the necks* of our leaders. They know no other way out of this terror but to take their own lives (pierced with sorrows). This is devastating. We saw this same spirit upon Judas. He loved Jesus but allowed the "love of money" to consume him. In the end, his conscious would not allow him to keep the money or his life. This spirit is one of the most demonic and destructive on the face of this Earth, and it has now consumed our pulpits. It begins with desiring wealth, which leads to all kinds of evil spoken in the verse above. Manifestations of other spirits include, but are not limited to, greed, lust, pride, arrogance, entitlement, oppressive and suppressive behavior: talking down to people, manipulation, deceit, threatening, and sense of superiority. These are all characteristics of Satan himself!

Deceitful prophets are prophesying increase, increase... give and God will give you *increase*! How can you prophesy the increase of God to a rebellious and unrepentant people? You keep them in bondage and sin by not preaching the full counsel of God's Word, the Word that is able to transform their lives and pull them out of the pits of hell. Instead, you keep preaching, teaching, and prophesying *more, increase, abundance, rain, blessing, favor, prosperity*... more, more, more... stay in your sin, just keep giving MORE! There are spirits behind this kind of financial and economic manipulation and deception.

"I have been a giver my entire life. My parents instilled the *gift of giving* in my heart at a very young age. Even when I didn't have money, I would make things for people: my parents, my sisters, my friends, my teachers, and my pastor. I sowed my time as a teenager serving in our Youth Ministry. I loved to see people smile. Upon getting my first job, it was instinct to give. I knew the Word of God and there was no hesitancy whatsoever to tithe and give. Shortly thereafter, things began to change drastically in our pastor's demeanor and lifestyle. We weren't a huge church nor were we a small congregation; we pretty much knew everyone and any radical change, people noticed.

Our pastor was never the "begger" when it came to tithing and giving of offerings. He taught it as the Word of God offered it and encouraged people to give as God led them to give. He began spending a lot more time preaching on tithing and giving of offerings. Every Sunday from that point, it progressively became worse. His tone became harsh and it was evident that he and his wife's clothing and jewelry had become *flashier*. They had driven the same car for as long as I can remember. Not that they couldn't buy a new car, but it was quite an expensive make of car, something people in our community simply did not buy. When a financial goal was not met, he would begin to ask for offerings at the beginning and end of service. It was clear to many that he was now reverting to twisting scripture and playing on people's emotions to give more. Several people voiced concerns and were met with verbal attacks. He stated, "How dare you question my hearing from God. If God tells me raise an offering, I'm going to raise an offering!"

Several families left the church, and he grumbled even the more, because now, he was losing "tithers". He would blame the devil and would even tell us we were being manipulated by the devil into not giving. It eventually became so bad; he would tell people they were going to hell for not giving what God was commanding them to give. My family left the church, as well. Sadly, he lost the church several years later. It is so sad to see pastors falling into this trap of "prosperity". It is definitely not the Gospel Jesus preached or lived." ~*Jen*, Ohio

We need to pray for our pastors, but even more than that, we need to stop enabling them through spiritual ignorance and immaturity. Don't keep complaining about them begging for money, stop giving it to them! We are *feeding the dragon*. Don't go to the conferences, stop buying their "self-help" books, and stop believing lies about 'God' saying 100 people need to give $10,000.00! Let them fall into the hands of a loving God. Repentance will come one way or another, and it will begin with our spiritual leaders. They brought the world into our sacred assemblies, now it's time for them to get it out. Many will suffer great consequences for their deceit and manipulation of God's people, but His grace is available. As they humble themselves and repent, He will lead them once again. There are many good pastors that simply fell into temptation and took on this evil spirit of mammon. We can't love God and love the wealth, fame, and fortune of this world. We will have to ultimately choose between the two... choose wisely!

HIRELINGS & CHARLATANS

When we trade the call of God for a career, we subsequently open a Pandora's Box that is almost impossible to close. Due to the explosion and exploitation over the last few decades of this *celebrity* spirit, the spirit of mammon, we are seeing masses flock to pulpits all around the world. Many desire a platform that will produce for them financial gain, immediate fame, and ultimate power. You cannot go anywhere in the "church world," without seeing someone that has taken on the title of pastor, apostle, prophet, evangelist, teacher, minister, bishop, overseer, missionary, reverend, preacher, seer, intercessor, prophetic psalmist, dancer, artist, etc., etc., etc. The modern church has become *big business* and is attracting the world in droves, not for spiritual maturation, but for fast money. The world has found that Christians are givers, and they will believe almost anything as long as Scripture is attached to it, sadly.

A *hireling* is defined as a person who works purely for material reward. They have no spiritual, moral, or personal investment in the role; they simply come for a paycheck. A hireling seeks his own. He is fully detached emotionally, mentally, spiritually, and physically from all aspects of his position. All he sees is *dollar signs* and will do anything to keep that financial flow going. Sadly, and unfortunately, this is not the world we are discussing… this is the Church! There are more hirelings in the Church today, than true spiritual leaders. Their doctrine is prosperity. They love to twist and pervert scripture, in order to excuse their wealth, status, and power. Hirelings are quick to spew out scriptures that are totally self-interpreted. They are prideful, arrogant, brash, and self-entitled. Nowhere do we witness the heart of a servant in the life of a hireling. He cares for nothing, other than himself and what he can get from you.

"The hireling fleeth, because he is an hireling, and careth not for the sheep." John 10:13

Hirelings are very easy to spot within the Church. They are flashy and sport the absolute *best* and most *expensive* in everything from the shoes and clothes they wear to the cars they drive and the homes they purchase. They refuse to live beneath the "favor" of God upon their lives. They truly believe God's favor and anointing lies in material wealth… they are deceived. Many refuse to travel unless it is first-class everything, from ground transportation (limousines and private cars) to and from airports, hotels, and events, to first-class seating on airplanes. Some even refuse to fly on commercial flights and take private jets from one city to the next. Two very well-known spiritual leaders appeared on a Christian television program discussing this very topic. My heart sank as I listened to these men, that I've heard others refer to as *generals of the faith*, usurp their spiritual authority as a means to demean and degrade other human beings as inferior, and they, superior.

These were their statements, paraphrased, "God told me to buy this jet. You can't 'talk to God' while flying commercial." He proceeded to state that his mentor, another well-renowned pastor, faced unsolicited requests for prayer when he flew on public airliners, "agitating his spirit." This pastor then stated, "You can't manage that today, in this dope-filled world, getting in a long tube with a bunch of demons. It's deadly." The other pastor stated that God told him directly that he was to purchase his jet. He stated that he couldn't "risk his anointing" flying commercially. Is this the example our Lord and Savior, Jesus Christ provided for us? Jesus/Yeshua was found amongst the sinners of His day: the tax collectors, the prostitutes, the thieves, and yes, the demon-possessed. Did He call these souls a "bunch of demons"? Did Jesus feel He was *above* those He was called to heal and deliver? Absolutely not! Sadly, one of these pastors stated that if Jesus was alive today, He'd do the same thing.

It sickens me to see such deception in the name of God. These are not pastors/shepherds; these are *charlatans* preying on the spiritual ignorance of their massive following. A *charlatan* is described as a person practicing quackery or some similar confidence trick or deception in order to obtain money, fame, or other advantages via some form of pretense or deception. The spirit of a charlatan is much more deceptive than that of a hireling. A hireling will tell you outright that they are simply *here for the job*. A charlatan uses deceptive schemes and tactics to lure people and trick them into giving them money. A charlatan will twist, manipulate, and pervert God's Word to get what they want out of innocent people. A charlatan simply put... is a fraud!

"For such are false apostles, deceitful workers, transforming themselves into apostles of Christ. And no wonder! For Satan himself transforms himself into an angel of light." 2 Corinthians 11: 13-14

We do not have to look very far from the so-called *prosperity* and *prophetic* churches to find a charlatan. Masses of deceivers and dishonest people flock to these types of churches, because they are keenly aware that these followers are spiritually immature and are merely seeking entertainment. They seek signs, wonders, and miracles, instead of intimate relationship with the Father. Jesus did not warn us of other false religions and/or spiritual leaders; He specifically warned us "there shall arise false Christs, and false prophets, and shall show great signs and wonders; insomuch that, if it were possible, they shall deceive the very elect." (Matthew 24:24) The only real way to detect a true charlatan is to compare what they say and do with what the Word of God says. Their fruit will reveal their authentic selves. The Bible tells us to "test the fruit" and to "test the spirit" of man to see whether they are of God.

"Beloved, do not believe every spirit, but test the spirits, whether they are of God; because many false prophets have gone out into the world." 1 John 4:1

THE ELEPHANT IN THE ROOM

God requires us to have a level of spiritual responsibility and discernment when it comes to false teachers and false prophets. We are not left ignorant to their devices, but we must seek His wisdom, not our own understanding.

"The state the global church has found itself immersed in today is almost nauseating. The search for authentic pastors/leaders in the modern-church structure today is like *trying to find a needle in a haystack*. The race to build the biggest church or to be the greatest preacher is well underway. The spirits of jealousy, competition, greed, and envy run rampant in churches all over the world. Pastors are bargaining and bartering with host churches to bring them to preach, overreaching other ministers that may charge a little more for honorariums. They are on the hunt for preaching gigs to line their deep pockets even the more.

The worldly slogan "securing the bag," has become a coin phrase of pastors traveling to different cities and countries weekly. They are now booking out their itineraries a year in advance. These people are not led by the Spirit of God, they are led by their fleshly and carnal wants and desires, yet *claim* God is leading them. The Church is inundated with hirelings and charlatans today, and honestly, they are being recruited as such. Church leaders know who to call to bring in the crowds, so they can *break the bank*. These are master manipulators and opulent orators.

Their charm and charisma hypnotize those under the sound of their voices. These charlatans are strategic, and they have learned how to study their targets. They cash in on emotional spiritualism and will talk you into leaving your inheritance to them if they could.   *~Rob*, former pastor Texas

There are several ways in which you will find pastors/spiritual leaders manipulating followers to give financially and to suppress them economically. Here are just a few that are prevalent in today's *church culture*:

❖ **Prophetic schools**
  • The emergence of prophetic schools and *schools of prophets* has become an epidemic in the modern church culture. No longer do we see the authentic hearing from God by spiritual leadership to anoint and release the "few" prophetic gifts/true prophets. Now, you can pay to have someone teach you *how to be a prophet*. These counterfeit schools are breeding grounds for witchcraft. They produce psychics, not prophets.

❖ **Spiritual fathering/mothering/mentoring**
  • We touched upon the abuse of spiritual fathering and mothering in an earlier chapter. We see great potential for corruption in this spiritual assignment when we reject and refuse

the wisdom of God offered in His Word. The flippancy and lack of reverence for our heavenly Father leads to idol worship of men. The Bible says call no man father upon this Earth. He is not speaking of earthly headship in the home; He is referencing spiritual leadership in the Church. Unfortunately, many are deceived by these charlatans posing as *spiritual fathers/mothers/mentors* seeking financial gain, status, and yes, worship. The more sons/daughters, the more they are "sowed" financially into monthly.

❖ **Bible colleges/classes**

- With the dwindling of church growth and attendance exploding in record numbers, pastors/spiritual leaders are seeking creative ways in which to recover their *financial losses* in tithes and offerings. The quick and easy way many are achieving this is through the offering of Bible classes, or in extreme cases, the forming of Bible colleges. People are *sold* an over-inflated résumé of degrees and offered over-inflated prices that are triple what the school actually costs. The profits from these schemes are astronomical.

❖ **Spiritual gifts training**

- Spiritual gifts are divinely imparted, not earthly taught. The gifts of God should be cultivated through relationship with Him in His Word and by the infilling of Holy Spirit, not formed by the mere teaching/training of men. So many are accepting/acquiring spiritual gifts they were never assigned to carry. This lackadaisical and erroneous view of spiritual training is leading many to be completely out of the will of God for their lives. Sadly, the initiators are unconcerned, as long as they are continuing to profit off the lack of wisdom and understanding of these believers concerning true, authentic spiritual gifting.

❖ **Healing rooms/gatherings**

- The Bible says, "Healing is the children's bread." The same way the teaching of God's Word and prophecy is free, so too, is the gift of healing. This spiritual gift is probably one of the most abused, aside from prophecy, in the Church today. We have witnessed some of the most absurd claims in the name of "healing" carried out in churches and conferences all over the world. People are punched, slapped, kicked, blown on, spit on, and thrown to the floor in spectacles *in the name of God*. Healing is *big business* for many false teachers. I have seen desperate people stand in lines with their life savings in their hand waiting to *sow their seed* for healing. I have also witnessed these charlatans refuse to lay hands on people for healing, or pray for them, unless a financial seed is given.

❖ **Conferences/concerts/events**

- Pastors/spiritual leaders have grasped on to these *cash cows* for dear life! In these massive gatherings, they can produce gross financial gain through registration fees, ticket sales, merchandising and memorabilia, multiple offerings, and vendors. Not to mention the masses that give online through live streaming these events.

- ❖ **Life coaching/Leadership training/Preaching itineraries**
  - Many pastors/spiritual leaders have joined the fast-growing field of *life coaching, leadership training and/or preaching itineraries*. These roles, in and of themselves, are not bad nor are they wrong, but the motives behind this supplemental income for spiritual leaders is deceptive and destructive. The biblical role of a pastor/shepherd is to remain in meditation of the Word and in prayer. Sadly, many have been deceived into believing God is taking them all over the world to preach, teach, and train, yet their congregations are left abandoned for wolves to devour. God's desire is not for pastors to travel all over the world; their position lies in the local church setting.

In these reckless decision-making ventures, many of these pastors/spiritual leaders have found themselves in tempting and compromising positions. You are seeing married men offering *life coaching* to divorced or single women and falling prey to adulterous affairs. You are seeing pastors consulting with worldly companies and firms that completely denounce Christianity, as well as moral compass and integrity for financial gain. We are also witnessing a huge spike in pastors traveling itinerantly to places God never led them to preach for financial gain, popularity, and influence.

❖ **Live videos**

- Social media has bred an insurgence of "online pastors" over the last several years. There is nothing wrong with encouraging believers all over the world, especially with so many spending hours upon hours on this platform. Unfortunately, many have abused this outlet for monetary gain and popularity. God has warned me against doing such videos and given me great wisdom on how to guard myself and guard others. There are so many false teachers and false prophets on these platforms promoting themselves, not God. Sadly, people fall for it and subsequently give financially into these schemes.

❖ **Corporate & Personal Prophecy**

- Prophecy is, by far, the most coveted gift in the Church today. Though the Bible clearly encourages us to seek to prophesy (1 Corinthians 14:1), its purpose, in context, is to encourage, empower, edify, and equip other believers with the Word of God, as well as through Holy Spirit. This is NOT the gift, or office, of the Prophet. Far too many today are "prophesying" falsely in an effort to obtain financial compensation for their *ministry*. This is not prophecy; it is more along the lines of predicting, as it does not come by way of or through Holy Spirit, but from the fleshly and carnal personal motives of charlatans.

I have witnessed these spectacles far more than I'd like to admit. I have been in church settings where "prophets" are *let loose* on congregations, walking through the aisles pointing people out to "give them a word". The words are so vague and void of the voice of God, yet people still fall for these shenanigans. People flock to altars with their checkbooks, ready and willing to give up their mortgage/rent payment for a *word from God*. These false prophets reveal not only the lack of authentic spiritual gifts within the Church, but also the immaturity and lack of discernment amongst those that called themselves born-again Believers.

❖ **Pastoral Appreciations, Anniversaries & Birthdays**

- Honoring and giving respect to those called by God to shepherd His people is one thing, making *idols* out them and *financing their livelihoods*, something entirely different. The word Holy Spirit dropped in my spirit over the last several years regarding spiritual leadership and financial abuse is *addiction*. These pastors have become addicted to honoring and the giving of gifts. *Honoring* has turned into idol worship and with it, spiritual manipulation in the form of financial/economic abuse.

Celebrations for our spiritual leaders are almost a weekly occurrence in the Church today. Pastoral appreciations, anniversaries, birthdays, and many other events are carried out for spiritual leaders, almost demanding that every church member *must* give financially toward these "gifts". If someone desires to personally give towards their pastors, they are more than welcome to do so, but doing so in a corporate fashion every year is an abuse of spiritual authority. Many spiritual leaders are now in a position of entitlement, waiting in expectation for these celebrations, because they know they will be receiving material gifts and/or financial compensation. This practice must end in the corporate church setting. It is not of God!

How is it even possible for so many people to continue to be victims of financial and economic abuse in the Church? Unfortunately, it is largely due to the twisting, manipulation, and perversion of the Word of God. Pastors/spiritual leaders have mastered the *art* of spiritual manipulation and deceit. They will pull one scripture, completely out of biblical context, and make it say what they want it to say. This is easily the most deceptive trait of false teachers/prophets; they *do not* know the Word of God or teach/preach the fullness of God through the collective canon of Scripture. Most believers cannot recognize the manipulation, because they do not know the Word, either. They will believe anything these charlatans tell them, simply because they attach a scripture to their message.

"Study to shew thyself approved unto God, a workman that needeth not to be ashamed, rightly dividing the word of truth." 2 Timothy 2:15

Another way in which people are manipulated and deceived financially by spiritual leaders is through celebrity and entertainment. Most churchgoers are not interested in obedience to God or true biblical suffering for the cause of Christ. They merely want to get to heaven, so they go to church on Sunday mornings, Saturday if they celebrate the Sabbath day. They are *checklist* Christians; they have a list of things they feel if they do, it will secure their spot in eternity. They rarely read or meditate upon the Word of God for themselves but would rather hear it out of a preacher's mouth. They are considered carnal, or worldly followers. They come to hear their favorite preachers, their favorite songs, and to sit in their favorite seats. These individuals are content with being *preached out of their seats* by charismatic charlatans. They love being entertained, and if they feel the pastor is not entertaining enough, they will go and look for one that will *tickle their ears* and give them *goosebumps*.

See, it is not only spiritual leadership that operates in deception; it is also carnal and worldly Christians that seek out these kinds of spiritual leaders to tell them what they want to hear. These people are not concerned about the morality and integrity of their spiritual leaders; they just want to be coddled in their sin. They do not desire repentance or a change of evil lifestyle; they simply want to hear that God is perfectly okay with them living in sin and choosing to live however they want to live. They are encouraged that God's grace will cover it all, no matter what they do and no matter how long they choose to do it. This spirit of compromising the truth leads to witchcraft in the Church, and ushers in the spirit of mammon, which is key in financial and economic abuse and manipulation.

"For the time will come when they will not endure sound doctrine, but according to their own desires, because they have itching ears, they will heap up for themselves teachers; and they will turn their ears away from the truth, and be turned aside to fables." 2 Timothy 4: 3-4

I have personally witnessed some of the most wicked acts committed by pastors/spiritual leaders on the hunt for financial prosperity and worldly fame. These men/women have spent months and even years planning and contemplating on how to gain wealth from the Gospel. A former pastor of ours stated that before he turned forty-years-old, he would be a millionaire. Sadly, many of his ventures to get to this place of prominence were at the expense of those that trusted him as a spiritual leader. He manipulated dozens of people, if not more, into joining a Christian Bible College and charged almost five times more than what it cost to enroll in the school. After contacting the dean of this school, it was revealed that dozens of files only had a $50.00 application fee inside: no payments and no grades whatsoever. I later found out that entire churches were scammed, as well. I watched a once powerfully anointed preacher turn into a success-driven motivational speaker seeking wealth, fame, and influence (the spirit of mammon). I don't share this story to demean or degrade anyone, and this is not personal, I have forgiven this man, but these stories must be shared in order to stop this financial abuse from happening to others in the Church. The Gospel is NOT for sale!

Unfortunately, many of these pastors have been deceived themselves by what true prosperity infers and includes, according to the Gospel. From the earlier testimony of the two well-known pastors calling commercial plane flyers "a tube full of demons," we see a corrupt and perverted view of how God *blesses* His shepherds, pastors, and spiritual leaders in the Church. These pastors own private jet (s) worth between 50-65 million dollars, and this does not include the airstrips, hangers, maintenance, and fuel to keep these jets flying. I know quite a few pastors personally that own private jets that fly them, as well as their children, from city to city. Most has nothing at all to do with the Gospel, but they are seen taking pictures celebrating birthday's shopping in the most expensive city districts in America.

This prosperity *gospel* is false doctrine and has led many spiritual leaders into corruption and perversion. These are carnal and worldly spirits counterfeiting as spiritual blessings from God. How is God blessing His "servants," while over half of their own congregations are on the brink of poverty? How is God giving His "shepherds" double-portions, while mere lay members are losing their homes, their cars, and their livelihoods? These are not pastors... they are charlatans! And they will use the Gospel in any way they can to continue *fleecing the flock*.

FINANCIAL/ECONOMIC ABUSE

As I have been a part of leadership in several of these megachurches, more than any other trick or scheme carried out by spiritual leadership, I would have to say the greatest of deceptions is that of the *church building*. The spirit of being the *biggest* or the *best* church in a city has found pastors building multi-million, even billion-dollar, facilities aimed at drawing in the largest crowds. These are not Kingdom churches; they are worldly empires. This is modern-day idol worship. Yes, these physical buildings have become the center of these pastor's lives, and subsequently, the love of many followers.

"My former husband, and pastor, was a kind, gentle, and compassionate man. He loved God, He loved the Church, and He loved his family. He wanted nothing more than to preach the Gospel and lead precious souls to the Lord. When I met him, he had just graduated from seminary and all he ever talked about was preaching and witnessing to the lost. He was not fascinated about the *title* of pastor, or even concerned about building or obtaining a large, magnificent church. He simply wanted to share the Gospel, which he did every day in the streets of New York City. For several years, this was his "pulpit". He was a *street preacher*. He ministered to the homeless, the prostitutes, the pimps, the drug dealers, the drug addicted, and the mentally ill. Many came to trust him and some even gave their lives to Jesus and got off the streets.

One winter day, he was out passing out food and blankets, and a very well-known pastor in our city walked up to him with his *entourage* and asked my husband if he was a preacher. He said, "Yes sir, I am." The pastor told my husband that his name was being spoken of throughout the city as transforming the lives in this area. My husband laughed and said, "Pastor, I am only doing my part." This pastor invited my husband to speak at his church, to let people know what God was doing in the streets of New York City. My husband told him he'd have to pray and seek God if He wanted him to do this, and the pastor laughed, saying, "If God sent me out here in these streets to you, which He did, then that is your answer." My husband never did anything unless he was sure God had spoken to him. There was something so unsettling in this man's demeanor, yet he was absolutely convincing. My husband agreed and I wish I could say this was the start of a beautiful connection and opportunity for my husband to walk into his divine calling.

After a year of joining this church and my husband working alongside of this pastor, I no longer recognized the man I described in the beginning. He was now obsessed with ministry. It was no longer about the lost souls in the streets; he did not even want to do street ministry any longer and wouldn't be caught dead mixing with the "sinners" out there. His reputation had grown exponentially, and he was now traveling all over the world preaching. He was rarely home anymore and even when he was in town, he was always at the "church" until late at night.

My husband's taste had changed drastically. He was now buying the best suits, watches, and shoes. He would not eat anywhere except extravagant and expensive restaurants. He would not fly anywhere unless he was flying first-class. This once kind and compassionate man had turned into a harsh, egotistical narcissist. He began lashing out at me and our kids for no reason at all and would leave us at home to go and preach at church. We would have to catch the bus to the church. I am sure you know where this is heading.

After some time, I found out he was having an affair with the church secretary. He wouldn't even discuss it with me and said he was divorcing me. He wasted no time at all; as soon as we were legally divorced, he married this woman. There is not enough space for me to share, in depth, what took place in my life after he accepted this pastor's *invitation to ministry*. It was an invitation from the devil himself. I no longer know the man I see today. The only thing I continue to hear over and over in my spirit is that "he sold his soul to the devil". Money and fame are his priority, not Jesus. I pray for him every day that he will repent and turn back to his first love before it's too late. *~Myriam*, NYC

In the opening scripture to this chapter, it states that if we are not faithful in the unrighteous mammon (money) how can God trust us with the true riches. This scripture alone reveals to us the Father's heart

concerning what is taking place in spiritual leadership in today's church. It shows us that the true riches in God's Kingdom is not money, wealth, and fame. In fact, the Bible states that money is *least* in the Kingdom. The Father understood clearly what the *love of money* and *fame* produce in the hearts of people. I have heard more pastors quote this phrase than any other: "The Bible doesn't say money is evil, it says the *love* of money is the root of all evil." They are correct in their statement, but their hearts are far from the pure intent of the scripture. In fact, they use this scripture, and many others to excuse, or justify, the massive wealth they have accumulated. Their hearts are corrupt. Their minds are corrupt. Their spirits are corrupt. They are deceived and they are deceiving.

"Do not lay up for yourselves treasures on earth, where moth and rust destroy and where thieves break in and steal; but lay up for yourselves treasures in heaven, where neither moth nor rust destroys and where thieves do not break in and steal. For where your treasure is, there your heart will be also." Matthew 6: 19-21

Wisdom is crying out from the Word of God. May we humble ourselves and submit to its truths.

Chapter 8

Physical & Sexual Abuse

"It is actually reported that there is sexual immorality among you, and such sexual immorality as is not even named among the Gentiles..." 1 Corinthians 5:1

For far too long, the Church has remained silent on the atrocities of sexual abuse, molestation, rape, sodomy, and the outrageous spiritual abuse that has taken place within its walls; those *associated* with the name of God. It is only recently coming to the forefront, not because the Church has taken responsibility and accountability for it, but because of our hypocrisy, the world is exposing it and God is allowing it. Throughout the last decade, we've seen the victims of the Catholic church finally coming forward and confronting their abusers. Many of these priests have committed suicide, leaving many of their victims to the same demise. Since 2004 over 3400 cases of abuse were reported in the Catholic church with 2572 addressed with lesser penalties, while 848 priests were defrocked. In Australia alone, 4,444 people reported they had been abused at more than 1,000 Catholic institutions between 1980-2015[viii]. Clearly this is not taking responsibility for the thousands of years of sexual and spiritual abuse, but more of a *scapegoat* issue, as many of these priests were already dead, or had committed suicide. And it has come to the light that many of these perpetrators were once victims themselves. This darkness has plagued the Church for centuries, and because of the "nature" of the sin, it is seen by most as an abomination, a sin greater than all. So, we can see why it has been *hidden* away and why victims are pretty much *silenced* from ever telling anyone.

Out of those almost 8,000 sexual abuse cases, statistics reveal that many turned to lifestyles that were heavily influenced by unhealthy sexual practices, pornography, and yes, even homosexuality and other forms of sexuality. Most of the reported cases are from men, and not women, though the women abused as children were by the opposite sex, not the same sex. If we understood the spiritual implications of sexual abuse in the context of homosexuality, we could clearly see our enemy's evil intentions to destroy what God created in Adam and Eve in the Garden. His desire is to pervert the purity of Creation, especially man. He is the giver of life; we are the recipient and birther of life.

Just in the last few years have we seen the spike in lesbianism, transgenderism, and other forms of sexual identity. But in my experience, as I have had many I know living as homosexuals and lesbians, each has identified sexual abuse in their childhoods. But even more, the sexual abuse stemmed from someone in spiritual authority in their lives... yes, the Church.

These precious children are taught about a loving God that sent His only Son to die on the Cross for their sins. They are mesmerized by His love at very early ages. For their own spiritual leaders to pervert the Word of God to manipulate, intimidate, and control the very essence of their lives is the real abomination! But instead of addressing, exposing, and dealing with these abusive spiritual leaders, we choose to attack and condemn the victims of these heinous acts. We have swept it under the rug for so long due to fear and intimidation that many of these children, who could have been healed at young ages, are now convinced they were born this way and that it was God's will they were used as sexual toys for grown men.

The very men that sexually abused many of these boys did their perverted deeds in closed church offices, under the veil of spiritual authority, and then stepped into a sacred pulpit to preach the Word of God; condemning the very acts they had just committed themselves? How do you think these children's perception of God was, and is? How twisted their thoughts were of a loving Creator considering such darkness? Now, with many years of living these lifestyles, they have grown to accept the darkness as their *normal*. I am, by no means, collectively placing all those living as homosexuals, lesbians, transgender, or other classifications in the same box. I am only speaking of those that were sexually abused, molested, raped, and sodomized as children by those in trusted spiritual authority.

Thousands, possibly millions, have fled the Church altogether, and many have rejected God completely due to being sexually abused by priests and pastors. Again, a greater abomination! The same way in which these priests and pastors used the very Word of God to control, manipulate, and abuse their victims, we, too, are now using that very same Word to condemn them once again. Where is their hope? Where is their justice? We want to throw the Bible down their throats condemning their sin, but they can only see their abuser sitting with his feet crossed in his Stacy Adams and Armani suit or in his long white robe with a cross hanging around his neck, smirking and not saying a word. Does God love the abuser more than the abused? Is there some sort of *rank* in the Kingdom where the elite are exempt from correction, rebuke, responsibility, and accountability? Let me promise you this is what they think and feel, many times. And therefore, many have committed suicide, because the very institution that should have stood up for them, abandoned them. Consequently, many have left the confines of the Church and walked away from the hope of eternal life with Father God. The greatest abomination!

"I grew up in the Catholic Church. My family were devout Catholics; we faithfully attended Mass every week. Most Catholic families are extremely strict and disciplined, especially non-American or non-western believers. It is our way of life, and it is passed down throughout our generations. The first time I was touched by my priest, I was around five years old. I was definitely uncomfortable, but we were taught never to question these two people: our parents and our priest. It began with him fondling my genitals and he placing my hand on his; he would say to me, "It feels good doesn't it? God gives us pleasure. He loves us and wants us to feel good." This continued for about six months or so, on and off, when he introduced the act of sodomy. It began with him "kissing" my genitals and then performing oral sex on me. He said again, "This feels good, right?" I could not deny it, though something deep within me knew this was wrong, it did feel good. He then asked me to "kiss" his genitals and do exactly what he did to me. I almost threw up, but he asked me to take a deep breath and try again. I did, and this continued for about another few months. I wanted to tell my parents, but he told me to keep this a secret between us and God. He said it was a "special relationship" that only we needed to know about.

This priest was telling my parents that he felt I was called to be a priest and he wanted to mentor me at a young age, so I would remain pure and innocent (what a joke!) After about a year, he finally penetrated me sexually. I was so scared at this point. It hurt so bad, and I asked him why he would hurt me. I thought it was supposed to "feel good". I thought he loved me. I was crying and he said to me, "This is covenant. When covenant starts, it will hurt a little first, then you will begin to feel the pleasure." I was sexually abused, sodomized, and raped by this priest from the age of 5-13; eight years of my life, I was being tortured sexually and spiritually.

I started having demonic dreams about a year after this started. I cannot even begin to speak of the horrors I saw almost every night during this time. I tried to kill myself at least three times during this eight-year period. My priest would tell my parents that this was "normal" for those *called* into the priesthood at a young age. He said that the devil's goal is to place seeds of doubt, unbelief, and fear into the lives of God's servants. He told them he would begin to give more "in-depth" counseling and prayer for me during our *sessions*. Boy, did he! He began to physically abuse me after my first suicide attempt. He told me I was his property and how dare I try to "break our covenant". I would apologize profusely so he would not hit me anymore. Unfortunately, due to the constant sexual abuse and horrific nightmares, I tried two more times to take my life. I was admitted into a mental hospital for several months each of these times, only to get out and go right back to the abuse.

At the age of thirteen, I finally found the courage to tell my parents what was happening to me. They did not believe me and pretty much rebuked me, asking me how I could say such things about a *holy* man of God. I explained, in detail, what he was asking me to do to him and what he was doing to me. I told them about the nightmares and the reason, the real reason, why I had tried to take my life, not once, but three times. My mother finally believed me. I believe my dad did too, but he would not admit it. He completely rejected me and told me never to mention this to anyone and if I did, he would kick me out of his house. He never looked me in my eyes ever again. He never hugged me or told me he loved me after this day.

I wasn't sure if my parents confronted this priest, but my "sessions" ended, and I never heard from him again. We stopped going to the Church and my parents divorced. I have two younger brothers and I didn't know if this was happening to them, too. My life completely went out of control. I was now *gay*, or had I been all along? I knew nothing else since the age of five. This was my reality. From the age of thirteen until around the age of twenty-five, I had more homosexual partners than I can count. The nightmares persisted, yet not to the extent when my priest was sexually abusing me. I started to get really sick and my mother took me to get tested, and sure enough, I was diagnosed with full blown AIDS. I started using drugs to dull the pain, as well as to try and stop the dreams (night terrors). I had become heavily addicted to heroin and went into crazy rages. In one of those drug addicted rages, I tried to kill myself again… this was my last attempt. My mother admitted me into a mental hospital where I remained for two years.

Upon being released, my mother shared with me that multiple families had brought charges against this priest, the parish, and the diocese. There were dozens of priests under investigation for sexual abuse. I was numb. I really did not know how to feel. This man was probably in his late seventies or early eighties by this time. There were no *formal* charges brought against these priests, many simply moved to other parishes, and yes, a few committed suicide in light of their abuses being exposed. Though my mental health is pretty stable now, I wish I could tell you that I am completely healed of this nightmare. Unfortunately, I am not, and millions of children and adults around the world are not, as well. We take it day by day. *~Anthony*, Italy

"Flee sexual immorality. Every sin that a man does is outside the body, but he who commits sexual immorality sins against his own body." 1 Corinthians 6:18

When will we finally choose to confront the *roots* of this immorality? We hear the condemnation of these abuse victim's sin as being *perverse*, but what about the *perversion* of the spiritual leaders that sexually abused them and stole their innocence? The carnal, worldly, and flesh-filled manner in which we address sexual abuse victims in the Church has revealed much to me. One, the Church is in denial and in need of great repentance. The evil one has set up shop in our holy, sacred assemblies. Witchcraft is now being released, because of the rebellion and sin running rampant in spiritual authority. We must blame someone, right? So, let us take the spotlight off the abuser, and put it on the abused. Absolute insanity! Two, how do we think we can commit spiritual adultery with the world and not be stained by it? Many of these pastors *rub elbows* with immorality daily. They have entered these "high places" not being sent by God and have fallen into its temptations and lusts.

Because of the *familiarity* with these spirits, demons will laugh at a pastor or priest that tries to cast it out, because they are "familiar" with them. Again, the conversation must be had. Until there is true repentance within the Church, from our spiritual leaders, and subsequent accountability, many will remain in bondage. This holds true for much of what has been done in the name of "Christianity". Many times, I have been ashamed to be called a *Christian*, because of the great atrocities committed in the name of our Lord Jesus Christ/Yeshua HaMashiach. But as I have grown and experienced life, as well as the *machine* of organized Christianity, I am more and more convinced of the true, authentic love of God. It must be preached. It must be seen. It must be lived, so the world will see who He really is and draw unto Him.

I can do nothing but apologize for the hypocrisy and arrogance of the "religion" that has been exalted above a relationship with our Heavenly Creator. My sin is no worse than yours. We were all eternally separated from Father God, because of sin. God does not love me more, because my sin was *lying* and yours may have been *murder*. For us to pick homosexuality as the ultimate sin and mount a Crusade against them reveals who we are, and it resembles nothing that Jesus stood for. His *love* is what drew people to Him. His non-judgment of them caused something inside of them to experience the ultimate love of God. Yes, He spoke to the sin within many, but it was ultimately between them and God. As followers of Jesus Christ, we minister the Truth, in love, led by

Holy Spirit. Jesus said He spoke nothing, unless His Father spoke it. He did nothing, until Father God released Him to do it. It was the wisdom of God that drew the *outcasts* of society. It was undeniable!

I submit the Church is lacking the wisdom of God in this hour and has been for quite some time. God's desire is that not one soul would perish. It is not our job to judge humanity. It is our job to love them. Yes, we are called to judge spiritual things, so first things first. We must *first* judge ourselves! We must *first* take responsibility and accountability for the thousands, possibly millions, of people sexually abused within our walls and we must repent and ask them for forgiveness. I know many living today have not been the perpetrators, but those of us who are *spiritual* must take on this responsibility. Judgment begins with *us*!

I know this is a hard word, but again, the conversation must be had for God to heal, deliver, restore, reconcile, and redeem His people. Yes, we are called to love the person and hate the sin; confront the spirit and not the man, but revictimizing these sexually abused people is evil. I am also quite aware that the true, authentic Gospel of Jesus Christ/Yeshua HaMashiach is offensive. None of us want to hear things that convict our hearts, so until the day He returns, we will be persecuted for spreading the Gospel, but I would rather be persecuted for preaching the unadulterated Word of God with love and by His Spirit and be backed by Him 100%, instead of doing it my way and having His hand of protection removed from my life. Let's do it His way, so He can be glorified throughout humanity.

I watched the movie *Spotlight*.[ix] My heart aches deeply for so many around the world that have been molested and raped by the very people that were supposed to protect them. Over 249 priests molested and raped over 1000 victims in Boston alone. Cases were brought about in almost every state in America and countries all over the world against Catholic priests. But what about the many, many others in churches all over the world? I've heard multiple stories of molestation and rape within the Church, amongst Believers in Jesus Christ/Yeshua HaMashiach. Children exposed to pornography, homosexuality, and demons of all sorts. Many have committed suicide or turned to drugs to escape the pain and guilt, voices we will never hear again. Others have been exposed to unnatural sexual relationships that now have them questioning their identities.

The majority of these pedophiles are never prosecuted. They are protected and *covered* by the Church, while many are placed in other churches or parishes around the world to molest and rape again. The cycle is devastating. Many of these priests were, themselves, molested and raped as children. Now, the victims are also carrying on destructive behavior. In speaking with a molestation victim this week, the revelation of their molester also being molested, and the multiple children affected both past and present, opened my eyes even the more to these generational curses and strongholds. As in this case in Boston, healing and deliverance cannot come, unless it is brought to the light. The generations of secrets covered up by families and the Church allows this perversion to continue to destroy children's lives, but we must understand the enemy loses his power over our lives when he is exposed. He tries to hold us in bondage to fear, guilt and shame, but God wants us free from the darkness. I'm not talking about the Church; I am speaking of God, our Creator. He wants to heal, deliver, and set us free from generations of dying in silence.

"I was raised in the COGIC denomination of Christianity. My family has practiced this way of life, yes it an absolute *way of life* for many, for hundreds of years. Our tradition, and in my eyes, religion, is steeped in sexual abuse of young boys. It is so rampant in the black church and especially within our denomination. I can only speak for me and my experience traveling around the country as a minister of music within this sect of Christianity. I was singing in the choir as early as age four and playing the piano since age five. I was groomed to be a minister of music, but more importantly, *groomed* by grown men as their *play toy* for a total of fifteen years, that I can remember. Many of my cousins, friends, and other church boys were a part of a ring of sexual abuse within our church and our denomination. We were passed around to visiting pastors to our church, as well as brought to hotel rooms where pastors were staying during church conventions.

People ask me all the time if my parents knew about this sexual abuse and I have to be honest; I know my father did, because he was one of the sexual predators. My mother was always very sad and at times, very angry. My father abused her physically, as well as me and my sister. I believe she knew, but was silenced by my dad's physical abuse, as well as the *code of silence* within our denomination and even our culture. As I have traveled ministering in music since the age of fifteen, I saw, witnessed, and experienced some of the most perverted things going on behind closed doors in these churches/conventions/concerts. Homosexuality is a *staple* of these events and guess what, everyone knows it! It is simply not talked about. The Gospel music community is infested with this perversion and *many* of your favorite pastors are living secret homosexual lifestyles.

I left the church, altogether, when I was thirty years old. I was an openly practicing homosexual but extremely broken and I believe, mentally ill. I was suicidal and began drinking heavily to the point of drunken stupors just to *leave my reality*. I can't even stand the thought of walking into *any* church at this time in my life. I still believe in God, the true God, and I pray that one day I will be able to heal and forgive. I'm just not there right now. ~*Jay*, California

When we remain silent amid such devastation, we are just as guilty as the pedophiles. When we cover up and keep these men/women in power, we pull the trigger ourselves, we push the abused off the bridge, and we stick the needle in their arm. It's time for accountability, as well as healing and deliverance on all sides. With God all things are possible.

Over the last decade, we have witnessed a greater level of exposure concerning sexual abuse in the church. It seems as if weekly, there is a new story of infidelity or sexual abuse reported amongst spiritual leaders. No matter if it is a consensual affair involving a pastor, this is still considered abuse of spiritual authority and it is rampant within the Church today. There are pastors/spiritual leaders being caught in sexual affairs and sexual abuse, and being sent away to other churches, in an effort for the *dust to settle* and then returned, as if nothing happened. Unfortunately, these rogue pastors are continuing their spree of sexual abuse in these new locations. Where is the accountability? Where is the responsibility? Are not these spiritual overseers just as accountable for allowing this abuse to continue without any repercussions? Sadly, most will receive no consequences whatsoever and continue preaching as if nothing happened.

There is an ongoing investigation into churches in the Pacific Northwest and sexual abuse involving pastors, pastoral leaders, and their children, also pastors. Dozens of victims have come forward from several different churches seeking justice, yet have been denied, de-meaned, dehumanized, demonized, and some destroyed emotionally, mentally, psychologically, and spiritually by these so-called spiritual leaders. The demonic circle of influence amongst these churches extends far beyond the Pacific Northwest; there is a network of pastors/churches that continue to back and support these spiritual/sexual abusers. They will continue to bring them into their network of fellowships to preach to their congregations, even knowing of their sexual misconduct. Their deceit: "We cannot judge them, only God can judge. We forgive them, love them, and restore them. The gifts of God are without repentance. They are still anointed by God. You can judge them, but we will love them." Guess what? The scriptures they quoted are absolutely biblical, but unfortunately, they are twisted and perverted in demonic deceitfulness!

So, are we simply releasing sexual deviants back to rape again because it's not our job to *judge them*? Are we letting these people go, because they were once anointed by God to preach? Are we handing over our sons and daughters to these pedophiles because God loves them and forgives them? Simply because many of these pastors/leaders can preach with great charisma and charm and bring in hundreds, thousands, and even millions of people, we will *look the other way*. The Church has completely lost its way! We have become hubs where rapists, molesters, perverts, and all sorts of sexual predators are allowed to roam. We have failed God and failed His precious people.

"I served as an assistant to one of my pastor's staff members while I was a teenager. He was cool and we always joked around with the other staff all the time. He was like a big brother to me. We all hung out, even with my parents, and went to the movies, ate out, and traveled to other states when there were church conferences. We were truly a family. About a year into being his assistant, he began to make weird statements to me like, "You have really grown up to be beautiful." I laughed and thanked him, even though it felt weird. I brushed it off. The next time, he was trying to move passed me in the office, and he put his hands real low on my waist to get to the other side, but it was more like him caressing me. I did not like it and was like, "Dude... you couldn't wait for me to move?" He laughed and said, "Girl, it ain't that serious." So, we laughed. I began doubting if I was just being too obnoxious or something, so I let it go.

One night, my parents had to be at a church function, and we were at the church still working on some final details for a huge church conference we were hosting that week. My parents asked if he could take me home, and he said of course. I was hesitant because of the things I had been feeling, but said to myself, "Girl, snap out of it. It ain't even like that!" Well unfortunately, it was like that. About thirty minutes after my parents left, and he was sure everyone was out of the church, he locked the door to the office we were working in and began to fondle me. I began to scream, but he told me no one was in the church. He said, "Scream as loud as you want, that turns me on even more." He ripped my shorts off of me and began to rape me. He raped me on and off for two hours. He then forced me to perform oral sex on him.

After it was over, he made me go and wash up in the bathroom in the pastor's office. There was a shower in there. He told me to scrub really good all over. I was numb from crying and screaming. I felt like I was in a dream. While I was in the shower, he took my cell phone and texted my parents that I was on my way home and that everything was good. He took some sort of glass cleaner and cleaned my phone after he used it. He then texted my dad from his phone and told him he was about to drop me off at my house. I could not believe all of this was happening. When he dropped me off, he told me that no matter what I said, no one would believe me and that there was no evidence to prove it. He told me that he knew I liked him, and he had known for a whole year that I wanted this, so we could keep this going, as long as I was quiet. I didn't say anything. He made me kiss him before I got out of his car.

I went in my house and ran up to my room crying. I was so mad and angry at my parents. How could they not see this and how could they trust this man to be alone with me and take me home? When my parents got home, they could see that I had been crying a lot. My eyes were so red, and I was still shaking. They asked what happened, and I began screaming at them that he raped me in the church office. My mom was like, "What do you mean… you just texted me and said everything was good and you were on your way home?" I told her that he sent that text while he made me shower in the pastor's office. She could not believe it. She just said, "This doesn't make any sense!" My dad, on the hand, took his keys and ran out of the house. He believed me. He drove to his house and "beat the crap out of him". Of course, he told my dad that I was lying. He did admit to having sex with me but told him we had been having sex for almost a year. He did not believe him.

When he returned home, he took me to the police station and then to the hospital to be checked. Of course, there was none of his DNA on me, from the outside, but they saw the tear marks, traces of blood, and the bruising on my thighs. I had never had sex before he raped me. They took samples of skin from underneath of my fingernails, as well. They also swabbed my mouth, as I told them I was forced to perform oral sex. He was arrested but bailed out of jail by our pastor. We could not believe this was happening. The pastor called us liars and told my parents I was "fast" and that everyone knew I had been having sex with this man. We later found out that he had sexually assaulted many other young girls in other states.

Parents NEVER leave your children alone with people you really do not know. I don't care if they *call* themselves a Christian. I blamed my parents for a very long time. My relationship with them really suffered, and I did not trust anyone! There are some very sick people in this world, and they are in the Church. *~Anonymous*, Virginia

Strongholds of Physical & Sexual Abuse and the Slave Trade

You won't hear much about sexual abuse from the black community, as you will in Catholic circles, because in the "black church," they do not talk about these things. It is *taboo*, because of the horrors that most of their ancestors lived through during slavery. Yes, I believe there are deep strongholds of sexual perversion in the black community that are a direct result of systematic sexual abuse dating back to slavery. The atrocities of sexual perversion during the time of slavery, though not widely discussed, bled down throughout the generations of the black church. The things they were told by these pastors as being the *reason* they were to be their *sexual slaves* was a direct correlation to what the slaves were told by their captors. These slave owners twisted and manipulated scripture in order to not only keep an entire ethnic group in bondage physically, but they also used scripture to mentally, psychologically, and sexually torture, manipulate, and abuse their "slaves". Submission does not equal slavery, yet we saw this evil forced upon millions of souls.

The massive rape of women for sexual pleasure, as well as conceiving in an effort to produce lighter-skinned children to work in the households, was done all in the name of "God". These slave masters literally rewrote an entire version of the Bible. The Slave Bible,[x] originally titled *"Parts of the Holy Bible, Selected for the Use of the Negro Slaves, in the British West-India Islands,"* was originally published in London in 1807 on behalf of the Society for the Conversion of Negro

Slaves, an organization dedicated to improving the lives of enslaved Africans toiling in Britain's lucrative Caribbean colonies. They used the *Slave Bible* to teach enslaved Africans how to read while at the same time introducing them to the Christian faith. Unlike other missionary Bibles, however, the *Slave Bible* contained only "select parts" of the biblical text. Its publishers deliberately removed portions of the biblical text, such as the exodus story, that "could inspire hope for liberation. Instead, the publishers emphasized portions that justified and fortified the system of slavery that was so vital to the British Empire."

Regrettably, there were much more sinister and insidious acts carried out by these slave traders/owners upon the enslaved Africans in the four hundred plus years of systematic slavery. The indescribable physical torture enacted upon these people is something that will never be erased from our history. Beatings, lashings, burning, branding, cutting off of limbs (mutilation), castration, "smoked alive" (suffocation from smoke inhalation), cooked/seared below a fire, animal torture (dogs), feeding bodies alive to alligators, sexual torture with inanimate objects, ripped by the stretching of limbs in chains, lynching, hanging, and being burned alive. The sexual perversion and demonic violation of these men/women's bodies for unnatural sexual pleasure, as well as for "sport" is nothing short of inhumane. Yet, these atrocious acts were hidden behind the veil of a *pseudo-Christianity*, a twisted religious belief. These slave traders/owners (masters) were not, by any means at all, operating underneath of the banner of the true, authentic Gospel of Jesus Christ (Yeshua HaMashiach). They had a *god...* the god, or *spirit of mammon*.

Their goal was complete domination and elitism as a *race* of people. They not only annihilated almost an entire ethnic group from the face of the Americas, the native Indians, but they subsequently enslaved and tortured another entire ethnic group, native Africans, in the lands of the Americas.

Devastatingly, this spirit of enslavement has continued, long after slavery was abolished in America, in the systematic racism so prevalent amongst people of color in the United States of America and abroad today. The formation of religious extremist groups like the KKK, Skinheads, and neo-Nazi's all lay claim in some form to the *religion of Christianity* and believe they are a superior race created by God. The spiritual connotations of this evil run very deep within the soil of this nation and around the world. Evil exists and sadly, it has been masked behind the cloak of *good*.

The Evil of Abortion & Eugenics

Even the genocide of *abortion*, and the founder of *Planned Parenthood*, formerly the *American Birth Control League*, Margaret Sanger, sought to control the population through eugenics. *Eugenics* is the practice or advocacy of improving the human species by selectively mating people with specific desirable hereditary traits. It aims to reduce human suffering by "breeding out" disease, disabilities, and so-called undesirable characteristics from the human population. Sanger was a devout Catholic and formed clinics in many low-income areas to distribute birth control methods for the less desirable, mainly that of abortion. Here is a statement she made concerning ministers helping them achieve their ultimate goal:

"The ministers work is also important and also he should be trained, perhaps by the [Birth Control] Federation [of America] as to our ideals and the goal that we hope to reach. We do not want word to go out that we want to exterminate the Negro population and the minister is the man who can straighten out that idea if it ever occurs to any of their more rebellious members." ~Margaret Sanger

Some argue that Sanger's words were taken out of context, but her strong beliefs of population management through birth control, abortion, and sterilization clearly reveals the direction her organization leaned towards in the black community, the disabled of society, and the population as a whole. Unfortunately, this mindset can lead to the idea that there is a superior race and all others need to be exterminated, as in the case of the Holocaust. Adolf Hitler believed in the idea of eugenics.

Here are several other quotes about sterilization, segregation, elimination, and extinction:

"Apply a stern and rigid policy of sterilization and segregation to that grade of population whose progeny is tainted, or whose inheritance is such that objectionable traits may be transmitted to offspring."[xi] ~Margaret Sanger

"... these two words [birth control] sum up our whole philosophy... It means the release and cultivation of the better elements in our society, and the gradual suppression, elimination and eventual extinction, of defective stocks -- those human weeds which threaten the blooming of the finest flowers of American civilization."[xii] ~Margaret Sanger

The World Health Organization (WHO) estimates an annual of 40-50 million abortions are performed worldwide. Of that number, an estimated 25-36% is African American or people of color. Statistics reveal that 4 out of 5 abortions performed are that of people of color. Planned Parenthood has pushed these 'birth control measures' heavily in the black community and sadly, the Church is being used to implement this genocide, or as some have coined, "The Black Holocaust".

The atrocities of physical and sexual abuse in the confines of the Church is beyond what we will ever know looking in from the outside. Yes, there are millions of testimonies all over the world from those subjected to the abuse of those in spiritual authority, but how many countless more will we never know about? How many were threatened into silence? How many were not believed by their loved ones? How many were admitted into mental hospitals? How many committed suicide? How many of these spiritual leaders committed suicide and left their abused scarred for life emotionally, mentally, psychologically, sexually, and spiritually because their story could not be fully verified?

Missionary & Humanitarian Organizations

The most humble and generous people I have ever had the pleasure to meet in my life are *missionaries/humanitarians*. Their life's work is to help the less fortunate and forgotten around the world. Many have sold everything they owned, left their careers, and ventured into unknown territories to spread the love of Jesus Christ/Yeshua HaMashiach. They have chosen to live amongst those they have been called to serve. They learn the language, the culture, and eventually become family to these precious souls around the world. Sadly, this most unrecognized assignment in the Body of Christ has become tainted over time by opportunists.

From the earliest records of missionary/humanitarian work in third-world countries, as well as war-torn nations, there have been horrific discoveries of physical and sexual abuse carried out by those that *say* God sent them to these people. Due to extreme poverty, language barriers, and systematic oppression in these countries, these people are easy targets and prey for sexual predators, and yes, they come *in the name of Jesus Christ/Yeshua HaMashiach.* They come with bibles in their hands telling them how much God loves them, yet they manipulate these unsuspecting people for their sexual gratification. Even during the earliest of slave trade, Christian missionaries met with tribal leaders in

Africa offering *Jesus/Yeshua* to these tribes, all the while planning and plotting to destroy them from the inside out. Yes, I believe fully in my faith, the Gospel of Jesus Christ/Yeshua HaMashiach, but I do not believe God desires us, as missionaries/humanitarians, to go in and wipe out people's entire cultures. He created them and gave them their identity. Who are we to tell them they need to change? Who are we to go in and disrupt entire ways of life and culture? No, we are called to share the love of Jesus/Yeshua with a lost and dying world. We allow Holy Spirit to do the rest in people's lives. But sadly, this is not the heart of the majority in today's church culture when it comes to missionary and humanitarian work and aid.

I have traveled all over the world doing missionary work and helping to aid in humanitarian efforts. I have witnessed the most inhumane treatment in the name of *missionary work*. People love to bring their cameras for photo-ops to show the world their *love and generosity* towards the outcasts of society, but when those camera's lights go out, there is an entirely different world that you will experience. Not only are these opportunists on vacation, living it up in five-star hotels and restaurants, and taking extravagant excursions, but many of them are taking part is major sex-trafficking rings within these countries. The easiest and most unnoticeable of ways to enter these countries is through the Gospel.

There are many non-profit missionary organizations, as well as humanitarian aid organizations, that are *smokescreens* for major drug and sex-trafficking rings all around the world. There are also major church conventions that have been taking place in some of these countries for years. Well-known preachers travel from all over the world to preach and teach at these churches, not only to rake in as much money as they possibly can through manipulation and deceit, but many of them are getting *sexual favors* offered to them by their host pastors in the form of *sex slaves*, both male and female.

"From as early as I can remember, I was given to visiting preachers for sexual pleasures. I was told it was God's will for me to make them happy, as they have traveled thousands of miles to bless us with God's word. My parents, and many others, were paid money to keep silent. We were brought by security guards late in the night to these preacher's hotel rooms to give them whatever they wanted. At times, physical violence did occur, especially when we did not want to do some of the things they were asking us to do to them. I have been hit with fists and with bottles, and the sexual acts I have done are shameful.

Many times, the following day, we were told to carry these preacher's bibles and personal belongings wherever they went, and to make sure they had water and fruit on the table next to where they sat in the church. In my eyes, we were their *slaves*. It was not only us girls, but there were boys, as well. Honestly, the boys were their favorite. Many nights, I would hear screams from other rooms where boys and girls were being sexually tortured. This carried on in my life until I was thirteen years old. I was not only raped by traveling preachers, but by multiple men in my church, including my pastor.

I ran away from home at that time and lived in the streets for years. I became a prostitute to provide for myself, and now my children. I always ask myself, "Is there really a God? If so, why did He allow this to happen to me?" I don't know who to trust anymore. These Christians are always coming into villages and cities over here, and I just walk away from them. I don't know who to trust anymore. ~*Mary*, Nigeria

I have interviewed many believers all over the world from China to Africa, the U.S.A. to Europe, and all in between, and to see this happening all over the globe is alarming. Many would not allow me to share their stories of sexual/physical abuse in this book because of fear, guilt, or shame. Many stated they tried to tell others about their sexual abuse, but they were threatened with physical violence and their families were threatened, as well. They said they were demonized by their pastors/spiritual leaders, who were accused of raping young boys for years, while the Church remained silent. Enormous events are planned every year where hundreds of thousands, even millions in some cases, come to witness signs, wonders, and miracles from these charlatans. False teachers, false prophecies, false healings, and false signs, wonders, and miracles are all a front for fame and fortune. But just as the American

NFL Super Bowl is a front for sex-trafficking, so are these demonic church conventions, prophetic conferences, and healing services all over the world. In the shadows, young girls, boys, women, and men are being sexually tortured for the insidious sexual pleasure and gratification of perverts and pedophiles masked as spiritual leaders.

I had a conversation with a spiritual leader that has traveled globally for the better part of his adult life. He was someone I had trusted spiritually for almost eleven years. He shared with me the evil of sexual abuse and homosexuality rampant in the African church. Obviously, it was the direct result of hundreds of years of sexual torture during the slave trades and colonization periods. He stated it had exploded in the Church in Africa, but that due to gross power and control, these pastors are not being held accountable or responsible. He said they are like "mob bosses" in that they resort to threatening their victims into silence. I was devastated to find out that he, the man that voiced these atrocities to me, traveled to minister for one of these very pastors accused of pedophilia and sexual abuse. I confronted him and he gave me every excuse in the book as to why *God* had led him to go. I understand fully well why he went; the influence this pastor/church has in this region is astronomical! How much is our soul worth?

How can this be? How can we call ourselves believers, or followers of Christ, and operate in such deceit and wickedness? The sexual and physical abuse imposed by spiritual leadership upon God's people all over the world is an absolute travesty. In my opinion, it is the greatest act of perversion and witchcraft we can ever witness on this Earth. Light pierces the darkness. We must continue to speak concerning these atrocities committed against God's people by those in spiritual leadership and authority. Don't be afraid to open your mouth and speak what has happened to you; one man led the way for thousands/millions to speak out and be healed and delivered. How many children can be saved from sexual abuse, molestation, and rape, because you were brave enough to take your life back? Don't allow the devil to steal, kill, and destroy the rest of your life or someone else's.

I am praying, interceding, uprooting, and pulling down generational curses and strongholds of spiritual abuse in every form. I will continue to be a *voice for the voiceless*, both alive and no longer here with us.

Chapter 9

The Mass Exodus &
The Return of the Scattered

"The word that came to Jeremiah from the LORD, saying, "Thus speaks the LORD God of Israel, saying: 'Write in a book for yourself all the words that I have spoken to you. For behold, the days are coming,' says the LORD, 'that I will bring back from captivity My people Israel and Judah,' says the LORD. 'And I will cause them to return to the land that I gave to their fathers, and they shall possess it.'" Jeremiah 30: 1-3

Many have walked away from the Church over the last several decades. People no longer trust the spiritual leadership set in place in most churches around the world today. The Church was once viewed as a safe haven, a place of non-judgment, and a place of unconditional love. Though you may not hear many say or admit this, people still want something that is *sacred* and *holy* in this world. They knew they could run to the church when the world around them was caving in, and knew that when they came, God would be right there waiting for them with open arms. The examples they once saw in their pastors or priests were that of holy men, not perfect, but committed to the cause of Christ and set apart for the work of the Kingdom. There was a standard set for these spiritual leaders, and many adhered to those principles. Sad to say, those numbers have dwindled exponentially over the last several decades and due to the gross sin taking place in our pulpits, people are leaving the Church in droves.

Church scandals are becoming all the more common and the chaos and confusion that arises from them are leading many to simply leave the Church altogether. I have experienced this in several churches that I attended in the past. One church, after the infidelity of its pastor was exposed, began rapidly declining in waves. Many pastors, elders, and members left immediately due to the nature of the scandal. Others trickled out periodically as the carnality grew in the pulpit. Once he was removed as pastor of the church, many more left and never returned. Some joined other local churches, while many others have not yet returned to the Church at all. I have had the opportunity to speak with many of these believers, and sadly, they no longer trust "pastors". They have witnessed the absolute callousness of these spiritual leaders and the spirit of entitlement they carry regarding spiritual abuse and sin. They have seen, firsthand, the overseers of these rogue pastors release them back into these pulpits after countless affairs and sexual perversion. Many have said, "I can do bad all by myself." They understand fully well that God is not amid this chaos and confusion.

"The Gallup Poll[xiii] as of 2018 revealed the number of Americans attending church is down to an all-time low of 50%. U.S. church membership was 70% or higher from 1937 through 1976, falling modestly to an average of 68% in the 1970s through the 1990s. The past twenty years have seen an acceleration in the drop-off, with a 20-percentage-point decline since 1999 and more than half of that change occurring since the start of the current decade."

"According to the Barna Group[xiv], in spite of America's "Christian" self-description, there is a growing sense among North American Christ-followers that the culture is changing faster than we can keep up with or respond to—and we're not always sure how to live faithfully in a world that feels like it's headed off the rails. Not too many years ago, church attendance and basic Bible literacy were the cultural norm. Being a Christian didn't feel like swimming against the cultural current. But now?" *Churchless*[xv] confirms that "the world has, indeed, altered in significant ways during the last few decades. It's not just your imagination. Real data confirms how drastically the moral, social, and spiritual lives of Americans have changed and are continually changing."

We understand the ever-changing landscape of the world and the decline in moral accountability and responsibility, but what happens when these statistics are now describing even the Church? The Church was formed to be the salt and light of the Earth.

"You are the salt of the earth; but if the salt loses its flavor, how shall it be seasoned? It is then good for nothing but to be thrown out and

trampled underfoot by men. You are the light of the world. A city that is set on a hill cannot be hidden. Nor do they light a lamp and put it under a basket, but on a lampstand, and it gives light to all who are in the house. Let your light so shine before men, that they may see your good works and glorify your Father in heaven." Matthew 5: 13-16

Our *salt* is losing its flavor and our *light* is dimming, and in many cases, being extinguished altogether due to the blatant hypocrisy of spiritual leadership in the Church. Another church I was a member of about eight years ago also found itself in the midst of sexual scandal. This church has been in this community for almost thirty years. Pastors that began with this church were slowly leaving to form their own churches in the city or in other states. Some members I spoke to have left and don't know where to turn. They feel betrayed and let down by pastors who were once their dear friends. I hear many pastors and churchgoers attacking these precious believers stating that if they truly knew and loved God, then they wouldn't leave the Church simply because a pastor or spiritual leader has fallen into sin. They accuse them of not being "Christians" in the first place or being weak and immature for walking away from the Church.

We must clear up this misconception immediately. God *does not* require or command us to stay in a toxic and contaminated spiritual environment. In fact, there are many scriptures that warn us against such people, including false teachers and false prophets, and encourage us to surround ourselves with like-minded believers, people of *like faith*.

"Do not be unequally yoked together with unbelievers. For what fellowship has righteousness with lawlessness? And what communion has light with darkness?" 2 Corinthians 6:14

This includes not only unbelievers outside of the Church, but also those within the Church that do not follow after righteousness and practice lawlessness, especially our spiritual leaders.

"But now I have written to you not to keep company with anyone named a brother, who is sexually immoral, or covetous, or an idolater, or a reviler, or a drunkard, or an extortioner—not even to eat with such a person." 1 Corinthians 5:11

This is a very serious command. It is clearly understood that such an individual has the capacity to contaminate the entire congregation with their recklessness and rebellion. Remaining underneath of such spiritual leadership is detrimental not only to our spiritual well-being, but also to our familial relationships. Rogue pastors/spiritual leaders are like a *cancer* that has the power to infect all under the sound of their voices. After the removal of the pastor mentioned earlier, it was revealed that many of the men under his leadership were also having extramarital affairs and mass divorce occurred in this church. Entire families were ripped apart and even to this day, most cannot even comprehend that they were the victims of gross spiritual abuse. They simply accepted their "fate," as they perceive it, and have moved on with their lives…

some still serving in this very church and some who are still friends with this pastor. Many of these wives I have spoken to personally, and their lives have been destroyed. Their children are broken and lost. What travesty!

Yet, we want to tell them that they should not leave the church. We accuse them of being oversensitive and overreacting. No, they have every right to leave such a destructive atmosphere! Those that remain I am more concerned with, as they are clearly blinded by deception and denial. The twisting, perverting, and manipulation of Scripture holds them in bondage to these false teachers and charlatans.

"For I know this, that after my departure savage wolves will come in among you, not sparing the flock. Also from among yourselves men will rise up, speaking perverse things, to draw away the disciples after themselves." Acts 20: 29-30

"Was I dreaming? When it was revealed that my pastor was having an affair, I refused to believe it. He was such a powerful preacher and his passion for the Word was infectious. His influence was far-reaching all over the world. I understand that people fall into temptation and that God is merciful and will forgive us when we truly repent with our whole hearts. This man was not only unrepentant, but he became outrageously arrogant and erratic. His demeanor shifted from being a loving pastor to an egotistical tyrant. He became so harsh and defensive about every-thing. He took absolutely no responsibility for his actions and blamed everyone else for what was happening to *him*. He was the perpetrator, but instead of humbly asking for forgiveness from his congregation, he used the pulpit to attack those who were "plotting to destroy his life".

I could no longer remain under such a toxic and narcissistic spiritual leader. I could no longer sense the Spirit of God in our Church. It became so carnal, worldly, and flesh filled. Other pastors and leaders, not only in our church, but all over the world, were standing with this man and excusing away his sin. Many others and I were extremely angry with how this man was getting away with this blatant evil. How were these people comfortable with this man preaching to them and their families? How were other pastors still inviting this man to preach to their congregations? My heart grieves deeply for this church and many other churches around the world. Churches are emptying out in masses and people do not know where to turn anymore. *~Patricia*, North Carolina

God is very serious about the welfare and well-being of His people. Many feel that people are simply walking away from the Church, but in many cases, God Himself is leading people away from these false teachers, false doctrines, and false signs, wonders, and miracles. God is protecting His people from deceitfulness in our pulpits. Holy Spirit is warning people to run and not to look back. The same way God told Lot and his family to flee Sodom and Gomorrah, He is speaking to His people to escape the apostate church before it is too late. *Apostasy* is the formal disaffiliation from, abandonment of, or renunciation of a religion by a person. It can also be defined within the broader context of embracing an opinion that is contrary to one's previous religious beliefs. The modern-day church has progressively turned apostate and adopted many forms of spirituality and religion. The rejection of the scriptures as holy and inherent and the subsequent adopting of carnal and worldly paradigms within the Church has produced a pseudo-Christianity.

This prototype is not only forcing the true, authentic believers out of the Church, but it is also drawing the non-believer, the uncommitted, to a place of compromised and fruitless religion. These people are only coming for the entertainment and to hear a watered-down version of Christianity. They're seeking a *good word* and *good music*. They are not at all concerned with their eternal salvation, and even if they are, it is getting to heaven without any earthly obedience to God or His Word. They do not desire accountability or responsibility, and these pastors/spiritual leaders are catering to their demands, so they can keep their seats full and their pockets overflowing.

Yet, we are now dealing with the massive scattering of believers all over the world that are leaving organized religion, and some, the faith altogether. We are at a dire crossroad and in desperate need of true, authentic shepherds to gather these broken, wounded, hurt, and devastated believers. God is calling His shepherds out of the organized church in this hour. Many are not comprehending what is taking place, and instead of consecrating themselves and seeking to hear the voice of God, they are running away and following all sorts of desperate paths. If you are a pastor that has left the church due to the gross spiritual abuse and corruption so rampant in today's church culture, please seek God on His will for your life and for the lives of millions all around the world. These false teachers/preachers/prophets will receive consequences for their actions. God will not allow this to go unpunished.

"Woe to the shepherds who destroy and scatter the sheep of My pasture!" says the Lord. Therefore thus says the Lord God of Israel against the shepherds who feed My people: "You have scattered My flock, driven them away, and not attended to them. Behold, I will attend to you for the evil of your doings," says the Lord." Jeremiah 23: 1-2

As I have witnessed this *mass exodus* of believers leaving the organized church over the last ten years, though I know the Word of God prophesied it, I felt in my spirit that much of its leading is directly from the Lord Himself. Those that know God intimately and are in relationship with Him through the Word and by Holy Spirit cannot remain in these lifeless and spirit-less churches. They are dry desert wastelands. I know personally what this feels like. I have sat in churches where the energy is extremely high, the pastor is shouting, and people are jumping to their feet, but here I am, sitting in my seat dumfounded wondering what he said that has caused them to jump and shout. I have literally wept at the things I have heard many of these pastors preach; carnal and worldly rants and attacks against people, and people find this encouraging or empowering? These are flesh-filled tirades, not Spirit-led exhortations. People's flesh is being catered to and God is nowhere amongst us. I cannot tell you how many stories I have heard similar to this where people have become fed up with these church shenanigans. Can we blame them? I know I cannot, and I will not remain in such a compromised place of religion. We cannot grow or mature spiritually in these carnal atmospheres and God does not expect, require, or command us to remain in such apostasy.

"I thought it was just me. I left my church of twenty years due to perversion and corruption in the leadership. It didn't just happen once, but on multiple occasions, our pastor had been caught in adulterous affairs. Time after time, he was released back into the pulpit. Each time, his preaching progressively became brash; his arrogance pierced through my soul and my spirit. I knew I had to leave, because I was becoming more and more anxious and depressed. I could not sleep most nights, as I prayed heavily for what was taking place in our church. That day came and it was like my heart was being ripped out of my chest. Before he could even open his mouth, I heard the Lord say, "Guard your heart." I immediately began interceding right there in my seat. As he began to speak, I could see the pride, the arrogance, and the controlling spirit upon him. He spoke these words, and I calmly grabbed my bible, my purse, my coat and I walked out of this church after twenty years and never returned.

"This is my church! God ordained me to lead this church and no one has the authority to remove me. My personal life is none of anyone's business and either you can submit to my authority or you can get your stuff and get out!"

I did just that, without hesitation and without offense, and as I walked out of the doors of the sanctuary, I heard multiple footsteps behind me. I turned around and at least forty to fifty people walked out with me! It wasn't just me! Though I had a bit of anxiety leaving, it turned to absolute peace. I knew this man was no longer being led by the Spirit of God; he was being led by his flesh and the enemy of his soul. Sadly, many pastors and churches in our area new this man well and followed his carnal ways and teachings. I haven't found a new church home since and it seems to be a hopeless search. I love God deeply and continue to pray and meditate on the Word every day. In fact, I have not been this close to Him in my entire saved life. My relationship with God has blossomed tremendously.

I do deeply desire more fellowship with like-minded believers and seek God for His perfect will for my life. I am seeking out those relationships through my community and volunteering wherever I can find a need. I know God will lead me. ~*Karen*, Oklahoma

More and more, we are witnessing faithful and committed believers leaving the confines of the Church. These are not rebels or fair-weather Christians; they are submitted servants that have given their entire lives in service to God and His people. Nothing has changed but their location. God would rather His children seek Him with all their hearts privately, than to be abused by spiritual leaders in a corporate setting. I hear people condemning others for walking away from "church" when they have no idea the hell they have been through. Don't pray for them to find another church; pray their relationship with the Lord remains intact! He will lead them. But is this God's doing?

Is He gathering His people *from* the corrupt church system and gathering them *to* His true, authentic Ekklesia? The original Greek meaning of the word *ekklesia* means to "call out". It was not until later that its origin was changed to mean "assembly, congregation, council, or convocation." Is God *calling His people out* of Egypt and *calling them to* the Promised Land of truth? Is He gathering His people to His Kingdom?

"We are witnessing the greatest exodus out of the organized church in modern history. We all know Scripture and knew this was prophesied, but to actually witness it with your own eyes is astounding! Go into any church around the world, whether small or mega, and you will see masses of empty seats. Sure, with the emergence of social media today, pastors can manipulate cameras to make us believe they are packed to the rafters, but this is simply false. I travel globally, so whenever I am away from home, I usually find a local church to go and worship. I have been in several churches, both in the U.S. and overseas, where the pastor asks the people to move in closer to the front to fill up the empty seats in the first three to four rows. One pastor literally told us to do this, because he was live streaming and he needed it to look as if the house was packed. He also told us to be energetic; to shout "Amen" and to clap loud when we heard something that *hit us*. Mind you, I had been in these churches in previous years and they were overflowing to capacity.

There is no question the Church today is in tragic decline, both morally and numerically. Whatever God is doing, I pray He does it quickly. ~Jonathan, WA

THE ELEPHANT IN THE ROOM

"For thus says the Lord God: "Indeed I Myself will search for My sheep and seek them out. As a shepherd seeks out his flock on the day he is among his scattered sheep, so will I seek out My sheep and deliver them from all the places where they were scattered on a cloudy and dark day. And I will bring them out from the peoples and gather them from the countries, and will bring them to their own land; I will feed them on the mountains of Israel, in the valleys and in all the inhabited places of the country. I will feed them in good pasture, and their fold shall be on the high mountains of Israel. There they shall lie down in a good fold and feed in rich pasture on the mountains of Israel. I will feed My flock, and I will make them lie down," says the Lord God. "I will seek what was lost and bring back what was driven away, bind up the broken and strengthen what was sick; but I will destroy the fat and the strong, and feed them in judgment." Ezekiel 34: 11-15

Chapter 10

The Truth Revealed: Exposing Sin in Spiritual Leadership

"Also He said to them, "Is a lamp brought to be put under a basket or under a bed? Is it not to be set on a lampstand? For there is nothing hidden which will not be revealed, nor has anything been kept secret but that it should come to light. If anyone has ears to hear, let him hear." Mark 4: 21-23

As we continue to hear of the exposure of "spiritual leaders" in the Church today, happening at rapid rates mind you, we hear so much confusion, and honestly ignorance, coming from the Church. On one side, many stand up for these leaders due to a lack of knowledge concerning biblical correction and rebuke. They "coddle" these leaders and literally "cheer them on," feeding their pride, arrogance, disobedience, entitlement, and rebellion. They refuse to see that if this is not dealt with privately, it will be exposed openly. And please understand that most of these cases have, indeed, been addressed privately, but have been absolutely rejected by not only the perpetrators, but their *circles of influence*, including their "spiritual fathers and mothers". People are literally covering the sins of these leaders, and not holding them biblically accountable as God commands.

"Them that sin rebuke before all, that others also may fear." 1 Timothy 5:20

This biblical principle is a safeguard against rampant sin within the Church. When other believers see that there are consequences to our sin, especially within spiritual leadership, which is supposed to be our example, then they are more likely to adhere to biblical standards. Sadly, we are living in a time where biblical rebuke is almost non-existent. Why? Because our spiritual leaders, themselves, are immersed in blatant sin and rebellion.

"Moreover if your brother sins against you, go and tell him his fault between you and him alone. If he hears you, you have gained your brother. But if he will not hear, take with you one or two more, that 'by the mouth of two or three witnesses every word may be established.' And if he refuses to hear them, tell it to the church." Matthew 18:15-16

These are some very serious warnings in Scripture that the Church has almost altogether refused and rejected. What happens when we neglect this command of God? We allow these rapists, pedophiles, adulterers, and yes, abusers back into the pulpit to do this again! But read the last verse, Matthew 18: 17. It says,

"But if he refuses even to hear the church, let him be to you like a heathen and a tax collector."

Are we truly hearing this? This is the greatest of rebuke! Yet, we want to water down the Scripture so as not to *offend* or *judge* someone. God has already judged it by His Word! But we have become so tolerant and as a dear mentor one shared, "a weak bunch of Christians!" If we openly obeyed the Scriptures, people would fear God and truly repent and turn away from their wickedness and be healed and delivered from this perversion. Do we really care about them? If we did, we would allow God to deal with them as only He is able. We are standing in the way of God's correction, chastisement, and rebuke. I promise you; you don't want to be caught in that place. You will suffer grave consequences, as well. Step to the side and pray for them and pray for God's refining fire to purge them of this perversion. And for those "spiritual fathers and mothers" releasing and returning these leaders to authority, the *blood* of their victims is upon your hands! You have directly and indirectly led God's people astray and if you do not repent, the Bible says,

"But whoever causes one of these little ones who believe in Me to sin, it would be better for him if a millstone were hung around his neck, and he were drowned in the depth of the sea." Matthew 18:6

223

See, we no longer believe the very Word we are preaching! Instead, we manipulate and pervert it to say what we want it to say. There is also a warning for this:

"For I testify to everyone who hears the words of the prophecy of this book: If anyone adds to these things, God will add to him the plagues that are written in this book; and if anyone takes away from the words of the book of this prophecy, God shall take away his part from the Book of Life, from the holy city, and from the things which are written in this book." Revelation 22:18-19

We must faithfully and wholeheartedly administer and render the Word of God our final authority if we are going to call ourselves spiritual leaders, pastors, or shepherds of the Gospel of Jesus Christ. If we refuse, we are not only leading God's people astray, but we are also hindering the world from coming to Him through His Church. But, let me promise you, He will draw His people with or without you! I had a dream a very long time ago and I saw pastors falling dead in pulpits across the world. I prayed and interceded so heavily, as this was long before God began speaking to me about spiritual abuse, perversion, and corruption in the Church. Not too long ago, the dream returned to me and these scriptures were given to me:

"Then Nadab and Abihu, the sons of Aaron, each took his censer and put fire in it, put incense on it, and offered profane fire before the Lord,

which He had not commanded them. So fire went out from the Lord and devoured them, and they died before the Lord." Leviticus 10:1-2

The judgment God pronounced upon His people before He sent the sacrifice of His Son was swift. It was understood that sin in the camp had to be eradicated immediately, so others would not assume they could so flippantly do as they pleased. The cancer had to be cut off before it was able to spread to the rest of the camp. Unfortunately, due to the errors of *rightly dividing the Word of Truth*, the Church has adopted the "hyper-grace theology," which assumes God's grace covers all our sin without need of repentance or earthly consequence. These spiritual leaders, false teachers, are turning the grace of God into a license to sin.

"What shall we say then? Shall we continue in sin that grace may abound? Certainly not! How shall we who died to sin live any longer in it?" Romans 6: 1-2

7 Signs of a Hyper-Grace Church

1. The preachers never speak against sin.
2. The lead pastor never takes a cultural stand for righteousness.
3. The Old Testament is almost totally ignored.
4. People are allowed to teach and lead ministries who live immoral lives.
5. The lead pastor speaks often against the institutional church.
6. The lead pastor only preaches positive motivational messages.

7. Key members of the church are regularly living sinful lives with immunity.

Those attending a hyper-grace church will most likely be involved in more loose living and sexual sin, due to the fact that sin and judgment is not preached. When God's commandments are refused and rejected, moral decline is inevitable.

"Now Eli was very old; and he heard everything his sons did to all Israel, and how they lay with the women who assembled at the door of the tabernacle of meeting. So he said to them, "Why do you do such things? For I hear of your evil dealings from all the people. No, my sons! For it is not a good report that I hear. You make the Lord's people transgress. If one man sins against another, God will judge him. But if a man sins against the Lord, who will intercede for him?" Nevertheless they did not heed the voice of their father, because the Lord desired to kill them." 1 Samuel 2:22-25

As we continue to read down to 1 Samuel 4:11, Hophni and Phinehas were killed and the Ark of the Covenant, the presence of God, was captured. What do we get from this? When spiritual leadership outright defames the name of the Lord through habitual sin, with no repentance or consequences, we hinder the voice, presence, and protection of God in our corporate gatherings. He will not meet us! Healing, deliverance, and salvation are stifled by the gross sin in our pulpits. Do we truly understand that many people coming to church day in and day out are not born again? Why? Because of the unrepentant hearts of our spiritual leaders, the true Gospel of repentance is not being preached or administered by and through the Spirit of God. This is a devastating revelation the Lord revealed to me in great intercession. We also run the risk of causing young believers to run from God, and even seasoned ones, to leave the church.

Could God be holding back His greatest hand of judgment upon His Church, sending His messengers of warning for us to repent before it's too late? I know many don't believe this can happen today, as Jesus Christ became the ultimate sacrifice for our sins, but God is yet speaking concerning spiritual corruption and perversion. The church is in a very crucial state and until true, spiritual leadership repents and gets back to the foundational teachings of the Word, we will continue to see a great crumbling taking place in our pulpits.

"If we say that we have fellowship with Him, and walk in darkness, we lie and do not practice the truth." 1 John 1:6

I heard over seven years ago that many well-known spiritual leaders would be brought down from the pulpit. God revealed several of them to me in dreams. One has already been removed, yet after just a short period of time, was restored to pastoring God's people. Another was never removed and continues as if he has done absolutely nothing. God is sending judgment upon the Church today. He is a loving, gracious, and merciful God. He heals, delivers, sets free, saves, restores, and reconciles, but He also corrects, chastises, scolds, breaks, and rebukes those that are His. The dispensation of grace has been so misused and abused by the Church today that we have replaced the entirety, the fullness, of God's Word with pure deceit and manipulation, all in the name of *Grace*. God calls us all to restoration of fellowship through forgiveness of sin, but He is *not* calling for restoration of these people to leadership or pastoral service. How do I know this? Let's take a look at the Word of God. All these national and spiritual leaders were replaced by God in some form or fashion through sin, either in disobedience or outright rebellion:

- ❖ Adam
- ❖ Moses
- ❖ Saul
- ❖ David
- ❖ Samson
- ❖ Eli
- ❖ Elijah
- ❖ Judas
- ❖ and many kings and leaders throughout the Bible

Whether by judgment, replacement by rapture, succession or death, all these leaders' disobedience led to being stripped of natural and spiritual authority. None were restored to leadership, but God rather raised up another who would obey and carry on His plan and will. God's judgment is always just and leads to the working of His perfect will for humanity. One scripture that floored me is revealed in Corinthians:

"Turn this man over to Satan for the destruction of the flesh, so that his spirit may be saved in the day of the Lord." 1 Corinthians 5:5

Are we more concerned with a spiritual leader's reputation on this Earth or are we rather determined to ensure his eternal name in the *Lamb's Book of Life?* God is not concerned with the temporary pleasures of this life; He is fixed upon our eternal salvation. We become so enamored with someone's *celebrity* that we completely forget about their possible eternal consequences. In speaking so boldly for Christ and for the Truth, I had to quickly come to terms with and count the costs of losing temporary earthly friendships in an effort to salvage that which is eternal. We cannot continue allowing these rogue and rebellious spiritual leaders *free passes* to continue sinning in our sacred pulpits and subsequently harming the people of God.

We are in one of the darkest hours in the Church, a time of great chaos, confusion, manipulation, deceit, and carnality. A time of rebellion has found itself upon the people of God once again. We have allowed the world to influence every aspect of our sacred meetings. Demonic and satanic spirits have crept their way in through disobedience and set up shop in our pulpits. The people of God are 'puppets' in the hands of masterful orators and deceitful dignitaries. Agendas are the mark of these ministries, or better called today "movements". They are focused on their *brand* and as their lives depend upon it, will protect it at all costs, including outright disobedience to the voice of God.

We are witnessing pastors/leaders who have preached over four decades now moving away from bold teaching and preaching on Truth. Instead, we find ourselves emotionalized by a "shouty" speech designed to over-emotionalize our experience and propel us to give. Sermons are laced with overindulgence in letting our *haters* know who they are and sneaky *drops* that are designed to tear down others in the Body of Christ and using their weaknesses as a means to lift up our accomplishments.

I have personally witnessed attacks from the pulpit that are in no way from the Spirit of God. I see a *mob-like* spirit upon our leaders today. They are becoming more and more controlling (the Jezebel spirit) and seek to recruit those who will stand with them and agree with everything they say and do. These are "yes" men and women, those who are too afraid to tell you the truth about yourself in fear they will lose a *title* or *position* within an organization. Spotlight and acknowledgement are more important to these people than the well-being of their leader. They inwardly disagree with what they see and hear, yet their knees shake when it's time to confront their leader with truth. These are *Ahab* spirits... enablers. They are just as bad as the leaders they secretly disagree with, because they will entertain deceit and manipulation and allow many others to be affected by withholding the Word of the Lord.

God is calling these spirits out of His Church in boldness! These modern day, corporate *Egypt's*, though highly profitable and marketable, are not above the judgment of God. Many have been warned by God and

His prophets, as well as have been put on *display* by our government, yet through ungodly covenants, they have appeased them through great compromise. So many have sold out to this world, so as to keep their fortunes and have allowed a worldly spirit to enter our places of Worship. For God to tell us to *turn them over to Satan for the destruction of their flesh* is an eye-opening revelation of His love and His sovereignty.

One thing which stood out to me here is that God, though He does not send evil upon anyone, does have authority to allow Satan to release it (as we clearly see in Job). But more than we see judgment here, we see ultimate love. When God sees us spiraling into sin, He will allow our *flesh* (natural lives) to be taken, so our spirit may be saved for eternity.

I had a person very dear to me who lived the homosexual lifestyle. He contracted AIDS and was dying. He gave his life to the Lord, but asked God this question, "God, if You save me from dying, I will give up living this way and serve You totally." Well, God saved his soul, but did not save his earthly life. God's ways are truly higher than our ways and His thoughts than our thoughts. I cannot begin to tell you completely why God didn't allow him to live, but I know we often try to *bargain* with God knowing we cannot keep the promises we make to Him. In great prayer, I heard the Lord say, "I love him too much to keep him here."

I often wonder if this was the case with Judas. Though he betrayed Jesus, his remorse, in the end, moved me to tears for our brother. We have penned Judas as the *ultimate evil*, yet the Word reveals his repentance. He went back to the high priests and threw back the silver. He was tormented and grieved at what he had done to His Lord to the extent of taking his own life. Did God allow *the destruction of his flesh*, so his soul and spirit could be saved? Only God knows the answer, but scripture lends great weight to God's ultimate grace over our lives, and it is not *releasing us in* this earthly life but *releasing us to* eternal life.

The Apostle Paul in Corinthians is speaking directly to the Church, not the world. Paul was speaking of immorality being judged *within* the confines of the Church. Let's look at a few scriptures:

"And you are puffed up (arrogant), and have not rather mourned, that he who has done this deed might be taken away from you." 1 Corinthians 5:2

Paul is revealing to us in this scripture that in their arrogance, they are not concerned about the impact of this person's sin in their fellowship. They are not worried about removing this *cancer* from among them. When this is allowed to continue over long periods of time, people become desensitized to the sin. They no longer perceive it as important or dire.

"Your glorifying is not good. Do you know that a little leaven leavens the whole lump. Therefore, purge out the old leaven, that you may be a new lump, since you are truly unleavened. For indeed Christ, our Passover, was sacrificed, for us." 1 Corinthians 5:6-7

When we allow those in authority to continue in disobedience, and outright sin, we allow these spirits to overtake the entire church. I have witnessed complete upheaval, the removing of a pastor/leader of a church, and on the other hand, I have witnessed complete cover-up or acceptance of sin and leaving a leader in authority, or a restoration of authority to one found in outright sexual sin or moral disobedience. Many refuse to accept God's judgment upon them. Their pride and arrogance fuel their *need* to remain in spiritual authority, when in reality, there is nothing *spiritual* left. Several instances in the Word reveal God removing His anointing from a leader.

1 Samuel 15 (Read in its entirety) Verse 26:

"But Samuel said to Saul, 'I will NOT return with you, for you have rejected the word of the Lord, and the Lord has rejected you from being king over Israel." (emphasis mine)

Saul begged God to keep him as king, even after his disobedience, but through the prophet Samuel, God said, "NO!" Samuel revealed to Saul that God was preparing a new king, yet Saul contended for this *title* with his sword until the day of his death; the very sword he kept wielding at David, his successor, was the sword he fell by. Be very careful not to rebuke what God Himself is sending to correct you.

Another instance is the life of Samson:

"And she said, 'The Philistines are upon you Samson!' So he awoke from his sleep and said, "I will go out as before, at other times, and shake myself free!" But he did not know that the Lord had departed from him.'" Judges 16:20

Samson's disobedience to God left him to his enemies. He was *warned* three times before, and God allowed him to get free. In his arrogance, he just assumed God would always strengthen him and give him victory. His arrogance finally caught up with him. His strength, God's anointing, would be taken from him, but not until God's ultimate plan was fulfilled. We can arrogantly, as Saul and Samson did, think we have control of our destiny, but let me promise you, you nor I do. We can work alongside God to fulfill His plans through us, but when we outright disobey Him and choose a life of sin, He can and will strip us of authority. When we refuse correction, chastisement or rebuke, He can and will turn us over to Satan. Not for eternal judgment, but for temporary judgment, so others will understand fear, or reverence, for the Lord.

"Those who are sinning rebuke in the presence of all, that the rest also may fear." 1Timothy 5:20

I am afraid we have moved so far away from Biblical teaching that this no longer matters to us. When a pastor/leader falls into sin and is allowed to remain there, or is restored there, it sends a message that one, I don't have to worry about sin in my life; God will *give me grace* if He gave my pastor grace, and I can live how I want to without consequences. Two, it reveals that the Bible is no longer our final authority. Many will say it is an outdated text, yet still manipulate its passages to suit their specific needs, wants, or desires. Either it is all truth or its not? *"Let not that man think he will receive anything from the Lord. He is a double-minded man, unstable in all his ways."* (James 1:7-9)

God is bringing judgment upon the Church. It will begin with us first, His people, and when we humble ourselves, receive it, and repent, He will then heal this world and bring many to His saving knowledge.

"For the time has come for judgment to begin at the house of God; and if it begins with us first, what will be the end of those who do not obey the Gospel of God." 1 Peter 4:17

God loves us so very much, and that love goes much deeper than temporary grace; it is an *eternal grace* that may not save us from this world but will save us to eternity. It's time to set our houses in order! I write this because God is grieved by the Church and what it is doing not only to His people, but to society and this world, as a whole. He is grieved by the misrepresentation of His name for fame, fortune, glory, and status. For those that have the power and authority to stop this, yet refuse and keep these sexual predators and pedophiles in our pulpits, here is a clear warning for you:

"Now the Lord came and stood and called as at other times, "Samuel! Samuel!" And Samuel answered, "Speak, for Your servant hears." Then

the Lord said to Samuel: "Behold, I will do something in Israel at which both ears of everyone who hears it will tingle. In that day I will perform against Eli all that I have spoken concerning his house, from beginning to end. For I have told him that I will judge his house forever for the iniquity which he knows, because his sons made themselves vile, and he did not restrain them. And therefore I have sworn to the house of Eli that the iniquity of Eli's house shall not be atoned for by sacrifice or offering forever." 1 Samuel 3: 10-14

God not only pronounced judgment upon Eli's sons, but also upon Eli because he did not "restrain" his sons from their wickedness. He allowed them to continue in their sin and disobedience to God. These spiritual leaders think they are getting away with this rebellion, but God is keeping a clear and precise record and will offer judgment in due season. Sadly, the masses underneath of this spiritual leaders are the ones truly suffering. The Church is hindered tremendously by this spiritual recklessness and rebellion, and God's Spirit is not free to flow in these churches. His *glory has departed* many congregations today due to spiritual abuse and manipulation.

"Then she named the child Ichabod, saying, "The glory has departed from Israel!" because the ark of God had been captured and because of her father-in-law and her husband. And she said, "The glory has departed from Israel, for the ark of God has been captured."

People ask me often, "Deborah, why is God allowing this to continue? If He sees what these spiritual leaders are doing, why is He not stopping it?" First, we must understand that God gives us all *free will*. Free will is the ability to choose between different possible courses of action unimpeded. Free will is closely linked to the concepts of moral responsibility, praise, guilt, sin, and other judgements which apply only to actions that are freely chosen. This is the choice to live either by the principles of God's wisdom, His Word, or by our own moral constructs, or ideas. God does not force us to live morally. He gives us His Word as a blueprint, but it is our choice to follow it, or not. Unfortunately, those in spiritual leadership, though commanded and required by holy Scripture to live after these precepts and principles, are choosing not to follow the very Word they preach/teach. It is outright hypocrisy!

Secondly, God's grace, His true grace, is still actively working in all our lives to bring us to a place of heartfelt repentance. The Bible says that "it is His goodness that leads to repentance." I know we typically choose to *weigh* sin and feel that spiritual leaders should know better and that their judgment should be swift and harsher. Well, this thought is absolutely correct and justified.

"My brethren, let not many of you become teachers, knowing that we shall receive a stricter judgment." James 3:1

237

"I love the Church. I believe in the Church. It is a beautiful organism of love, grace, justice, and mercy, but there are some things disturbingly wrong with the American church, particularly some threads of the evangelical church. I know of at least four instances recently, and in the not so distant past, where congregations have given literal standing ovations to the Senior Leader for acknowledging abuse of power, abuse of people, and general misconduct. This is not the time or the place for a standing ovation (if ever).

For those who have been wronged, abused, or maligned, this is re-traumatizing them. Why a standing ovation? The American church has become a cult of personality and a cult of organizational pride in many cases. Their "church" is the best and does things the "right" way. Their identity becomes attached to the charisma of the Senior Leader, rather than identifying with the greater Church at large. Something has to give and change." *~Pastor*, Chicago

We must also understand that God did not send His Son into this world to condemn us, but to save us, and that is the authentic idea of *unlimited grace*. His unlimited grace is given to secure our eternal place, or position, not to provide us a license to continue in our blatant sin. We

must understand the difference, but we must also know what the Word of God reveals to us will take place, and yet is, in the last days.

"But know this, that in the last days perilous times will come: For men will be lovers of themselves, lovers of money, boasters, proud, blasphemers, disobedient to parents, unthankful, unholy, unloving, unforgiving, slanderers, without self-control, brutal, despisers of good, traitors, headstrong, haughty, lovers of pleasure rather than lovers of God, having a form of godliness but denying its power. And from such people turn away! For of this sort are those who creep into households and make captives of gullible women loaded down with sins, led away by various lusts, always learning and never able to come to the knowledge of the truth. Now as Jannes and Jambres resisted Moses, so do these also resist the truth: men of corrupt minds, disapproved concerning the faith; but they will progress no further, for their folly will be manifest to all, as theirs also was." 2 Timothy 3: 1-9

Trust God's Word! He clearly tells us that they will *progress no further* and that *their folly will be manifest to all*. But this is God's assignment, not ours. I had to really allow Holy Spirit to minister to me and teach me the deep things of Scripture as I was dealing with great frustration, bitterness, and anger concerning the spiritual abuse I not only witnessed but experienced myself. I had to allow Him to give me *His heart*, so I was not out of His perfect will. I could not effectively and wholeheartedly intercede or speak to these atrocities in His name if my heart was not right and if I did not fully understand His wisdom concerning it. This was a period of great spiritual growth in my life. Please understand that God is deeply grieved with the spiritual abuse, perversion, and corruption in the organized Church and He will bring swift and harsh judgment upon those that have harmed His people.

Spiritual leaders are not above correction or rebuke, especially when they abuse the pulpit in which they were called to preach the unadulterated truth of God's Word, as well as to maintain the character and attributes of Holy Spirit. Attacks across the pulpit and even behind closed doors, as well as threats both directly and indirectly are not from God. Understand that these are defensive measures/mechanisms these spiritual leaders take in order to bully those that are calling out their rebellion. How can we sleep at night knowing we have attacked God's precious people? How can we stand in the stead of God in the earth realm and treat His children with such guile and disrespect and call it Him?

We are witnessing a rise in this type of *spiritual leadership* in the church today and it is literally tearing people and yes, churches, apart. It deeply saddens me that men and women called of God can turn so far away from the Word and His Spirit that they have no remorse when attacking God's children and no conscious as to continue doing so. I have asked myself often, "Have we all but thrown the fear and reverence of God out the window? Will God ever intervene?" His Word brings great comfort and assurance that He is yet, indeed, sovereign.

"My heart within me is broken because of the prophets; all my bones shake. I am like a drunken man, and like a man whom wine has over-

come, because of the LORD, and because of His holy words. For the land is full of adulterers; for because of a curse the land mourns. The pleasant places of the wilderness are dried up. Their course of life is evil, and their might is not right. "For both prophet and priest are profane; Yes, in My house I have found their wickedness," says the LORD. "Therefore their way shall be to them Like slippery ways; In the darkness they shall be driven on and fall in them; For I will bring disaster on them, The year of their punishment," says the LORD. "And I have seen folly in the prophets of Samaria: They prophesied by Baal and caused My people Israel to err. Also I have seen a horrible thing in the prophets of Jerusalem: They commit adultery and walk in lies; They also strengthen the hands of evildoers, so that no one turns back from his wickedness. All of them are like Sodom to Me, and her inhabitants like Gomorrah." Jeremiah 23: 9-14

The allowing of blatant and public sin in our pulpits by these spiritual leaders without consequence is causing a desensitizing toward sin in the global church. The pride, arrogance, and spirit of entitlement, the thought of being *untouchable*, is rampant in churches all over the world. Their sin is becoming even more evil and sinister, and these are the ones we have chosen to cover us and our families spiritually. Do we understand the ramifications of this spiritual negligence? These are the men praying over our marriages, praying for our children, praying for our health, and praying for our destinies. Don't simply allow a man to lay hands on you because he is a "famous" preacher, or because they tell you they are anointed and called by God. If they are living in unchecked sin, they have no business whatsoever laying their hands on anyone. Many of their hands are drenched in the blood of the saints and contaminated with sin. God is exposing this deceit.

Our Father in Heaven is not silent nor His eyes dim concerning the blatant spiritual abuse going on in the Church today. The deep-seated sin within the ranks of spiritual leadership is causing an implosion within the Church, but God will surely turn it around for His good. He sees all, and He will enforce as He sees fit and in His perfect timing. Trust Him and continue interceding that these spiritual leaders will repent and turn back to Him.

Chapter 11

Justice vs. Judgment

"But he who is spiritual judges all things, yet he himself is rightly judged by no one. For "who has known the mind of the Lord that he may instruct Him?" But we have the mind of Christ." (1 Corinthians 2: 15-16)

In today's Christian culture, one word that is probably the most overused and misunderstood is "judging". All too often, you hear offended and defensive people throwing out the saying, "Judge not lest you be judged." So much chaos and confusion has infiltrated the Body of Christ that most Believers automatically assume someone is passing judgment upon them. What most Christians don't understand, and what most pastors/spiritual leaders refuse to acknowledge, is that we who are "spiritual" are called to *Judge* spiritual things. We are mixing judgment with judging. If spiritual things are not "judged," then anything and everything will be accepted as Biblical. And the sad reality is, most of those calling people who judge spiritual matters "haters" or "criticizers"

are the ones who are most likely in error in some aspect of their spiritual walk. When we judge spiritually, Holy Spirit will convict the Believer. So spiritually immature people, instead of receiving correction from the Spirit, attack the one who has judged spiritually by the Spirit of God.

"However, we speak wisdom among those who are mature, yet not the wisdom of this age, nor of the rulers of this age, who are coming to nothing." (1 Corinthians 2:6)

This is happening at alarming rates in the Church today. Spiritual *hierarchy* demands honor, loyalty and respect, yet refuse to open themselves up for correction or receive from someone sent by God to help them. Instead, they surround themselves with weak imitations of "spiritual" people, so they remain the *one* in authority. If anyone questions the validity of spiritual practices, that do not line up with the Word of God, they are rebuked and accused of questioning their authority. I really need to make a note here how very dangerous *spiritually* this is for anyone. We cannot choose who God uses to speak the Truth into our dark situations. We cannot surround ourselves with those *we* feel are "qualified" to prophesy into our lives. On both ends, we are shortchanging ourselves, because something will be compromised due to familiarity. The Church must get to the place of operating solely by the leading of Holy Spirit, and the gifts of the Spirit flowing freely and in order.

1 Corinthians details the gifts of the Spirit, their unique functions and assignments, and their purpose in ministering to the Body of Christ. In

operating fully in these Ascension gifts within the Church, we tap into a realm that lacks nothing regarding justice and judgment. He is our Advocate! An *advocate* is defined as to speak or write in favor of; support or urge by argument; recommend publicly.

"My little children, these things I write to you, so that you may not sin. And if anyone sins, we have an Advocate with the Father, Jesus Christ the righteous. And He Himself is the propitiation for our sins, and not for ours only but also for the whole world." 1 John 2: 1-2 (emphasis mine)

It truly breaks my heart that the Body of Christ has been almost crippled in the area of *justice and judgment* due to lack of knowledge and wisdom, as well as fear. Jesus Himself left us the Promise of Holy Spirit; He did not leave us alone. His Word provides the blueprint with which we, as followers of Christ, are to conduct business within the Church, amongst believers. I find, often, that most people who have yielded themselves to Holy Spirit and opened up themselves to the gifts of the Spirit within, are labeled by others who have chosen not to, as "too spiritual," and yes, even judgmental. It is devastating to experience such judgment from those called your brothers and sisters in the Lord who, if they stopped for one moment to discern spiritually, would see that it is a loving God who sends such *gifts* into our lives and into our churches. LOVE propels them to seek God intimately and therefore propels them to speak the Truth. The Truth, even in the Church, is not popular, especially when it steps on the toes of spiritual leadership. Instead of accountability, we mask our sin, iniquity, and go on with church *as usual*. But how can we, with integrity and authentic anointing, do this? Sorry to say, we can't. It is pride and arrogance, almost rebellion (witchcraft), that perpetuates the audacity to call upon God to supernaturally infuse our lives while in outright disobedience. He is no puppet, and let me promise you, He will not be mocked! We have traded holiness for perversion and call it *anointed*. It is time for those who are *spiritual* to judge spiritual things.

"These things we also speak, not in words which man's wisdom teaches but which the Holy Spirit teaches, comparing spiritual things with spiritual. But the natural man does not receive the things of the Spirit of God, for they are foolishness to him; nor can he know them, because they are spiritually discerned. But he who is spiritual judges all things, yet he himself is rightly judged by no one. Who has known the mind of the Lord that he may instruct Him? But we have the mind of Christ." 1 Corinthians 2:13-16

"I was sexually assaulted by my pastor at a church convention I traveled to with him while I was working as his administrative assistant on staff at our church. I traveled all over the world with this man for several years. Protocol was always followed and there was always a man on staff that traveled with us, usually his security. This particular trip, his security was with us, but due to the state we traveled to being his family's home, he took some time to go spend with them. I was staying in the same hotel as my pastor and the same hotel the church convention was scheduled to be hosted. He called me to bring him his speaking itinerary for the weekend. I told him I would email it to him, but he insisted I bring it, because he needed to go over some logistics with me. I told him I would meet him down in the hotel lobby, but he told me he was not feeling well and wanted to rest up as much as he could before the following day's opening session. This was not an issue, as I had been asked to do this before, as his security was always there. I went up to the room and he answered the door. I asked where his security was, and he told me he had gone to spend some time with his family that lived there. I was very hesitant, but I proceeded to enter the room and stood at the door. I handed him the itinerary and we began discussing his speaking schedule.

After about ten minutes, we were done, and I told him I would see them in the morning. He got up to "walk me out," even though I was right beside the door sitting on a bench. As I went to open the door, he grabbed my hand. He proceeded to tell me how he has been attracted to me since the day he saw me. I told him this was not appropriate. One, he was my pastor, and two, he was married. He then began to tell me he was not happy with his wife and that they were getting a divorce. I explained to him that I was sorry for them, but I was not interested in him. He then pushed me away from the door and told me I knew what I was coming to his room for, and that I was going to give him what he wanted. I screamed, but he lunged toward me and pinned me on the floor. He proceeded to rip my clothes off me, and he raped me. I was devastated. He knew no one would interrupt him, as his security would always call him before coming back to his room.

He threatened if I told anyone, he would tell them that we were having an affair the entire time I was traveling with him and that his security would vouch for him. He also told me that he would fire me and that he had a very good team of lawyers that would *rip me to shreds.* Upon returning home, I contacted the police and a lawyer. I was not concerned about losing my job, because as far as I was concerned, this man violated me and was no longer, in my eyes, my pastor, or a pastor, at all! And I knew the truth… that is all that mattered to me. It was evident he had done this before due to his response. Unfortunately, my rape case was dismissed, as not only was I served with a suit of slander against this pastor, but his lawyers did exactly what he said they would do to me: *ripped me to shreds.* They completely turned this around on me stating that we had been having an affair for over a year, and that every time we traveled, I was with him in his hotel room, according to his security detail. They stated I conjured up this rape case for financial gain.

This is the state of the church today. Pastors are treated as *gods* and conduct business like the *mafia*. There are so many sexual predators and pedophiles in our pulpits, but we *look the other way* and let them continue abusing innocent people. Yes, this pastor is still preaching in his church today and he is still married. Unless or until God intervenes, this will continue taking place in the Church. *~A broken woman*, FL

I often get calls, texts and emails from discouraged believers who have been ostracized and even asked to leave their churches, some kicked out of their fellowships and their entire family attacked by members, and even across the pulpit by their pastor. I once could only advise, or counsel, them to hold fast and trust the Lord. To submit to God and serve Him, regardless of what was being done, erroneously, to them. But now, I can honestly relate to their plights. So many have not only left the Church but have given up on God completely. This is so tragic and devastating. I now refer to them as "spiritual casualties" of war. There are so many out there and yet many still sitting silently in the Church afraid to speak what God is telling them to speak because of the fear of rejection. Yet there are others who privately speak out, but go silent in public, because they are afraid of losing titles, positions, status, and connections. NO TITLE or "connection" on earth is worth disobeying the Lord! The only connection I am afraid of losing is to God, by way of Holy Spirit, through my disobedience.

I had a dream several years ago concerning this very thing. I saw a council, a Biblical council, with seven judges sitting behind a huge granite desk. From my view, they looked like the stone figures in Black Hills National Forest, *Mount Rushmore*, of four of our former presidents. They were enormous in my eyes, yet there was an absolute sense of peace and order about them. As I looked away from them to my left, there were pastors/spiritual leaders standing in long lines waiting for their "court hearing". They had no lawyers/attorneys; the council would be their judge and jury, and they were enacting biblical judgment and justice according to the Scriptures. I heard in my spirit multiple times after this dream that God was restoring judges, seasoned leaders full of wisdom, integrity, and moral compass, in the Church.

I had no idea how quickly I would see this, or if I would even witness it in my lifetime, but sure enough, there was a panel of pastors/leaders formed by Dr. Michael Brown to weigh allegations of spiritual abuse, particularly sexual misconduct, regarding Todd Bentley, founder of Fresh Fire Ministries[xvi]. Dr. Brown is a radio host, author, apologist, professor and noted proponent of Messianic Judaism, Christian Zionism, and the Charismatic Movement. Dr. Brown and several church leaders all over the United States came together after hiring an investigator that interviewed multiple witnesses that accused Todd Bentley of sexual abuse. This minister had been accused in previous years and released back into ministry.

Here is a portion of this council's findings, and subsequent biblical judgement based upon months of review:

***

"As followers of Jesus, we delight in God's mercy and grace and believe in the power of restoration and forgiveness. At the same time, we recognize that God's Word holds leaders in the Church to high standards, since they serve as representatives of Christ Himself. The question before us is this: Does Todd Bentley, founder of Fresh Fire Ministries, live up to those standards? Is he qualified to be a recognized leader in the Church?

The signers of this statement are leaders in ministry who were asked to review a matter that invokes these beliefs, and to judge the fitness of a person for ministry according to biblical standards and the leading of the Holy Spirit. In conducting such investigation there are limits on what can be known with certainty, but we look carefully at long-term track records and the accumulated testimony of many witnesses.

The opinion we have reached here is theological, answering the question: Does Todd Bentley, founder of Fresh Fire Ministries, live up to the high standards required of those who serve as representatives of Christ? Is he qualified, according to our understanding of biblical standards, to be a recognized leader in the Church?

As part of this process we sought to hear Todd's side directly, but he declined to answer a list of 60 questions compiled by the investigator after initially agreeing to respond. (Todd required the investigator to submit the questions through his attorney, after which he ceased communicating with Dr. Brown or the investigator.)

Based on our careful review of numerous first-hand reports, some of them dating back to 2004, we state our theological opinion and can say with one voice that, without a doubt, Todd is not qualified to serve in leadership or ministry today. There are credible accusations of a steady pattern of ungodly and immoral behavior, confirmed by an independent investigator's interviews dating from 2008 up through 2019, along with other testimonies dating back to 2004. And while we only took into account first-hand reports, there are many other second and third-hand reports repeating the same accusations, often from people in different parts of the country (or, world) who had no connection between them, other than their interaction with Todd." (You can read further the link provided in the Bibliography.)

***

"Do you not know that the saints will judge the world? And if the world will be judged by you, are you unworthy to judge the smallest matters? Do you not know that we shall judge angels? How much more, things that pertain to this life?" 2 Chronicles 6:2-3

Unfortunately, because there is no set agreement with the global church on these "biblical councils," and Todd Bentley is not under the spiritual covering of Dr. Michael Brown or any of the other spiritual leaders on this council, Todd did not receive the biblical judgement agreed upon, rightly so, by this spiritual leadership council, and might I add by many spiritual leaders and believers all over the world, as well. The spiritual leaders that were and are over this man's ministry have refused and neglected to take this man out of global ministry. They are enablers to this man's spiritual and sexual abuse, as is every single pastor/leader around the world that continues to allow him to "minister" in their churches and/or events. Sadly, he received a *slap on the wrist* in 2004, which led to him being able to abuse once again. *Justice* was not administered for those abused by this man and *judgment* was brushed under the rug within the Body of Christ, once again.

We look at the scope of pedophilia and rape cases within the Catholic Church over hundreds of years, possibly centuries, yet we have not witnessed much in the form of *justice* for these millions of abused believers. How many will we never know about? How many have committed suicide because of the guilt, shame, and the unbelief of those they entrusted to believe them? I know, personally, many victims of spiritual abuse within the Church and the years, even decades, they have suffered in silence, because someone did not believe them, or they have been threatened into silence.

Many of these pastors/leaders continue this cycle of spiritual control, manipulation, intimidation, and abuse because they know they can get away with it and that their "covering" will protect them. It is absolutely reprehensible to know that there are spiritual overseers that, instead of holding these leaders accountable and bringing justice to the abused, are simply sending them on vacation only to have them return to do it once again. We have become *open doorways* to sexual abuse and every sort of evil due to the lack of accountability, responsibility, and biblical justice and judgment in the Church.

Revenge verses Justice

"Beloved, do not avenge yourselves, but rather give place to wrath; for it is written, "Vengeance is Mine, I will repay," says the Lord." Romans 12:19

We must allow the Father to *work out His wrath* upon the evil we see so prevalent in the world today, as well as in the Church. I understand completely the desire for justice, especially for the spiritually abused, but God knows better than us. We must trust His leading. Here are five key differences between revenge and justice:

1. Revenge is predominantly emotional; justice primarily rational.

2. Revenge is, by nature, personal; justice is impersonal, impartial, and both a social and legal phenomenon, as well as spiritual.

3. Revenge is an act of vindictiveness; justice, of vindication.

4. Revenge is about cycles; justice is about closure.

5. Revenge is about retaliation; justice is about restoring balance.

We want people to pay for what they have done to us and to others. We want to see them suffer the consequences of their actions. In many cases, we would rather they not even be upon the face of the Earth any longer, especially for such horrific abuses they have forced upon people. The Bible tells us that we can get angry, but that we should not let that anger turn to sin.

"Be angry, and do not sin": do not let the sun go down on your wrath, nor give place to the devil." Ephesians 4: 26-27

Instead of allowing God to pass or pronounce judgment upon someone, and bring His ultimate justice, we rather desire to get our revenge. What does this do? Well, it brings that judgement upon us. We are to keep our hands clean and our hearts pure. Only God knows the best for each of us. When we grasp these principles, we are better able to allow God to *repay*, according to His wisdom.

"I wanted him to suffer. I was sick to my stomach when I found out how many women he had sexually assaulted in our church throughout forty years of ministry, and our marriage. Some of these young women were teenagers at the time. How did I miss it? How did I not see any of this coming? I guess I was so caught up in serving God's people and serving alongside of my husband that I was not able to see what was right underneath of my nose. Strangely, our marriage and our intimate life was great. I went over every scenario I possibly could in my mind to make excuse for why he did these horrible things, but I could not find one.

It wasn't until my son walked in on him in the basement watching pornography that the pieces of the puzzle began to come together. My son shared with me what he saw his dad doing, and my heart sank. I did not even know how to confront him, so I waited until he was gone, and I went into the basement to see for myself. What I found was beyond comprehension! My husband had been videotaping these sexual assaults for years. He not only had pornography, but he had his own personal archives of sexual abuse. I could not breathe! I became nauseous and let out this horrific scream. My son came running down the steps and just held me in his arms. He was eighteen at this time. This could not be real. Was I dreaming? I truly wish I could tell you it was and that all is well, but it was absolutely not. My life shattered right before my very eyes.

It took me a week to confront my husband. I went into a deep depression almost immediately. I could not get out of my bed, and I could only tell him I was sick. I left all the videotapes where they were, until I was able to deal, in some way, with this and approach my husband. That night finally arrived and when he came home, I was sitting on our couch with these "boxes" of pornography and recorded sexual abuse. I had only viewed a few, as I could not stomach sitting there watching all these videos. I recognized a few of the women, and girls, in these videos.

Some had long left our church, and I now know why. Why hadn't they come forward? My heart was sick and my heart pounding out of my chest. It was like he had seen a ghost. My husband, in our entire forty years of being married, never once yelled at me nor had we had a heated argument of any kind. He turned into someone I have never seen right before me, and the words that came out of his mouth were foreign to our marriage. I was so scared and afraid he was going to do something to me, until our son and daughter walked through the front door.

Both looked confused and even frightened. They asked if we were okay and my husband shouted for them both to go to their rooms. My son was not leaving. He was adamant that he was going to stay with me, as he knew what this was about, and he was not going to allow my husband to do any harm to me. My husband was at a boiling point. He went to grab for the boxes and my son pushed him out of the way. They began to fight, and I had to call the police. Upon their arrival, I not only had to see my husband in handcuffs, but my son, as well. My daughter was devasted and had no idea what was going on… she was sixteen at the time. I had no other choice; I turned the boxes over to the police and turned my husband in for sexual abuse.

You would think this could get no worse, but upon the police contacting me after all the videos were viewed, one tape revealed that my husband had sexually abused our own daughter when she was just a little girl. I lost it! I wanted to kill him! It wasn't until long after his trial and his conviction that I was able to finally talk to my daughter. She told me she thought it was a dream. She was only three or four years old, and evidently, he did not carry on with this past the time she was five years old. My husband was convicted of sexual assault, rape, sodomy, child abuse, child endangerment, child rape, and multiple counts of possessing child and adult pornography. He received life in prison with no eligibility for parole. Most of his victims were contacted, the ones that we knew, and many others came forward after hearing of his arrest and conviction. Multiple lawsuits were filed against the church, as well as my family. We lost everything! But I lost everything the day I found those boxes.

It took me years to get over the thought of killing him. I envisioned how I would do it if I ever saw him again. I had to pull myself together, so I proceeded to seek out mental and psychological help. I hadn't been to church in years and did not want to even step foot into any church. I was not only embarrassed, ashamed, and guilt-ridden, but I was angry with him and angry with God. How could He allow this to happen? The hate was consuming me. It was eating me alive. How did I not see what was inside of this man? My husband? My friend? My children's father? My pastor? How could I not protect my precious baby girl? Or any of these precious girls and women I was responsible for in our church? The weight was too much to bear. I tried to take my own life while inside of a temporary mental facility that I checked myself into for help. They found me in time, and I was admitted to a psychiatric hospital.

I was there for a year in intense therapy. Upon my release, I felt as if I had finally awakened from this nightmare. I was numb, but I was well on my way to healing. I had to forgive myself and yes, I had to forgive him. I didn't want to, but I knew if I didn't, this hate would kill me. He has been in prison for ten years now. My children refuse to visit him, and I am not even sure if I ever will, either. My daughter found a very good church where she has been receiving counseling for several years. Even though she does not remember much about her abuse, the findings of her father's dozens and dozens of sexual assaults scarred and haunted her for years.

Forgiveness doesn't release the one that harmed you; it releases you from a lifetime of hate. I no longer desire revenge. God has provided the justice and the judgment. I leave him in the hands of God. ~*Anonymous*, IL

Justice and judgment will eventually come for all that have been harmed by spiritual leadership in this world. Whether it is now on the face of this Earth, or eternally, may we allow God to be the final Judge and enact justice for His people.

"The Lord is longsuffering and abundant in mercy, forgiving iniquity and transgression; but He by no means clears the guilty, visiting the

iniquity of the fathers on the children to the third and fourth genera-
tion." Numbers 14:18

This chapter speaks of judging and bringing justice in spiritual things and situations, not judging people. It is going to take a truly mature Body of Believers to walk in this kind of accountability. The Bible tells us that if we judge ourselves, we will not be judged. (1 Corinthians 11:31) Our justice is nothing compared to what the Father is able to render in His wisdom. As Believers, it is beneficial for us to make it right within before we are put on display without. I wish I could say we didn't have to experience this, but sadly, we are already here. I intercede greatly that we will receive the loving correction of our Father, so we can bring His name glory, not reproach. May God help us.

Chapter 12

Deliverance for the Abusers: The Truth Shall Set You Free

"You are of God, little children, and have overcome them, because He who is in you is **greater** than he who is in the world." 1 John 4:4 (emphasis mine)

God calls us to live free from the sin that "so easily entangles". As Christians, we are promised power and strength when we call upon God to deliver us from spiritual attacks and Satan's schemes to bind us whether to an addiction, emotion, thought, relationship, finances, or other strongholds.

God has shown me great demonic strongholds on our spiritual leaders, *chain-like* shackles imposed upon them, because they refused to stand boldly in the face of compromise and even persecution. Some, in fact, have gone so far in the ways of the world that many believers have questioned their actions and are rebuked for doubting their spiritual authority. These spiritual leaders are under great demonic influence and bondage, and we must intercede for God to remove the scales from their eyes, break the chains off them, humble them, heal them, deliver them, and then restore them back into His *fellowship* within the Body of Christ. This restoration is not in the position of spiritual authority over anyone. Far too many are manipulating the scriptures, in order to keep these spiritual leaders from any sort of accountability or responsibility. If there is to be any true deliverance for these spiritual leaders, then they need to be removed from these positions of authority immediately.

Upon accepting such positions of spiritual authority, one must count the costs of this role in people's lives. It is not something to be taken lightly or haphazardly. Our recklessness will eventually produce consequences. We must also understand that God sees things from a higher perspective. His ways are higher than our ways and His thoughts are higher than our thoughts. Though justice and judgment will be carried out, His grace is still sufficient for healing, forgiveness, redemption, deliverance, and reconciliation. With God, it is both: judgment and justice, but also the restoration of the abuser. His desire is that not one will be lost. We seek the temporary; He seeks the eternal.

So many believers refuse to see the deeper things going on in the spiritual realm. They only see what's on the *surface*, and therefore have no power and authority in the spiritual realm to effectively intercede and war on behalf of our spiritual leaders. Many say they pray for their pastor/spiritual leader every day, but are you praying carnal, flesh-filled, selfish prayers or are you praying according to the will of God through His Holy Spirit's leading for their lives? Are we covering our spiritual leaders from the demonic onslaughts sent against them? Are we interceding for the temptations that plague our spiritual leaders, especially in this time of great deception? Are we weeping and travailing, and praying in the Spirit for God's Church in the earth realm? We are not fighting mere earthly battles; we are warring in the Spirit for that which is eternal.

"For we do not wrestle against flesh and blood, but against principalities, against powers, against the rulers of the darkness of this age, against spiritual hosts of wickedness in the heavenly places. " Ephesians 6:12

We have a real enemy and it is not spiritual leadership, no matter how demonic their abuse toward us or others may have been. I know, in our flesh, we want them to suffer, but we must understand that for them to carry out the insidious things they have done, there is something *hidden* deep below the surface that is driving this evil. Over the last three years of traveling the globe conducting interviews with spiritual leaders and ministering to many of them, God has revealed their own childhood abuse from their spiritual leaders and family members, as well. I prepared to be shut down immediately by each and every one of them, yet I chose to go anyway, praying and interceding that God would soften their hearts and open doors of honest communication. He did just that. Very few refused to discuss spiritual abuse, but many stated they had been praying and waiting for someone to come. These spiritual leaders have held decades of secrets, some personally and others regarding spiritual leaders they knew that had been abusing for years.

After hours of tears, prayers, and repentance, many of these spiritual leaders were delivered from the years, some decades, of guilt and shame. Most had been sexually abused themselves as children and have spent their entire lives in psychological torment. Not having had a chance to see justice or judgement in their own lives, the cycle of abuse continued through their own position of spiritual leadership. Is this an excuse for their abuse? Absolutely not! It is, however, an explanation of the abuse and an open door of communication to end these demonic cycles of abuse in the Church.

"In the confines of the Catholic Church, there are *codes* set in place to guard priests that have committed sexual, physical, psychological, and spiritual abuse. The abuse runs so deep within our religion, dating back centuries. I will not go in depth in my response, as you have heard most of the hidden things I have shared with you, but there are spiritual practices and rituals that many priests go through in order to get positions in the Catholic Church. These rituals are nothing short of evil, many of which are sexually initiated and bonded. They are sealed with oaths that are designed to be for life.

DELIVERANCE FOR THE ABUSERS

Some priests never venture into the sexual abuse of their parishioners, though the numbers are astronomically high for those that do carry out these abominations. The ones that don't simply desire the prestige of the title of *priest*. It is more about their status in society. Unfortunately for me, my initiation had been marred before I even stepped foot in the darkness of that room. I had been sexually abused by my priest for twenty years, eventually leading into a mutual homosexual relationship. This is *by no means* abnormal in the Catholic Church. It is very widespread. So, the *sexual initiation* was not too difficult for me. It was what I knew.

After close to ten years in the priesthood, the priest that sexually abused me and hundreds of other young boys was exposed and convicted. I was numb. I did not think I would ever see this day. I had conflicting feelings. One, he was my abuser; two, he had become my lover. I eventually found out I was one of many he was carrying on homosexual relationships with during this period. After his arrest, I took a long sabbatical. So many emotions rushed to the surface in my life. I spent a good period of time under psychiatric care. It dawned on me that the abused had now become the abuser. My priest and many before him had also been sexually abused. This atrocity runs throughout generations of the priesthood. After much therapy and counseling, I was adamant that it would stop with me. I have, indeed, had thoughts of sexual relationships with young boys. I guess the relationship that developed with my priest held me back, so to speak, from acting on those thoughts.

THE ELEPHANT IN THE ROOM

I made the decision to walk completely away from the priesthood. I had to protect the innocent from my years and years of abuse. I could not guarantee, at that time, I would not eventually do this to someone else. I have remained under psychiatric care, and I am walking through my deliverance. I know we want to *demonize* the Catholic priesthood, and rightfully so… their sin is inexcusable. But for those that see deeper into the darkness of systematic sexual and spiritual abuse within our religion, please, I beg of you, pray for their deliverance! If one priest can be delivered, can you imagine how many young boys can be protected from this evil. *~Former priest*, Boston

There is a common phrase we hear often within counseling and psychological circles, "Hurt people, hurt people." In the testimony above, "The abused became the abuser." This systematic, as well as generational, cycle of spiritual abuse in the Church must be exposed once and for all. We must break these cycles, in order for healing and deliverance to come for all involved. No matter how we view it, God desires that both the abused and the abuser are healed and delivered. "Statistics reveal among 747 males, the risk of being a perpetrator was positively correlated with reported sexual abuse victim experiences. The overall rate of having been a victim was 35% for perpetrators and 11% for non-perpetrators. Of the 96 females, 43% had been victims but only one was a perpetrator."[xvii]

These statistics are so alarming. The enemy is truly targeting our husbands, our fathers, and our brothers in an effort to taint and pervert the male authority in our homes, in society, and in our spiritual communities. Again, this is much deeper than most are willing to acknowledge. I am not downplaying the severity of this gross spiritual abuse, but for us to get to a place of ultimate healing and deliverance, we must get to the root of these atrocities and tear down these strongholds, so this does not continue to happen to others.

"One of the major freedom keys in my recovery was realizing that the definitions of love and relationship that were taught to me (by example) were wrong. The key was to realize that relationship conducted that way is dysfunctional and is never going to work. As long as I tried to function within that sick dysfunctional system, I could not heal. And because I could not heal, there were parts of the cycle of abuse still being passed on. I had to face the fear of standing up to it. If the truth was going to set me free, then I had to find the truth." ~*Darlene Ouimet*, Founder of "Emerging from Broken"

If you are a spiritual leader that has found himself/herself in the dysfunctional cycle of spiritual abuse, in any form, now is the time to find out the truth concerning your life and the plot of the enemy to destroy you. The truth is the only thing that will set us free.

THE ELEPHANT IN THE ROOM

"Then Jesus said to those Jews who believed Him, "If you abide in My word, you are My disciples indeed. And you shall know the truth, and the truth shall make you free." John 8:31-32

It is not too late to right the wrongs you have committed against God and His people. You do not have to live any longer in the torment and torture you have endured for so many years. God desires to heal you and to deliver you from your suffering. Yes, there are consequences to the abuse you may have inflicted on others, but through heartfelt repentance, God is able to restore you into His Kingdom. Hiding behind these pulpits is not going stop the torment. You have a real enemy and just because he *offered* you power, riches, and fame does not mean he is not going to require your eternal soul in the end. What will it profit you to gain the whole world and lose your soul? It is not worth it!

Many pastors/spiritual leaders are afraid to leave these circles of compromise and corruption. They know very well it is not of God but are so caught up in the perversion and corruption that they do not know how to get out. Fear is holding many of them hostage, because the same way these leaders manipulate and intimidate their followers, they do the exact same to anyone that does not stand in agreement with their deceit. Yes, there are leaders threatening one another, turning on each other, in self-preservation. I have witnessed some of the most unbelievable situations amongst these pastors/spiritual leaders. This is no way to live, especially as those that call themselves followers of Christ. This is bondage, not freedom.

"Now the Lord is the Spirit; and where the Spirit of the Lord is, there is liberty." 2 Corinthians 3:17

Liberty in this scripture is the word *freedom.* This is God's heart and desire for you… His ultimate freedom. The Bible says He came to "set the captives free". If you feel you are being held captive by the enemy or by a system, whether of your own doing or not, I am here to encourage you that God is ready and willing to set you free from its grips. When He sets you free, no man has the power, authority, or control over your life.

"Therefore if the Son makes you free, you shall be free indeed." John 8:36

If you are ready to make this crucial step toward your freedom, you are going to have to set some safeguards in your life that will solidify your decision to walk in His perfect will for your life. Over twenty years ago, when I first began writing for the Lord and before I became a minister of the Gospel, Holy Spirit spoke to me to guard myself from the temptations that were sure to come in writing, as well as speaking, for Him in this world. As ministers of the Gospel, whether you are a shepherd over a flock: pastor (within the Church), or any sort of traveling minister (evangelist, prophet, teacher, etc.) there are standards and safeguards that God gives us in order to shield us from the evil temptations of this world, as well as from the enemy of our souls. Our Lord and

Savior was tempted just as we are, yet in no way did he sin or fall into the lies and deception of the enemy.

"For we do not have a High Priest who cannot sympathize with our weaknesses, but was in all points tempted as we are, yet without sin." Hebrews 4:15

Let's take a closer look at the enemy's temptation of Christ:

"Then Jesus was led up by the Spirit into the wilderness to be tempted by the devil. And when He had fasted forty days and forty nights, afterward He was hungry. Now when the tempter came to Him, he said, "If You are the Son of God, command that these stones become bread." But He answered and said, "It is written, 'Man shall not live by bread alone, but by every word that proceeds from the mouth of God.' Then the devil took Him up into the holy city, set Him on the pinnacle of the temple, and said to Him, "If You are the Son of God, throw Yourself down. For it is written: 'He shall give His angels charge over you,' and, 'In their hands they shall bear you up, lest you dash your foot against a stone.'" Jesus said to him, "It is written again, 'You shall not tempt the LORD your God.' Again, the devil took Him up on an exceedingly high mountain, and showed Him all the kingdoms of the world and their glory. And he said to Him, "All these things I will give You if You will fall down and worship me." Then Jesus said to him, "Away with you, Satan! For it is written, 'You shall worship the LORD your God, and Him only you shall serve.' Then the devil left Him, and behold, angels came and ministered to Him.'" Matthew 4: 1-11

Our Lord not only provided us the blueprint; He IS the blueprint! He clearly warns us what the enemy will send our way and provides the answer to his deception. SPEAK THE WORD! Read the scriptures and find out what his tactics are and speak the Word to those temptations as they surface in your life. Satan tried to offer our Lord what was *already* His! Our treasure is not in earthly things: titles, positions, wealth, fame, or influence. We are seated in heavenly places with Christ and our reward is eternal. Don't be deceived by this demonic *prosperity Gospel* or this evil *hyper-Grace theology*; they are smokescreens designed to blind you and deceive you into compromising your faith and selling your soul. Here are some ways in which the Lord spoke to me twenty years ago to guard myself against temptation, as I traveled around the world ministering the Gospel:

1. The Gospel is NOT for sale! IT IS FREE!

True, authentic minsters do not have speaking itineraries. We cannot be *booked*, and we will not be *bought*. We are sent by God, and He will provide for our every need according to HIS riches in glory by Christ Jesus/Yeshua HaMashiach. We DO NOT set honorariums! If someone decides to bless you, then leave that between them and God. God's Word and His gifts are FREE!

"Heal the sick, cleanse the lepers, raise the dead, cast out demons. Freely you have received, freely give." Matthew 10:8

2. Do not fly first-class.

The temptation to make ourselves feel as if we are more important than others is one of the enemy's oldest tricks. We are not afforded *special treatment* simply because we share the Gospel. Some pastors believe flying commercially invites *demons* into our lives, and that we need to isolate ourselves from the very ones that need the Gospel. No true minister is going to separate themselves from those they have been called to touch with the love of Jesus/Yeshua.

"Pride goes before destruction, And a haughty spirit before a fall." Proverbs 16:18

3. Do not stay in five-star hotels.

Most areas we travel to are either in third-world countries or in regions where the Gospel is not accepted by the masses. How can we, in good conscious, seek to stay in an extravagant hotel, while the masses of people we are ministering to are either living in dire poverty, or barely making ends meet? This was not our example, and it is highly disrespectful to the Gospel, as well as the precious souls we are sent to minister the love of God.

"When pride comes, then comes shame; But with the humble is wisdom." Proverbs 11:2

4. Do not eat in extravagant restaurants.

Many of the very people we are sent to encourage, equip, and empower are destitute and living in famine. Just trying to figure out where their next meal is coming from brings great anxiety and fear. Even if we travel to areas that are not impoverished, many of these everyday people cannot even afford to dine at some of these lavish restaurants. Who are we to feel so privileged? May we humble ourselves and seek only that which we need, not what we want or desire. This is not a vacation; this is ministry.

"And do not become idolaters as were some of them. As it is written, "The people sat down to eat and drink, and rose up to play." 1 Corinthians 10:7

5. Do not take photos or videotape; ministry is sacred.

The ministry of the Gospel is about Jesus/Yeshua, not about us. We are to minister His love to this lost and dying world and offer Him. Taking photos/videos of ourselves is counterproductive and serves no purpose in ministry, except to exalt us. On the other hand, taking photos/videos of those we are ministering to is abhorrent. Many of these people are struggling tremendously with dark issues, and for us to force a camera in their face, or to take photos/videos of these sacred moments is absolutely distasteful. These are holy moments between them and God. Stop stealing these precious moments from God's people for your own vainglory and self-promotion.

"And whoever exalts himself will be humbled, and he who humbles himself will be exalted." Matthew 23:12

6. Do not wear flashy clothes/jewelry/shoes.

We are not going to a runway show or a world-premier event; we are traveling the globe spreading the Gospel of Jesus Christ/Yeshua Ha-Mashiach. Again, some of these people live in poverty, so show them some kind of compassion and consideration as to not enter these gatherings wearing Armani suits and Stacy Adams, while laced with diamonds, gold, and expensive watches. They are children of God just like we are, don't make them feel less than who they were created by the Father to be… how did we get so far away from our Lord's example?

"… thus says the Lord God: "Remove the turban, and take off the crown; Nothing shall remain the same. Exalt the humble, and humble the exalted." Ezekiel 21:26

7. Do not meet alone with someone of the opposite sex.

This is self-explanatory, yet so many still make excuses as to how innocent things are and how God is *covering* them. God provides us His wisdom for a reason. If we refuse and reject it, then we are left to our own devices, and to the enemy's deception. Guard yourselves, your spouse, your children, your church, the name of Christ, and any potential individual that may think it's okay to carry on in this manner with you.

You are the spiritual leader; you will be held to a higher standard, as well as greater consequences.

"Abstain from all appearance of evil." 1 Thessalonians 5:22

8. Do not sit on pulpits/platforms.

There is a growing phenomenon in the Church today of ministers/guests sitting on the platform where pastors/clergy preach. This is not so new in the COGIC, Baptist, or Pentecostal church; it has been around for some time for these denominations. This trend has become an absolute spectacle, as ministers/guests are getting up and shouting and disrupting the preaching of the Word. They are drawing attention to themselves and causing the listeners to become distracted. Overall, this practice reveals a hierarchy within services, or more like a "who's who" in Christian circles. Well-known pastors invite their friends and colleagues, urging the worship of these spiritual leaders.

"... you shall not bow down to them nor serve them. For I, the Lord your God, am a jealous God." Exodus 20:5

9. Do not put your face on flyers, posters, or billboards.

When we draw attention to ourselves, we take the focus off Jesus/Yeshua and the message of the Gospel. This has become the norm in every sphere of Christianity. Our faces splattered all over social media and billboards around the country/world is a slap in the face of our Lord. God says He will share His glory with no man.

"I am the Lord, that is My name; and My glory I will not give to another, nor My praise to carved images." Isaiah 42:8

10. Do not market your ministry assignments.

Ministry is not entertainment. The world whether the music industry, film industry, or even corporations market their events so the masses can attend. When God calls a gathering, He not only *sends* His ministers/prophets/teachers, but He also *draws* those that need to be in attendance. By mass marketing our spiritual gatherings, we are not only promoting entertainment, but we are opening the doors for charlatans and frauds to enter and take advantage of God's people. This practice amongst pastors/spiritual leaders targets large numbers of people, so there is a higher chance of larger offerings, as well as products/merchandise sold. Do not be named among these deceivers. We need to get back to allowing Holy Spirit to lead us in our sacred gatherings.

"I say then: Walk in the Spirit, and you shall not fulfill the lust of the flesh." Galatians 5:16

11. Do not promote yourself/brand.

All too often in today's church culture, we are seeing the emergence of *branding*. A brand is a name, term, design, symbol or any other feature that identifies one seller's good or service as distinct from those of other sellers. Pastors and lay members alike are so consumed with their own *personal ministries* that the ministry of the Gospel has taken a backseat, or in some cases, is almost non-existent. This *branding* leads to pastors creating portfolios and press kits to send out for potential "ministry gigs". This is not of God... this is purely flesh and has nothing to do with building His Kingdom; it is building their own personal empires.

"But seek first the kingdom of God and His righteousness, and all these things shall be added to you." Matthew 6:33

12. Do not follow the crowds/what is popular.

All throughout the Bible, especially in the Gospels, we see Jesus/Yeshua and His disciples ministering in places that others would not dare be found. The crowds may have followed Him, but He did not follow the crowds. Our Lord went out in search of the orphans, the widows, the lepers, the demon-possessed, and the outcasts of society and even religious circles. You will not see many pastors/spiritual leaders today traveling to minister the Gospel to the *least of these*, because they do not have a "penny to rub together" to give financially into the ministry of these church leaders. Following the crowd, and what is popular, will definitely bring in the numbers, but it will not fulfill God's ultimate purpose in your life or for His Kingdom.

"Enter by the narrow gate; for wide is the gate and broad is the way that leads to destruction, and there are many who go in by it. Because narrow is the gate and difficult is the way which leads to life, and there are few who find it." Matthew 7: 13-14

The way of the righteous is a very narrow path. We must guard ourselves and purpose to make the Word of God our final authority in all matters of life. All of these points (not exhaustive) to keep ourselves safeguarded against temptation, if not heeded, can and will lead to much greater abuses in the lives of God's people. Disobedience is sin and if left unchecked, will lead to rebellion taking us down a path of devastation and destruction.

"For rebellion is as the sin of witchcraft, and stubbornness is as iniquity and idolatry. Because you have rejected the word of the Lord, He also has rejected you from being king." 1 Samuel 15:23

The Bible tells us in 1 John 2:16 that *"for all that is in the world—the lust of the flesh, the lust of the eyes, and the pride of life—is not of the Father but is of the world."*

Each of these were the areas the enemy tempted our Lord in, and each of us will be tempted, as well. It is up to us to *allow* the Word to guard us. It is a choice. We do not have to be enslaved in our hearts, our minds, or our bodies to anything or anyone. God gives us free will, but He also provides us with His supernatural wisdom to make the right decisions.

"Stand fast therefore in the liberty by which Christ has made us free, and do not be entangled again with a yoke of bondage." Galatians 5:1

The position of spiritual leadership is an honor and a privilege, not an entitlement. For God to trust us to lead His people is a gift, not a right. May we humbly, and with godly fear, walk in this calling with all reverence and respect. Do not allow the enemy to corrupt the high calling of God in and over your life. There are many things that people believe are *gray areas* when it comes to the Word of God. They use these "gray areas" as a license to do immoral things. We have enough wisdom at our disposal to know what is and what is not of God.

"All things are lawful for me, but all things are not helpful. All things are lawful for me, but I will not be brought under the power of any." 1 Corinthians 6:12

Ultimately, there are several questions you must honestly answer:

- ❖ Do you want to be healed from your childhood traumas?
- ❖ Do you want to be delivered from demonic oppression?
- ❖ Do you want to be set free from guilt, shame, and torment?
- ❖ Do you want to walk in absolute freedom in Christ?

As you answer these questions honestly, and begin to forgive your-self, you will be able, through heartfelt repentance, to receive God's ultimate love and forgiveness in your life. You will also be able to seek the forgiveness of those you have hurt, harmed, and abused. You may never hear it from their mouths, but you must be prepared to wholeheart-edly repent and accept the fact that they may never be ready to hear this from you, and also accept the consequences of your actions with humble, broken repentance.

Chapter 13

Authentic Repentance

"If My people who are called by My name will humble themselves, and pray and seek My face, and turn from their wicked ways, then I will hear from heaven, and will forgive their sin and heal their land."
2 Chronicles 7:14

We come to God often asking Him to forgive us for the things we do, which He absolutely does, but is He forgiving of "unrepentant" prayers? He revealed to me that forgiveness and repentance are two entirely different things. If we repented, we would not need to ask for forgiveness so often, as we are choosing to turn away from our sin. *Repentance* means to feel such sorrow for sin or fault as to be disposed to change one's life for the better; be penitent. *Penitent* is feeling or expressing sorrow for sin or wrongdoing and disposed to atonement and amendment; repentant; contrite. *Contrite* means being filled with a sense of guilt and the desire for atonement, penitent.

Each of these words: repent, penitent and contrite are words that reveal a *heart change* within a believer. It is a choice and a commitment, through genuine remorse for that sin. Are we sin-conscious? Have we adopted the world's way of viewing sin? Do we see gossip, bitterness, disobedience, and division as sin, just as we would murder, lying, fornicating, homosexuality, or theft? God began to deal with me several years ago regarding repentance. I was hurt by a lot of people, and the hurt was so deep that bitterness, resentment, and anger set in. Though I could hear the Spirit tell me to pray for and intercede for my enemies, as I did, I would find those feelings coming back up often. Why was this not going away if I was interceding for these people? The Lord shared with me that though I asked for forgiveness for the bitterness and resentment, I did not *repent*.

This blew me away! We read so often in the Word about "repentance" and it is something that we, as the Body of Christ, are not effectively practicing today. We are asking for forgiveness or a "pass" for our disobedience but are not remorseful for the sin and turning away from it.

Let's look at several very important scriptures on repentance:

JEREMIAH 31:19

"Surely, after my turning, I repented; And after I was instructed, I struck myself on the thigh; I was ashamed, yes, even humiliated, Because I bore the reproach of my youth."

AUTHENTIC REPENTANCE

JOB 42:6

"Therefore I abhor *myself,* And repent in dust and ashes."

EZEKIEL 14:6

"Therefore say to the house of Israel, 'Thus says the Lord God: "Repent, turn away from your idols, and turn your faces away from all your abominations."

HOSEA 6:1

"Come, and let us return to the Lord; For He has torn, but He will heal us; He has stricken, but He will bind us up."

JOEL 2:12

"Now, therefore," says the Lord, "Turn to Me with all your heart, With fasting, with weeping, and with mourning."

God is calling us to *repentance.* I was challenged not only by a loving Father, but also a Mighty God! He is calling His Church to a place of maturity; discipline, obedience, submission, order, power, authority.... a place of effectiveness. The spirit of "offense" is at its greatest in the Body of Christ at this very moment. We know the enemy wants not only to divide, but to discount the name and character of believers, as well as Christ. When we don't repent, and turn away from our sin, no matter how "small" we think it is, it begins to grow even larger. *"A little leaven leavens the whole lump.* " (Galatians 5:9) It seeps into every area of our lives and into our relationships, and ultimately, into the Body of Christ.

We find ourselves judging and condemning non-believers, because they won't repent and turn their lives over to God, while we who "call" ourselves believers refuse to repent ourselves for our disobedience, or sin, IN Christ? What does God say about this?

2 CHRONICLES 7:14

"If MY people who are called by MY name will humble themselves, and pray and seek MY face, and turn from their wicked ways, then I will hear from heaven, and will forgive their sin and heal their land." (emphasis mine)

"I lost everything: my wife, my children, my family, my friends, my position, my church, my integrity, my honor, my name… but more importantly, I thought I had lost Him, my Lord and Savior. I was deeply broken. It did not have to get to this point, but the lights, the cameras, the action, the fame, the wealth, the influence, the status, the red carpets, the private jets, the five-star hotels and restaurants, and yes, the women were a temptation I weakly gave into due to my pride, arrogance, and selfishness. It came like a whirlwind. I cannot even remember when this shifting began in the circles I was accustomed to being surrounded with, but it was like a *cancer*… it spread quickly.

AUTHENTIC REPENTANCE

I was part of the Charismatic/Prosperity/Word of Faith movement of churches. Yes, there has been a fast merging of these movements in the last few decades. It began in the early 1960s when me and most of my buddies from seminary were filled with the Holy Spirit. Our lives were changed dramatically and there was much evidence/fruit in the lives of those we led in our churches. We were now teaching and preaching on the gifts of the Spirit and encouraging our members to seek His fullness for their lives. It didn't take very long for some of our national leaders to grasp onto the idea that this could very well be a *cash cow*. Our annual leadership conferences changed drastically. They brought in marketing consultants, PR firms, business leaders from all walks of life, and financial experts, and pastors/ministry leaders from all over the globe were flocking to these conferences.

Everything changed. The pursuit of God and the call of preaching the Gospel slowly faded into the background. We were now being taught how to *brand* our name/ministry. We were building portfolios and press kits and sending them out all over the world for speaking engagements. Within six months, I was booked up an entire year in advance for preaching/speaking "gigs". Yes, this is how it was pitched to us in these conferences. The *wordage* is completely worldly, surely not what you would hear pastors, say forty or fifty years ago, speaking regarding the Gospel. My first year traveling itinerantly, I had "fans" at my hotel. In every country I traveled to, there were *church women* seeking to spend time with me. Of course, the first few years I battled these temptations, making sure there was always someone I could trust with me on these trips. But after a period of time, even the men that traveled with me were now having extramarital sex and some, affairs, with women in other countries. After the first sexual relationship outside of my marriage, it went downhill. Everywhere I traveled, I was with another woman. This carried on for seven years.

I had become so arrogant and entitled in my *position* as a pastor. It was no longer a call; it had become my career. And this was true for most of my friends that were pastors, as well. Trust me, everyone in our circle was doing the same thing, yet many of the wives never knew until much later. When my wife found out, it was through one of the women I had been having regular contact with, and it was a much deeper relationship than most of the others. She told my wife we had been having an affair for three years and that I had asked her to marry me. I had discussed divorcing my wife with her and possibly marrying again, but I later told her I was not going to marry her or leave my wife. She then proceeded to tell my wife about all my past infidelity, which unfortunately, I did share with her.

I am grateful this was all revealed, because I am not sure it would have ended well for me. I was spiraling out of control and the things I did during that time were unacceptable to someone called a *pastor*. I lost everything, but more importantly, I lost myself. Through all of this, I fell on my face in repentance not only to God, but to my wife, my children, my family, my friends, my church, and to those women I took advantage of during that period. It was not asking for forgiveness (I overused that grace in the first year after being exposed); it was deep remorse and grief not only for cheating on my wife and harming my children, friends, and church, but for disappointing and grieving my Lord and Savior, Jesus Christ. I abused my call of pastoral leadership and authority. I used His name to gain wealth, power, and influence, and I perverted and corrupted the Gospel.

There is still much grief I endure daily, and the loss in my life is overwhelming, but these are my consequences. I have wholeheartedly repented to God and yes, I do believe He has forgiven me. I can only pray that everyone else I hurt will someday find it in their hearts to forgive me, as well. Not so much for me, but for them." ~*Jeff*, S.C.

It *must* start with us! God is not going to do anything, until HIS people humble themselves, pray, seek His face and turn, or repent. Some of us are oblivious to true repentance, as it is not taught often anymore in our churches. We hear that God will forgive us, but we are not taught the "heart of repentance". God says that when we "hear" the Word, His voice, harden not our hearts, but be willing to do what it says the moment we hear it. If you, like me, thought that asking the Lord to forgive you of the bitterness, resentment, and anger that you allowed into your heart was enough, then I encourage you to wait a little while longer after asking Him to forgive you, because you will then hear instructions to *repent*, or seek atonement, for those sins, so that you don't have to repeat them again.

God needs us to mature. He needs us to get this! If we can grasp the intent of repentance, we can not only take ground that the enemy has stolen, but we can also conquer even greater ground for the cause of Christ in this Earth. Hebrews 6:1 reveals the peril of not progressing in Christ:

"Therefore, leaving the discussion of the elementary principles of Christ, let us go on to perfection, not laying again the foundation of repentance from dead works and of faith toward God."

I would be remiss if I did not share the fullness of God's Word with you concerning repentance. We know that the entire intent of the Prophets in the Word of God was to warn the people to *repent*. There was warning after warning in every letter that was written by the Prophets. Some listened and some did not. God has used men and women of God throughout the ages to be His mouthpiece in the Earth. They were not perfect by any means, but they simply chose to say *yes* to what God was asking of them. They availed themselves to "hear" what He was saying to them and subsequently "spoke" what they heard Him say.

AUTHENTIC REPENTANCE

Read these scriptures concerning those who, even after many chances and warnings, either chose not to repent at all, or chose to repent and it was too late. My prayer is that none of us are in that number:

HEBREWS 12:17

"For you know that afterward, when he wanted to inherit the blessing, he was rejected, for he found no place for repentance, though he sought it diligently with tears."

REVELATION 2:5

"Remember therefore from where you have fallen; repent and do the first works, or else I will come to you quickly and remove your lampstand from its place—unless you repent."

REVELATION 9: 20-21

"But the rest of mankind, who were not killed by these plagues, did not repent of the works of their hands, that they should not worship demons, and idols of gold, silver, brass, stone, and wood, which can neither see nor hear nor walk. And they did not repent of their murders or their sorceries or their sexual immorality or their thefts."

God is very gracious and merciful. He desires that not one would be lost, but we see that there is an "expiration date" for each one us. He is coming back for His Church and He tells us that it is a church with *no spot or wrinkle.* (Ephesians 5:27) I believe that His people will eventually understand the need of being "sin conscious," so that we don't have to keep asking for forgiveness. May we learn to repent, turn away, and move on to maturity, so that we can effectively let our lights shine among men that they would see our good works and glorify God in Heaven. (Matthew 5:16) God does not want us to stay babies forever; He now desires *sons*. We must allow the Word of God to become flesh, and dwell among us, or live within us, so He is able to guard us from the temptations of the world and from the enemy of our souls.

PSALM 119:11

"Your word I have hidden in my heart, that I might not sin against You."

I spoke with a dear spiritual mentor in my life and he asked: "Deborah, where can we find in history precedence where God used exposure of spiritual leadership as a means to bring healing and deliverance?" I explained to him from my own experiences where I have witnessed, even through great devastation and destruction, people repenting and turning back to the Lord; both spiritual leaders and those that followed them blindly. We see, through the exposing of the atrocities in the Catholic church, many of the abused finally getting closure in their lives. What would happen if the masses of these priests came to a true, authentic place of repentance? Repentance of this sort brings great healing and deliverance for generations past, present, and future. It pulls down demonic strongholds of insidious evil and witchcraft that have been hidden for centuries. So yes, there is a precedence, even it is starts today.

Why do we think Jesus/Yeshua and His disciples made it their top priority in spreading the Gospel? Repentance is powerful!

In today's church culture, we want to hear what God is going to do for us; what He is going to bless us with, and the gifts He will bestow upon us. We believe the Kingdom of God is all about the blessing, miracles, manifestations, and prophecy, instead of all about seeking Him, His love, His righteousness... His perfect will. For decades, even millennia, the Church, the people of God, have sought more for what God will do for them, instead of asking, "Lord, what is Your will?" In the age, or era, we are currently in, the Church age, or the age of the Spirit, we should be advancing the Kingdom of God with heartfelt humility, integrity, holiness, and righteousness. Instead, we have allowed the *blessing* of God to become more of a hunger than hungering after the Bread of Life, Jesus Christ (Yeshua HaMashiach) Himself. But what happens when the call is for *repentance*, not prosperity? A turning back to Him? We refuse to hear it... the desire for wealth and fame have consumed us and contaminated us.

Over the last 10-15 years, God has put a cry in my heart for repentance, true authentic repentance, before the Lord. With the emergence of the faith movement, as well as the prosperity and hyper-grace models of the Gospel, we have seen a decline in true, heartfelt repentant Believers in Christ Jesus. The faith movement teaches Christians that they can access the power of faith through their words; you can have what you say. This doctrine has much error in that if we do not have a surrendered and repentant heart, our asking becomes self-centered, instead of Christ-centered. Prosperity theology is the belief of health and wealth; the idea that it is God's will for every Believer to have financial blessing and that as we give financially to the Church, God will increase our material wealth. It proposes that God's way of making us happy is to provide financially and that sickness and poverty are curses. This, too, is error, as there are many Believers around the world in dire poverty yet are completely sold out to the Gospel of Jesus Christ (Yeshua HaMashiach) and have His joy dwelling within. Lastly, the hyper-grace theology, which contends that all sin: past, present, and future is already forgiven; that there is no need for confession or repentance. This completely goes against Scripture. It is truly a perversion of grace and a license for immorality.

"For certain men have crept in unnoticed, who long ago were marked out for this condemnation, ungodly men, who turn the grace of our God into lewdness and deny the only Lord God and our Lord Jesus Christ." Jude 4

The cry of John the Baptist was, "Repent of your sins and turn to God, for the Kingdom of Heaven is near." Matthew 3:2 Then, Jesus came preaching the same thing, "Repent, for the Kingdom of Heaven is at hand." Matthew 4:17 And then we hear the disciples' battle cry, "Then Peter said to them, "Repent, and let every one of you be baptized in the name of Jesus Christ for the remission of sins; and you shall receive the gift of the Holy Spirit." Acts 2:38 "Truly, these times of ignorance God overlooked, but now commands all men everywhere to repent, " Acts 17:30 We can even look back to the Prophets and see the underlying message of the Kingdom, "Therefore I will judge you, O house of Israel, every one according to his ways," says the Lord God. "Repent, and turn from all your transgressions, so that iniquity will not be your ruin." Ezekiel 18:30

The cry of repentance runs very deep and should be the message preached by every pastor in every church to every heart around the world. We have been so fashioned and deceitfully taught that the Kingdom of God is *things*. This is a twisting and perversion of the Living Word of God and it has deceived our spiritual leaders all over the world.

"The modern-day Church is at a crucial turning point. We have never seen such blatant disregard for truth, integrity, and moral compass as we have in the last several decades. The lack of humility, brokenness, and repentance amongst our spiritual leadership is beyond comprehension. The brazenness of these pastors has reached astronomical levels in Christian circles all over the world. We have allowed it and condoned it for so long, that it is now accepted and even celebrated in the Church. People actually applaud these perverted and corrupt leaders and have lifted them to "god" status. Their deliberate sin is excused away under the guise of *forgiveness* and *non-judgment*. They will dare you to try and remove them from these pulpits, and even if you succeed, they have already secured speaking opportunities all over the world that will sustain them for a lifetime. The Church, as we knew it, no longer exists. Everyone I speak with in Christian circles all over the world is seeing and sensing the great tide coming and are preparing. ~*Robert*, Spiritual Advisor, Christian Counselor, Australia

"But seek FIRST the Kingdom of God and His righteousness and all these "things" will be added unto you." Matthew 6:33 (emphasis mine)

Do you see this? God's Word is inexplicably precise in its content. The Kingdom of God is intentionally revealed as *separate* from the things; the "things" is NOT the Kingdom. The false teachings and doctrine that has sprung forth out of these movements has distorted and perverted the Word of God and our hearts. It has blocked us from complete brokenness and surrender to our Lord in repentance. We are seeking the things; the fame, the fortune, the affluence, the gifts, the manifestations, the blessing.... instead of the Kingdom, *the heart of God.*

As I traveled to Southern California in 2016, I had no idea what I was about to face. I knew it was going to be a tremendous move of the Spirit, as the intercession and warfare I experienced before I left was great. But what transpired left me even the more broken before the Lord, not in a bad way, but in a more alert and surrendered manner to what is hidden in the spiritual realm. Literally, as I stepped foot off the airplane, and touched the ground, I heard the Lord say, "There is blood on the hands of My people. Repentance is crying out from the grave." As I prayed over this word for several days, He revealed the insidious spiritual abuse of leaders in the Church, both past and present and that there was a "cry of repentance" coming forth from the graves of the abused, as well as the abusers, that have either died or committed suicide. I wept and travailed deeply this entire weekend. I could not shake this *cry of repentance.*

I am keenly aware that the enemy will place many distractions in our paths to keep us from a truly repentant heart: pride, arrogance, greed, fame, knowledge, and yes, even *grace.* As we saw previously, "hypergrace" theology blinds us to the need in our souls for repentance. Sin keeps us out of the presence of our Lord. If there is no repentance, there is no awareness of sin, and we are left accepting, agreeing with, and condoning anything and everything.

As I looked at what took place that weekend in Southern California, I was reminded that God is not impressed with crowds. He seeks and searches for the 1, the 5, the 10... the few that will wholeheartedly repent before Him and turn away from their sinful ways, to humble themselves and understand, truly understand, the Kingdom of God. You can discern an atmosphere of true repentance, a fresh wind of God, from an event that seeks to imitate a move of the past. We seek out big names, well-known pastors, prophets, singers, and musicians to be the *face* of a movement and we boast of miracles and manifestations and the like, in order to authenticate it. We must have videos and photos to "prove" what God did, but was this our model? Every time Jesus healed, He told them to go and tell no one. The proof is not in the proclamation, the evidence is in the living, breathing miracle walking when his feet have never touched the ground. The eyes that are now opened that were blinded from birth. The family on the verge of divorce now sharing their testimony with others struggling to stay together. The Church has made these pastors, prophets, miracles, manifestations, and gifts.... *idols*. Even Jesus/Yeshua refused to take the glory away from the Father. Repentance is crying out!

I believe we are, indeed, at a crucial turning point. We hear so many speak of *shifts* in the spiritual realm and that God is about to do a new thing, but I am here to prophesy to you that God will do *nothing* without a true, authentic move of repentance in the Church. We call for repentance, yet our hearts refuse to surrender to the very summoning ourselves. We mask repentance with a call to America, or the world, to repent. The devil is laughing at us, because he knows the true cry of a repentant heart; it causes him to violently tremble. We can fill churches and fill stadiums every day and call it God, but if there is no turning, *metanoia*, there is no repentance. As I spoke with one Christian leader, my heart trembled as the thought arose, "Are we really saved?" Are we *churched* or are we wholeheartedly repentant and surrendered to the One who gave His life for us? Are we willing to die for the cause of Christ? Is this a game to us or is it a laying down of our lives for Jesus Christ/Yeshua HaMashiach?

AUTHENTIC REPENTANCE

I have surrendered my life in intercession. The things God has shown me and revealed to me are life transforming. I have learned that many Believers refuse to delve deeper into the spiritual realm to see as God sees, to hear as God hears, and to love as God loves. They are satisfied with surface-level Christianity: the buildings, the pastors, the lights, the music, etc., instead of becoming living epistles... literally allowing the Word to become flesh within us. As the prophets of old cried out to the nations for repentance, they included themselves in those cries. They were not exempt because they were prophets; they were surely not perfect, but they could be trusted. God knew they would obey. If we are to stand before this world crying out for repentance and a turning to God, we must be on our faces, as well. The Church must repent to God for the atrocities we have allowed within the walls of His holy tabernacle. We must allow Him to tear down everything we've erected in our buildings, as well as our hearts, that have replaced Him. We must be willing to let go of our idols if we are to truly call ourselves followers of Christ. We must be able to repent not only for our personal sins, but the sins of our forefathers; the hidden things we've carried with us for generations that we have yet to repent for and yet to allow God to heal.

"I was verbally, emotionally, mentally, and physically abused all of my childhood. From the time I can remember, I was being punched, kicked, hit in the head with belts, and slammed against walls. Most of my childhood is a blur, either due to physical injuries or by me blocking them out completely. The injuries I sustained from this child abuse are inexcusable, and at one point, almost unforgiveable! I have Traumatic Brain Injury (TBI) that has resulted in psychotic episodes ranging from anxiety, depression, to thoughts of suicide; my brain was like jelly. I have had to see neurosurgeons, brain specialists, and neuro-pathic/naturopathic doctors to help me maintain brain health. I have a Deviated Septum from my nose being broken. I am legally blind in my left eye from blows to my head. I lost hearing in my right ear due to excessive blows to my head, as well. I have had two stapedectomies (ear surgeries) which replaced the stapes bone with a prosthetic. Every one of my ribs were broken, and easily break now due to the extent of my abuse. I have belt scars on my legs and derriere to this day. I had multi-ple black eyes and there was much emotional abuse as a toddler being left alone for hours, and sometimes all day, in a playpen. If I cried, I would get smacked. The emotional, mental, and psychological scarring will probably live with me for the rest of my life in some way.

I was born into a Jewish family. My father was a bridal salesman and traveled often selecting high-end bridal gowns for a boutique in New York; he was rarely at home. He was also a compulsive gambler at the horse races. My mother, a stay-at-home wife and mother, was extremely abusive to me and I believe very unhappy. I had two brothers, one now deceased from AIDS and another that is battling drug addiction. I lived this hell for so many years. It wasn't until I finally chose to leave my home at sixteen years old that I was able to escape the abuse. My dad disowned me at the age of eighteen as I sought to learn of his Jewish background growing up. He died when I was twenty-one.

I converted to Christianity only a year earlier at the age of twenty and I was completely excommunicated from my Jewish family, and my mom constantly mocked me; they wanted no part of me whatsoever. Fortunately, I had several families in my life since I was fourteen that supported me until I was around thirty. I married at thirty-nine and suffered for years not being able to conceive children. I am confident it is because of the physical abuse in my childhood. I now look back and accept this as my *reality*, as I am not sure if the torture I experienced as a child would have crossed over into my children's lives. There is a permanent hole in my life due to not being able to have birthed children, but God has been faithful to give me many "spiritual children".

I have suffered abuse my entire life in one way or another, but I never expected to experience spiritual abuse in the Church, as well. I was a fragile woman: physically, emotionally, and mentally. Though I endured such horrific abuse, God led me to a place of great inner healing and deliverance and gave me a ministry to reach others that have endured such devastating things in their lives, as well. I was taught and trained by the very best and I am eternally grateful to them all. After several years, I was introduced to an opportunity to join a missionary/humanitarian organization. The things spoken over my life could only have come from God Himself. He spoke concerning my childhood abuse and told me that I would begin traveling with this ministry. There was tremendous confirmation, and I thought, "This is it! I am finally walking in the God-ordained purpose for my life. This is where I am supposed to be."

The first few trips were phenomenal. The freedom in ministering to people all over the world was life-changing for me. Suddenly, I was being told not to pray for people until I was told to do so. I was encouraged not to tell people I had a hard time seeing or hearing, due to my childhood physical abuse, because this would draw attention toward me. I only offered this because at some of these gatherings, the lights were dimmed and the noise would, at times, interfere with my hearing. I wanted to be sure I could hear them and see when necessary. I began to feel targeted by the leadership. After every gathering, we usually went out to eat. I was always seated at the end of the tables, so I would not be a part of the "important conversations". I felt like a leper in their presence.

There were several online platforms I was part of in this organization where Believers gathered to pray and discuss the missionary and humanitarian work. I was completely ignored, even when I responded with feedback, while every other person on the feed was greeted and recognized. This was heartbreaking for me and very traumatizing. What did I do to deserve this kind of treatment? I felt as if the abuse from my childhood was now following me into my spiritual life. I was told by our spiritual leader that I had a *waiting period* to see if I was *worthy* of him becoming my spiritual father. I waited two years, only for him to send me a voice message stating he was *releasing me.* I felt the overwhelming sense of rejection and abandonment once again. The anxiety, depression, and thoughts of suicide resurfaced greatly during this period. I began self-inflicting, causing harm to myself, and wanted my life to end. Gratefully, God sent someone into my life that drew me up out of this darkness, and began breathing God's Word into and over me, for the first time in my life. She was used by God to strengthen me, encourage me, equip me, and empower me to walk in my God-given gifts. She *saw* me as God sees me.

After four years of leaving this organization, it is clear the spiritual abuse I endured. Yet, I have forgiven them for the things done to me. There was no repentance offered in any form by any of them, and though I still see traces of the abuse amongst them every time I see them, God has allowed me to release them all. I understand in hindsight that for them to do such things to people reveals the deep, inner turmoil they are going through themselves. I pray for them and have left them at the foot of the Cross.

Ironically, I found my mother after many years of not knowing if she was alive or dead. I was sixty-four years old. We reunited on Thanksgiving of 2019 and it was surely not a loving reunion. I found out she was very sick and possibly dying. Our first visit, she yelled at me and stated some very mean things to me, even throwing water on me. I held my composure; God had already prepared me for this moment. She was suffering from Dementia, so one minute she knew me and the next, she didn't. I continued to drive nearly an hour away to visit her and my stepfather; yes, they were in the same state as my husband and me. Nothing but God. She began to soften over time, and I had the opportunity to share the love of Jesus with them both before they died, a week apart from one another. Many say *God works in mysterious ways*, but I am here to tell you *He works in magnificent ways*! There was a certain level of *closure* that took place in my life through all of this. Though I have much more to work through, I am grateful to God for where He has brought me from… there is *beauty in brokenness*! It is His doing and it is marvelous in my eyes! ~L.B.M, CA

Going through spiritual abuse, or abuse of any kind, never feels good or makes sense while you are going through it, but somehow, after years of forgiveness, inner healing, and deliverance, He is able to bring something beautiful out of that dirty ground. We may never hear the words "forgive me," or see any sort of repentance from our abusers, but we can be assured that our Father in Heaven is more than able to heal, deliver, restore, and reconcile for His glory.

AUTHENTIC REPENTANCE

I spoke with a dear sister in Christ that shared the story of her family. As a Jewish woman, now a transformed, Holy Spirit-filled woman of power and authority in the spiritual realm, she testified of how Holy Spirit led her to repent for her ancestors, that stemmed all the way back to the Pharisees that crucified our Lord and Savior, Jesus Christ, Yeshua HaMashiach. What power and authority! I wept as she shared what God had spoken to her and I could sense great chains breaking through her generations: past, present, and future. This is what repentance does, it brings freedom! Not the freedom to continue in sin, but the *chaphash* (Hebrew) of God. This word is in close relation to the word redemption. Jesus/Yeshua came to redeem us from the curse and to free us, literally cutting the chains of oppression off us and opening the gates of hell, causing us to walk freely out of bondage. This is what repentance does for the Believer, but the more the enemy can keep us locked in this *"pseudo-Gospel"* we are preaching, we will not have need of repentance. He reveals the hidden things in man's heart and exposes us to ourselves. This message is not a message for the *masses* ... it is for those that have *an ear to hear what the Spirit of the Lord is saying to His Church,* His people. Some will receive, some will reject and be offended.

"Enter by the narrow gate; for wide is the gate and broad is the way that leads to destruction, and there are many who go in by it. Because narrow is the gate and difficult is the way which leads to life, and there are few who find it." Matthew 7:13-14

Repentance... true, authentic, heartfelt, broken, humble repentance, from the Church as well as a nation, has the power to move the hand of God. It has the power to shift earthly outcomes. It has the power to transform the hearts of mankind. It has the power to stifle and destroy the works of darkness. There is no other way! With all the devastation and destruction we are seeing engulfing our world today, we are also seeing a rise in bitterness, resentment, anger, hate, blame, and divisiveness. This is not only in the world, but in the Church, as well. The Earth is in desperate need of repentance. It is crying out from depths. It is absolutely easy for us to pray for those we love, or for those we feel will *benefit* us in some way, but can we pray according to Biblical insight for those that have committed spiritual abuse of every form? Are we truly and heartfeltly praying and interceding for spiritual leadership in the Earth? Are we praying for their repentance?

"But I say unto you, Love your enemies, bless them that curse you, do good to them that hate you, and pray for them which despitefully use you, and persecute you; That ye may be the children of your Father which is in heaven: for he maketh his sun to rise on the evil and on the good, and sendeth rain on the just and on the unjust. For if ye love them which love you, what reward have ye? do not even the publicans the same? And if ye salute your brethren only, what do ye more than others? do not even the publicans so? Be ye therefore perfect, even as your Father which is in heaven is perfect." Matthew 5: 44-48

If we are not praying according to this Biblical blueprint, then we have *no power... no authority... no access* to the heavenly realm. Our prayers are not even getting passed our lips, and we wonder why we are still in many of the situations we are currently facing. Unless we pray, as our Father has taught us to pray, as our Lord Jesus/Yeshua Himself prayed, then we are of no use to the Kingdom of God. We must *die to self* in order to access the realm of authentic Spirit-led prayer and prophetic intercession. This is not a realm many that call themselves Christians have access to, and it is a devastating reality. So many feel they are operating in the anointing and will of God, when they are absolutely *blocked* from His presence due to unforgiveness, anger, bitterness, resentment, jealousy, pride, arrogance, disobedience, and divisiveness. God cannot and will not go against His Word. If we are going to be called followers of Christ, then we are going to have to simply *follow* His ways. We desire the benefits of His Word, without any authentic transformation or repentance in our lives. As we seek His will in these areas, we will begin to see a marked changed within spiritual leadership, and the global church, as a whole.

Prayer of Repentance for Spiritual Leadership and the Church:

(2 Chronicles 7:14- "If my people, which are called by my name, shall humble themselves, and pray, and seek my face, and turn from their wicked ways; then will I hear from heaven, and will forgive their sin, and will heal their land.")

Lord, we come before you in humble and broken repentance with our hearts bowed low. We have sinned against You, and You alone. We have condemned the world for their sin, while concealing our own. We are hypocrites Lord, forgive us for compromising and corrupting not only Your name, but our witness before man. We lie in "ashes and sackcloth" understanding that we have nothing to enter Your presence, except broken repentance. We are but filthy rags in Your holy presence. We cry out in sorrow and grief for our unrepentant hearts, our stench-filled pride and arrogance, and for turning our backs on our first love, You, Yeshua HaMashiach, Jesus Christ. We call out those sins, one by one, bringing to light those things we have tried to hide in the darkness, all the while judging the world for the very same sins.

Forgive us Lord for:

*Molesting our Children

*Incest

*Rape

*Abortion

*Adultery

*Fornication

*Lust

*Lying

*Stealing

*Hate

*Racism/Prejudice

*Murder

*Corruption

*Deceit

*Manipulation

*Intimidation

*Gossip

*Homosexuality

*Greed

*Gluttony

*Slothfulness

*Pride

*Arrogance

*Idolatry

*Jealousy

*Envy

*Division

*Discord

*Apostasy

*Revelry

*Lewdness

*Perversion

*Sorcery/Witchcraft

*Pornography

*Drunkenness

*Drug Abuse

*Compromising Your Word

*Taking Away and Adding to the Word

*Accepting/Offering Bribes

*False Teaching

*False Prophesying

*And any other sin we have committed against You 'O Lord.

We grieve, weep, and travail over our sins and they disgust us. We choose today to turn away from our sin Lord and turn to You. You are holy God/Yahweh and we desire to be as You are…HOLY. We surrender and submit our lives to You Father and to Your will. May we possess Your heart and Your ways, to turn away from our wickedness and toward holiness, so this world can see You. May we truly be the salt and the light to this lost and dying world. May they see the light within us and glorify You in Heaven.

Forgive us for not living the very Word we say we believe in and were saved by. Forgive us for not loving You with all our heart, our mind, our soul, and our strength and not loving our neighbor as ourselves. Forgive us for not praying without ceasing; not praying for those You have placed in authority, not praying for the lost and dying of this world, and not praying for one another. Forgive us for judging the world, instead of loving them to You. Forgive us for abandoning our marriages, our children, and our families. Forgive us for our selfish desires and not keeping the vows we vowed before You and man. Forgive us for not trusting You to reveal Your perfect plan through the covenant of marriage and for the beauty of life. Forgive us for thinking it is our choice to choose if a child lives or dies within our wombs; the very wombs you breathed life into. Forgive us for choosing the lies of the enemy above the truth of Your Word and Your Spirit. Forgive us for trading the natural use of our bodies for filth and perversion. Forgive us for not seeing our bodies as Your temple. Forgive us for not teaching our children the ways of Your Word and raising them up in the admonition of Your Word. Forgive us for not teaching them to guard their eyes, their ears, and their mouths. Forgive us for exposing them to the filth of this world and calling it *entertainment*. Forgive us for corrupting your holy altars with carnality, worldliness, and perversion. Forgive us for manipulating Your Word to control, intimidate, manipulate, and deceive Your people, robbing them not only of their finances, but of their dignity. Forgive us for desiring fame, fortune, and notoriety, instead of the Truth of Your Word and Your glory.

We humbly cry out today Lord in heartfelt, broken repentance and not only ask You Lord to forgive us for our sins, but we ask the world to forgive us for the hypocrisy we have shown before them. We humbly lay down our lives before God and man that Your glory may be revealed through us for the salvation of mankind.

In the name of Yeshua HaMashiach, Jesus Christ, we pray. Amen.

Chapter 14

The Rebirth of the Gospel:
THE REMNANT ARISING!

"Arise, shine; For your light has come! And the glory of the Lord is risen upon you." Isaiah 60:1

With all the devastation and destruction we have witnessed in the Church and the millions of lives all around the world that have suffered from the verbal, emotional, mental, psychological, physical, and sexual abuse of spiritual leadership, there is yet a *Remnant* arising out of the ashes of organized religion. Through all the hurt, pain, and betrayal, we are witnessing something truly supernatural taking place in the lives of the spiritually abused. We are seeing the *rebirth of the Gospel* of Jesus Christ/Yeshua HaMashiach, as in the early days of the spreading of the true, authentic Gospel. The Book of Acts is coming to life once again, right before our very eyes. As the land of Israel blooms in all her splendor in these last days, so, too, His Bride is blossoming, flourishing, and maturing, but not without great tests, trials, and tribulation. As the sprout breaks through the earth's surface with power and force, racing through the dark and seemingly impenetrable ground, seeking the light and glory of its Creator, so, too, God's *remnant* is springing forth out of the hardened soil of religious and spiritual abuse in great adversity, turmoil, and tragedy. The *rebirthing of the Gospel* is here, and *the Remnant is Arising*!

"The wilderness and the wasteland shall be glad for them, and the desert shall rejoice and blossom as the rose; it shall blossom abundantly and rejoice, even with joy and singing. The glory of Lebanon shall be given to it, the excellence of Carmel and Sharon. They shall see the glory of the Lord, The excellency of our God." Isaiah 35: 1-5

So much is stirring in the Spirit realm. God is positioning His people for an end times gathering... beginning with the *Outpouring of Holy Spirit* on His people. Many believe this "Outpouring" will be a remarkable move of the Spirit of God where He will impart and anoint His people with the Gifts of the Spirit and use them greatly in bringing souls into His Kingdom. Though this is true and Biblical, we are missing a crucial step to the prelude to this season, and that is the *shaking* and *awakening* of the Body of Christ. What we have witnessed within the Church over the last several decades is definitely revealing a *shaking* of spiritual leadership, as well as an *awakening* of the Body of Christ. Honestly, everything that can be shaken is being shaken in the Church.

THE REBIRTH OF THE GOSPEL: THE REMNANT ARISING!

The Bible speaks often about the Church being birthed in and through great persecution and tribulation. This was not only from the outside world, unbelievers, but also from the perverted and corrupt religious system of their day. We saw this take place in the lives of Jesus/Yeshua and His disciples, along with the followers of the Gospel. All that we see taking place in the Church today is merely a precursor to the *rebirthing* of the authentic Ekklesia of God, the *called-out ones*.

"...we must through many tribulations enter the kingdom of God." Acts 14: 22b

"God called me out of the Church in 2010. There was so much corruption in my church and many nights, I simply could not sleep going over and over in my mind if this was where God wanted me to stay. Many leaders would throw Scripture at me as to why I needed to submit and remain, but something within me knew I was leaving. When that time came, I was verbally abused and told I was not in the will of God. I was emotionally abused by leaders that used the Bible to tell me how evil I was, and that God would never forgive me if I left. I was mentally and psychologically abused as my pastor turned it all around on me and tried to make me think I was mentally ill. They put many of my dear friends against me and told them not to interact with me at all, even outside of church.

Upon leaving, I felt a huge burden lift from off my life. Not even a week later, God led me to a homeless shelter in my neighborhood and I began serving meals every week and ministering to these precious people. I have been at this shelter for ten years, and support in many outreaches in the city. I have never felt so free and so connected to God in my entire life. I feel as if I am making a difference in this world, instead of sitting in a church pew week in and week out watching my church worship their pastor. My heart aches for many of them. I pray they, too, will be able to see the truth one day. ~*Billie*/Louisiana

The birthing process is a beautiful gift and brings forth abundant life and joy unspeakable, but the journey to fruition is far from enjoyable. As the child is ready to come forth, there several stages that take place. In the first stage, contractions begin causing the cervix to open, or dilate. This leads the baby into the birth canal. Early labor can take many hours to even days for first-time mothers. Once active labor begins, contractions become stronger, closer together, and regular. Your legs might cramp, you may feel nauseated, your water may break, and you may experience increasing pain in your back. Active labor usually lasts between four and eight hours. Breathing techniques and relaxation are very important during this time to prevent discomfort.

The final stage of labor is called *transition*. It is intense and painful. Contractions will come closer together. You will experience pressure in your lower back and rectum. You will feel the urge to push. Sometimes, it is too early to push and if you do, it can cause swelling of the cervix, which can delay the delivery. Breathing helps to stop this urge of pushing too soon. When it is time for the baby to proceed through the birth canal, the mother will bear down and push in between breaths. This stage can last from a few minutes to a few hours; longer for first-time mothers.

Once that baby breaks forth out of the birth canal, through the cervix, it can be extremely painful. The head usually comes first, with the body following. As the baby is delivered, there is happiness and relief. You can hold your baby and experience unspeakable joy, but there is still a final stage of delivery and that is delivering the placenta. You can still experience contractions during this time, even though minimal, and you will push once again to release the placenta from your uterus. The uterus will continue to contract until it is back down to its normal size. "Through much preparation, and even pain, the result is *the miracle of birth*."[xviii]

The same can be said for the birthing, or rebirthing, of the Church in the last days. There is a deep weeping and travail coming forth from the abused and from the past generations that never received justice from their abusers. The word *travail* is defined as work especially of a painful or laborious nature, a physical or mental exertion or piece of work, agony, or torment. Many cannot understand the deep traumas associated with abuse. Unless you have experienced it, there is no way to fully comprehend what people endure daily. Yet, out of this travail is springing forth great hope, both for the spiritually abused, as well as the Church at large.

"For we know that the whole creation groans and labors with birth pangs together until now. Not only that, but we also who have the firstfruits of the Spirit, even we ourselves groan within ourselves, eagerly waiting for the adoption, the redemption of our body. For we were saved in this hope, but hope that is seen is not hope; for why does one still hope for what he sees? But if we hope for what we do not see, we eagerly wait for it with perseverance." Romans 8: 22-25

There is great hope for all that have endured the evils imposed upon you by those you trusted in spiritual authority, as well as those persecuted all over the world. God is able to heal, deliver, restore, and redeem all that was stolen from you. You are not alone. There are hundreds, thousands, and even millions around the world that are crying out to Him in the dark, cold caves of isolation. God is bringing them out in great healing, deliverance, forgiveness, and power! They will be the *ministers of reconciliation.* Whether you see justice carried out in this lifetime or not, there is not only a promise of restoration, but eternal justice for you!

"I was abused for so many years until the age of sixteen. I went from relationship to relationship after running away from home. My parents did not believe me that our pastor was sexually abusing me. They called me a slut and said that I was having sex with boys in school, which was not true. It was not until I left that in order for me to have a place to stay, I would have sex with guys, some leading to very brief relationships. At the age of twenty, I met a woman that "took me in" and began to help me heal from the years of abuse, neglect, and abandonment. She saw me as God saw me and did not judge me. She loved me back to God. I began traveling with her on missionary work to Central America. My life changed dramatically on these trips. I stopped looking so much at what I did not have in my life growing up and began to see that others had it way worse than me.

She died several years later, and I honestly did not know what I was going to do or where I was going to go. There was a trip already scheduled for both of us to go back to Central America the following month. I felt so conflicted. How could I go without her? After several weeks of praying, God sent me my confirmation. Not only was I going on this trip, but I would not return home. This would now be my home and these precious people would now be my family. I found my calling and to watch God touch people as He is doing in this remote region of the world encourages and empowers me to continue spreading the Gospel with love and compassion.

THE ELEPHANT IN THE ROOM

"The desolate land shall be tilled instead of lying desolate in the sight of all who pass by. So they will say, 'This land that was desolate has become like the garden of Eden; and the wasted, desolate, and ruined cities are now fortified and inhabited." Ezekiel 36: 34-35

This prophetic declaration is not only for the land of Israel, but for the people of God. The desolate land of your heart, your mind, your soul, and your body will be like the *Garden of Eden*. There is a refreshing, renewing, restoring, redeeming, and reconciling coming for you and all of God's children. None of us are exempt from the hurts and pains of this life. But with God, we have so much more than those that do not know Him. We have great assurance through our faith of His love, His peace, and His will being done in our lives on Earth, as it is in Heaven.

"My brethren, count it all joy when you fall into various trials, knowing that the testing of your faith produces patience. But let patience have its perfect work, that you may be perfect and complete, lacking nothing." James 1: 2-4

There is much being produced within God's people in this hour. Our brothers and sisters all over the world are being persecuted daily for their faith in Jesus Christ/Yeshua HaMashiach. In China, Iran, Nigeria, Pakistan, Iraq, Syria, and many other countries, there is great persecution with mass incarcerations, kidnappings, and killings of believers. With the Church being eradicated in many of these areas, we are witnessing an emergence of bold and courageous followers of Jesus/Yeshua. Their trials and tribulations are fueling their faith! We are seeing a very similar trend within the Church of those that have been spiritually abused. They have made the choice to take back their lives and refuse to allow anything or anyone to separate them from their Lord and Savior.

"Who shall separate us from the love of Christ? Shall tribulation, or distress, or persecution, or famine, or nakedness, or peril, or sword? As it is written: "For Your sake we are killed all day long; we are accounted as sheep for the slaughter." Yet in all these things we are more than conquerors through Him who loved us. For I am persuaded that neither death nor life, nor angels nor principalities nor powers, nor things present nor things to come, nor height nor depth, nor any other created thing, shall be able to separate us from the love of God which is in Christ Jesus our Lord." Romans 8: 35-39

This Remnant is rising in leaps and bounds all over the Earth. From the persecuted to the spiritually abused, God's *Ekklesia* is preparing and positioning themselves for the Great Outpouring, the Harvest of Souls, and the Second Coming of our Lord. They are not afraid of anything or anyone; they know in whom they trust. They know their eternal destination and will lay down their lives for the cause of Christ, at all costs.

"Blessed are those who are persecuted for righteousness' sake, For theirs is the kingdom of heaven." Matthew 5:10

THE ELEPHANT IN THE ROOM

Do you believe you are a part of the Remnant of God in the Earth? Have you surrendered and submitted to the inner healing and deliverance of abuse and persecution in your life? Have you committed to walking fully in the Spirit and allowing God to use you to reach the lost and dying of this world, even the abusers, the corrupt and perverse spiritual leaders, and those whose only desire is to see us wiped off the face of this Earth? Are you prepared to open your hearts once again to receive God's covering over your life and those He has divinely ordained to walk along this journey with you? Spiritual leaders, are you prepared to walk away from it all? Are you convinced that this corrupt and perverted religious system needs to be eradicated? Are you wholeheartedly repentant not only for the spiritual abuses you have committed, but also penitent for the centuries of abuse perpetrated under the veil of "God's love"? The time to decide is *now*!

"But I will gather the remnant of My flock out of all countries where I have driven them, and bring them back to their folds; and they shall be fruitful and increase. I will set up shepherds over them who will feed them; and they shall fear no more, nor be dismayed, nor shall they be lacking," says the LORD." Jeremiah 23: 3-4

Father God is opening the eyes of His people. He is removing the blinders. He is removing the scales from their eyes. He is melting the ice from their cold and hardened hearts. He is piercing through the fortified walls of hurt, pain, betrayal, and abandonment with vengeance.... He is snatching His people out of religion's grip. He is fortifying the persecuted and granting them supernatural armor for these last days. They are waking up, looking around, and are on a mission. They are now speaking up and crying out against this travesty of spiritual abuse and persecution in the Church. They are correcting and rebuking the lies, deceit, and manipulation. They are prophesying to the Church to Repent! Many are being harassed, blacklisted, and are now leaving the structure of organized religious "Christianity" ... some even being kicked out. They are leaving in masses. Where are they going? What will they do? Will anyone accept them? How can they ever live a true Christian life?

In traveling abroad, I have witnessed the emergence of cell groups, home fellowships, discreet gatherings, and underground churches. I have found that these assemblies are made up of former pastors, leaders, and life-long servants in their former churches. There are the marginalized and abused. There is the persecuted. There are also the delivered abusers. Each of them stated that God had *called them out* of the Church and *called them to* the true, authentic Gospel of Jesus Christ/Yeshua Ha-Mashiach. In all my communications with these precious believers, each stated that they had never in their lives experienced such freedom in Christ as they did now. I believe we are on the cusp of a *rebirthing of the Gospel* and are soon to witness His presence in ways we have never before experienced in the Church.

"For behold, the darkness shall cover the earth, and deep darkness the people; but the Lord will arise over you, and His glory will be seen upon

you. The Gentiles shall come to your light, and kings to the brightness of your rising. Lift up your eyes all around, and see: they all gather together, they come to you. Your sons shall come from afar and your daughters shall be nursed at your side. Then you shall see and become radiant, and your heart shall swell with joy." Isaiah 60: 2-5a

People's hearts are seeking after authenticity. They are searching for God/Yahweh in a dry and thirsty land. Their spirits are crying out to the God of Creation. The God of their salvation! Where are You Lord? In that *still small voice*, He whispers, "I Am here. Follow Me. I will show you THE WAY!" They are being led by Father God. They are following Him every step of the way. Holy Spirit is instructing and directing His sons and daughters. He is building His Church; His Ekklesia and the gates of hell shall not prevail against it! This entertainment and worldliness is not sufficient, it cannot satisfy the soul. It is not going to sustain the *true sons of God* in this Earth. Deep is calling unto deep. He is preparing His people, His Church... His Bride. An army who stands for righteousness and holiness. He will see His image and likeness in this Earth! He will be lifted up in our lives and He will draw all men unto Himself through His people. *The Remnant* is here, and I am excited at what I see!

The *rebirthing of the Gospel* is exploding all over the Earth. Pastors are leaving their pulpits, masses are leaving the organized Church, and the true, authentic Gospel is being released into the earth realm. The Acts 2 Church is and has yet been forming for several decades all over the globe. You won't see them on television. You will not hear of their accomplishments. You will not find their faces or their names on social media blasting what God/Yahweh is doing.

These *Remnant* are on their faces in heartfelt prayer and intercession and are rallying the angels of Heaven for a great awakening in the Earth. They are in the streets ministering to the homeless, the drug addicts, the orphans, the widows, the poor, and the outcasts. They are on the highways and byways spreading the love of Jesus Christ/Yeshua HaMashiach, not inviting people to "church," but inviting them to Christ! This Remnant has become the Word: walking, talking, breathing, living epistles of Christ reconciling the world to their Creator. They understand that time is short and will carry their cross until the day the Lord brings them home. They are clothed in truth, love, grace, mercy, boldness, courage, power, and authority. The Word of God is their final authority and they will preach and teach with the fire of Holy Spirit! Signs, wonders, and miracles will authentically follow them because the Spirit of God dwells within them and the Word of God is their banner... they *believe*!

The days are growing shorter and the world is increasing in darkness and evil ... the Earth is groaning and travailing for our Redeemer to deliver us and bring forth His final justice and redemption. Do not become weary in well doing for in due season, you will reap if you do not faint. (Galatians 6:9) Be strong and remain encouraged. We are not in this fight alone. The battle is not ours, it's the Lord's! Fix your eyes on eternity!

"Therefore we do not lose heart. Even though our outward man is perishing, yet the inward man is being renewed day by day. For our light affliction, which is but for a moment, is working for us a far more exceeding and eternal weight of glory, while we do not look at the things which are seen, but at the things which are not seen. For the things which are seen are temporary, but the things which are not seen are eternal." 2 Corinthians 4: 16-18

Conclusion

The intense pain and abuse suffered at the hands of spiritual leadership all over the world for Millenia has caused deep weeping and travailing in the hearts, minds, souls, and spirit of believers. The roots run so deep throughout our generations that lineal succession of spiritual leadership is destined, through powerful strongholds, to repeat the sins of their forefathers if we do not take a biblical stand against these atrocities. Whether the organized institution of Christianity repents or not, God's *Ekklesia* is moving full steam ahead! We will not wait another one-hundred, or even thousand years for the acknowledgement of their insidious abuse. We will speak the Truth, in love, and we will extend forgiveness to our abusers. Many will argue that they will forgive, not for the abuser, but for their own well-being. This is fine and truly a step of growth and maturity, but I am here, sent by the Lord, to tell you that it *is* possible to forgive our abusers for *their* benefit.

God wants to extend His grace and mercy *through* us to this lost and dying world. He desires to use us to set many of these spiritual leaders free from the years, even decades, of their own childhood abuse by those they trusted as spiritual leaders, as well as family members. This is much bigger than just our own abuse. This is multi-generational: past, present, and future. As we painfully remember the abuse of our past, may we seek to *see* others in their abuse, as well. Again, "Hurt people, hurt people," "the abused becomes the abuser," but let us be the "*healers that heal*". What happened *to you* had nothing to do *with you*. May we all commit to be the *bridge* between good and evil. May we all purpose to be the *light* in the midst of darkness. May we all seek to be the *ministers of reconciliation* in the earth realm.

"Therefore, from now on, we regard no one according to the flesh. Even though we have known Christ according to the flesh, yet now we know Him thus no longer. Therefore, if anyone is in Christ, he is a new creation; old things have passed away; behold, all things have become new. Now all things are of God, who has reconciled us to Himself through Jesus Christ, and has given us the ministry of reconciliation, that is, that God was in Christ reconciling the world to Himself, not imputing their trespasses to them, and has committed to us the word of reconciliation." 2 Corinthians 5: 16-19

About the Author

Deborah G. Hunter is a wife, mother, author, inspirational speaker, minister, philanthropist, and CEO & Publisher of Hunter Heart Publishing and co-owner of Hunter Entertainment Network. She has written seven books of her own, *Breaking the Eve Mentality, Raising Your Prophet, The Call of Intercession, The Wilderness, El Desierto, Stir Up the Gift*, and her bestselling book *Holy Spirit, the Promise Left for the Believer*. Deborah travels nationally and internationally on the mission to "Offer God's Heart to a Dying World" through the inspired gift of writing, personal testimony, and through the gifts God has placed within her. She serves as an avid philanthropist through her charity, *Stir Up the Gift*, dedicated to providing support for the needy around the world, including the country of Japan after the wake of the 2011 Earthquake/Tsunami that ravaged this country.

Deborah has been a born-again believer since the age of twelve. She was ordained as a Minister in Prophetic Gifting on July 7, 2007 in Kitzingen, Germany from International Gospel Church. She received her Bachelor of Arts Degree in Biblical Studies/Theology, Magna Cum Laude, from Minnesota Graduate School of Theology in 2010. She also travels globally with several missionary organizations ministering hope and providing help to those in need around the world.

Deborah is married to Chris Hunter, Jr., radio personality and CEO of Hunter Entertainment Network, a conglomerate of Christian media outlets, including record label, movie, book, and music production companies. They share in the raising of their three children together, Jade, Elijah, and Ja'el, and are the father and stepmother of three, along with four beautiful grandchildren. They reside in the majestic mountains of Colorado.

Bibliography

[i] *History Begins at Sumer*. Samuel Noah Kramer. Originally published under title: *From the Tablets of Sumer*: Indian Hills, Colorado. Falcon's Wing Press, 1956.

[ii] *Breaking the Eve Mentality*. Deborah G. Hunter. Hunter Heart Publishing, Colorado Springs, Colorado. 2004.

[iii] *Cult Formation*. Psychiatrist Robert Jay Lifton. Harvard School of Psychiatry. 1980.

[iv] *Diagnostic And Statistical Manual Of Mental Disorders* https://dsm.psychiatryonline.org/doi/book/10.1176/appi.books.978089 0425596 ©American Psychiatric Association.

[v] United Nations Resolution 96 (I). "The Crime of Genocide." 11 December 1946.

[vi] *10 Stages of the Genocidal Process*: Genocide Watch. https://www.genocidewatch.com/countries-at-risk.

[vii] Xenophanes of Colophon (c.570-478 BCE) https://www.ancient.eu/Xenophanes_of_Colophon/.

[viii] *Most Senior Catholic Charged With Child Sex Abuse Convicted* https://www1.cbn.com/cbnnews/cwn/2019/february/most-senior-catholic-charged-with-child-sex-abuse-convicted.

[ix] *Spotlight*. Production: Participant Media First Look Media Anonymous Content Rocklin/Faust Productions Spotlight Film. Director:

Tom McCarthy. Distributed by: Open Road Films. Release dates: September 3, 2015 (Venice) and November 6, 2015 (United States).

[x] *Parts of the Holy Bible, selected for the use of the Negro Slaves, in the British West-India Islands.*
https://www.museumofthebible.org/exhibits/slave-bible

[xi] Sanger, Margaret. "My Way to Peace," Jan. 17, 1932. Margaret Sanger Papers, Library of Congress 130:198.
https://www.nyu.edu/projects/sanger/webedition/app/documents/show .php?sangerDoc=129037.xml.

[xii] Margaret Sanger, "High Lights in the History of Birth Control," Oct 1923.
https://www.nyu.edu/projects/sanger/webedition/app/documents/show .php?sangerDoc=306641.xml.

[xiii] U.S. Church Membership Down Sharply in Past Two Decades https://news.gallup.com/poll/248837/church-membership-down-sharply-past-two-decades.aspx.

[xiv] *Do You Really Know Why They're Avoiding Church?*
https://www.barna.com/churchless/.

[xv] *Churchless: Understanding Today's Unchurched and How to Connect with Them.* George Barna and David Kinnaman. Tyndale Momentum, Carol Stream, IL. 2016.

[xvi] Official Statement from the Leadership Panel on Todd Bentley, January 2, 2020: https://askdrbrown.org/library/official-statement-leadership-panel-todd-bentley-january-2-2020.

[xvii] Cycle of child sexual abuse: links between being a victim and becoming a perpetrator.
https://www.ncbi.nlm.nih.gov/pubmed/11731348.

[xviii] *Stages of Labor and Birth*. The Mayo Clinic.
https://www.mayoclinic.org/healthy-lifestyle/labor-and-delivery/in-depth/stages-of-labor/art-20046545.